DICKENS

AND HIS READERS

ASPECTS OF
NOVEL-CRITICISM
SINCE 1836

BY GEORGE H. FORD

The Norton Library
W · W · NORTON & COMPANY · INC ·
NEW YORK

TO THE MEMORY OF

E. K. BROWN

1905-1951

W. W. Norton & Company, Inc. is also the publisher of
The Norton Anthology of English Literature, edited by M. H.
Abrams, Robert M. Adams, David Daiches, E. Talbot Donaldson,
George H. Ford, Samuel Holt Monk, and Hallett Smith; *The American Tradition in Literature,* edited by Sculley Bradley, Richmond
Croom Beatty, and E. Hudson Long; *World Masterpieces,* edited
by Maynard Mack, Kenneth Douglas, Howard E. Hugo, Bernard
M. W. Knox, John C. McGalliard, P. M. Pasinetti, and René Wellek;
and the paperbound Norton Critical Editions—authoritative texts,
together with the leading critical interpretations, of *Adventures of
Huckleberry Finn, The Ambassadors, Crime and Punishment, Gulliver's Travels, Hamlet, Heart of Darkness, Henry IV, Part 1,
Madame Bovary, The Red Badge of Courage, The Scarlet Letter,* and
Wuthering Heights.

PRINTED IN THE UNITED STATES OF AMERICA

1 2 3 4 5 6 7 8 9 0

PREFACE TO THE PRESENT EDITION

WHEN a new edition of a book represents what is essentially a reprint rather than an over all revision, the author's contribution for the occasion should more appropriately be styled a Postscript than a Preface. As traced in this book, the story of the relationship between Dickens' novels and his various reading publics had to terminate in the mid 1950's, and at that date I ventured to endorse Kipling's prediction about Dickens' novels tending to become, as time passed, more and more modern. If it could be demonstrated that since then the critical regard for these novels has been radically modified and that such a prediction was obviously a bad guess, I suppose the present Postscript would have to be expanded into a long additional corrective chapter. Happily there appears to be as yet no need for such drastic corrections. In 1962, one of the best Dickens' recent critics, J. Hillis Miller, spoke of what he called the "Dickens boom," and there are plentiful indications that its noise since 1955 has been steadily magnifying rather than diminishing. Manifestations of the boom are various. They include authoritative editions of Dickens' letters and speeches, studies of the various versions of his novels and the establishment of authoritative texts, fresh historical investigations into the Victorian political and educational backgrounds of his writings, and comparative studies such as Mark Spilka's *Dickens and Kafka*. Perhaps most significantly they include a number of distinguished critical studies featuring, in particular, a close reading of individual novels, the kind of reading recommended in the final paragraph of the following book. As for contemporary English novelists, the persistence of Dickensian influences are, as we might expect, much less evident, but we have had at least one outstanding example of these influences in the novels and stories of Angus Wilson, a writer who demonstrates how Dickens' modes of creating scene and character can be adapted, with striking effect, to contemporary fiction.

But a short Postscript is hardly the place for any full-scale review of recently published books and articles about Dickens.

What can be recommended as most useful for carrying forward the history traced in *Dickens and his Readers* are three books published in the 1960's: *Dickens and the Twentieth Century,* a collection of essays edited by John Gross and Gabriel Pearson; *The Dickens Critics,* edited by G. H. Ford and Lauriat Lane Jr. (which includes an extensive bibliography) ; and Ada Nisbet's impressive review of Dickensian criticism and scholarship which is included in *Victorian Fiction: A Guide to Research,* edited by Lionel Stevenson.

Finally some mention might be made of a Dickensian conference staged in 1962, for the circumstances of this unusual gathering might serve to indicate in what directions the discussion of Dickens' novels has been moving. In that year the Dickens Fellowship chose to cross the Atlantic in order to stage its annual conference. To Boston were invited four scholars and critics who were asked to air their views on the past and future status of Dickens' novels.* The pooling of resources represented by the harmonious exchange between an organized group of Dickensians and an assorted panel consisting of a biographer, a literary historian, a textual scholar, and a literary critic, was remarkable in itself. Most of all, as one of the panelists said, it exemplified how Dickens' variety of appeal related to a quality his writings share with those of only the greatest writers, the quality of inexhaustibility.

Rochester, New York　　　　　　　　　　　　　　　G. H. F.
October, 1964

---

* A transcript of the discussion, edited by Noel Peyrouton, was published in Cambridge, by the Charles Dickens Reference Center, under the title *Dickens Criticism.*

PREFACE

IN old age, George Eliot noted that while her body and health were declining, her "spiritual life"—the reputation of her novels among readers—was daily waxing more vigorous and hale. Such an awareness of the distinction between the existence of a work of art and the existence of its creator can lead (as Samuel Butler was led) to theories of immortality. Although what follows is not quite so ambitious, its starting point is a similar awareness. Abundant investigation has been devoted to the story of the man Charles Dickens, who lived from 1812 to 1870, but comparatively little attention has been given to the story of the flourishing of his novels, which have had their own form of existence from 1836 to the present. Especially in the midst of the present ardent revival of interest in Dickens, almost every year sees the addition of a biography to an already bulging bookshelf; yet studies of the way in which his novels have been received by readers are rare.

The conventional history of an author's reputation is often based entirely upon a study of reviews. In such a tidy concentration of the evidence there is obvious value, yet the results are sometimes rather dull and even misleading. What follows is based in part upon reviews but also upon diaries, autobiographies, letters, memoirs, and critical essays. My object has been to extend the history of Dickens' reputation beyond a listing of reviewers' notices into a more general study of novel-reading. What kinds of English readers have read Dickens' novels? What aspects have they enjoyed or failed to enjoy? What were they expecting from prose fiction? How did their reactions affect Dickens' own development as a novelist? In what ways have the appreciation and understanding of Dickens' work been influenced by shifts of taste, by the growth of new critical theories of the novel, and by the successful experiments of later novelists? These are the principal questions raised in the present study. There is a further question hovering in the background, to which the answer can be only implied and that by the whole book itself: Of what assistance to us now is a record of the earlier understandings (and misunderstandings) of Dickens' novels in enabling us to arrive at an adequate recognition of his achievement?

Almost every critic, diarist, or letter-writer of the past century and a quarter has had something to say of Dickens' novels, and merely to compile a list of references to his work in newspapers, magazines, and books during a single year in the present century would be beyond the reach of an investigator working by himself. In William Miller's *Dickens Student and Collector*, an unannotated list of titles stretches for over 280 pages, and, as those enthusiastic bibliographers Messrs. Calhoun and Heaney have indicated, a *selection* of 1200 more titles could be added to Miller's list if a team of twenty researchers were summoned to hunt for them. Although what follows does contribute several new items for such an ideally comprehensive compilation, it is of course not intended to be a substitute for a bibliography. Many classifications dear to the bibliographer are treated here as subordinate. For example, a seemingly endless quantity of writing about Dickens has been concerned with topography. Such writings, like the musical compositions based on his novels, seem an interesting sign of activity, but, for a book concerned with tastes and critical judgments, they are little more than a sign of activity. I have consequently discussed them only in passing.

But the major obstacle is not the quantity of the evidence; it is the diversity of the evidence, a diversity which depends partly upon shifts of taste and partly upon the variety of fare that Dickens provided for his readers. To offset these difficulties, as the Table of Contents indicates, I have tried to devise both horizontal and vertical perspectives. The normal horizontal perspective is provided by the general chronological arrangement. In addition, a vertical organization of the material is set up so that different aspects of Dickens' appeal to his readers may be isolated and treated as virtually separate entities when necessary. Such an ordering allows estimates from past and present to be more freely brought into juxtaposition, and thus some of the larger critical problems can be introduced into the earlier parts of the survey. For example, in the first chapter, there is a conventional summary of the reception of *Pickwick*, in appropriate chronological sequence, but there is also an attempt to range forward from 1837 in order to discuss the impact of a single feature of Dickens' appeal to his readers: his humor. In the fourth chapter, sentiment is similarly isolated, and at the same time, the early reception of *The Old Curiosity Shop* is described. The advantages of such a double perspective seemed to outweigh the obvious dangers which are involved in isolating a single phase of an author's work instead of constantly considering the total impression. Moreover, I hope that some of the later chapters, especially the seventh and twelfth, may restore a sense of the relationship of the parts to the whole.

This investigation has had to be confined to Dickens' readers and critics in England. To make a detailed study of his readers in America would require another volume, and I have not attempted to deal with them, in a comprehensive way, at all. When, however, there was a question of including critics as influential in England as Henry James, W. D. Howells, or Edmund Wilson, it seemed to me a hobgoblin kind of scrupulosity to pass them by. In the twentieth century, a system of lend-lease which caused the transplanting to England of Henry James and T. S. Eliot, and of reverse lend-lease which caused the transplanting to America of Aldous Huxley and W. H. Auden, poses nice problems for the more categorically-minded exponents of literary nationalism on both sides of the Atlantic.

Cincinnati, Ohio   G.H.F.
March 1953

ACKNOWLEDGMENTS

MOST of my investigation depended upon the resources of that huge literary Bank in Bloomsbury (as the British Museum was called by Philip J. Bailey). Also helpful were the libraries of the University of Cincinnati, Dickens House, Yale, Johns Hopkins, and the Victoria and Albert Museum. To Miss D. L. Minards of Dickens House I am especially indebted.

Among early publications, listed in the Bibliography, I derived most assistance in the initial stages from Blanchard's vigorous review of novel-criticism: *Fielding the Novelist*. Also useful was an excellent unpublished University of Illinois Ph.D. thesis by Carolyn Washburn, which provides an informative survey of the reviews between 1832 and 1860. Through oversight, a work which seems to bear most pertinently upon the subject, Irma Rantavaara's Ph.D. thesis, which was published in Finland, did not come to my attention until late in my own investigation. Happily, although parts of the two studies sometimes derive from the same basic sources, there is little overlapping, and I hope the two books may complement each other. I am also sorry not to have been able to profit from a short recent study of Dickens' later status written by K. J. Fielding, this book not yet having come into my hands.

Among more personal acknowledgments must be included my thanks to various graduate students who, for the past six years, have played a lively part in the development of this study. Assistance of a more material sort was provided by research grants from the Taft Fund of the University of Cincinnati, and I wish to thank Edwin Zeydel and other members of his committee for their persistently generous encouragement.

To Stephen Spender I am grateful for suggestions made after reading the manuscript of the later chapters, and to Professor Geoffrey Tillotson for some advice of very long standing. I also wish to thank Richard D. Altick, W. C. DeVane, Edgar Johnson, Miss Ada Nisbet, Lionel Stevenson, and Mrs. Jane Parker. My greatest debt, for help through all stages of the writing and editing of this book, is to my wife.

A NOTE ON THE FOOTNOTES

As an experiment in meeting some of the difficulties of documentation, a few of the supplementary notes, which may be of most interest to the general reader, are placed at the foot of the pages to which they belong. All others are located less accessibly, but more economically, at the end of the book.

The following abbreviations have been used throughout:

Dickensiana . . . . . F. G. Kitton, *Dickensiana* (1886)

Forster . . . . John Forster, *The Life of Charles Dickens*, ed. J. W. T. Ley (1928)

Gissing . . . . George Gissing, *Charles Dickens: A Critical Study* (1898)

Nonesuch . . . . *The Letters of Charles Dickens*, ed. Walter Dexter (Nonesuch Press, 1937-1938)

Speeches . . . . *The Speeches of Charles Dickens*, ed. R. H. Sheperd (n.d.)

When titles of books appear without the place of publication having been indicated, it is to be assumed that the book was published in London.

CONTENTS

for cheerfulness. Antiquarianism and *Drood*. Sensationalism and Dickens' contribution to development of mass entertainment. Narrower aims of later entertainers such as Collins. Divorce of later artists from mass of readers.

His reputed failure to provide psychological insight or religious questioning becomes a major flaw for sophisticated readers. Weaning away of such readers by later novelists. Reasons for prospering of Meredith and Eliot. Their anti-Dickensian concepts of fiction. Eliot's success before 1900 in uniting a public. Meredith's more exclusive followers. Their discrediting of Dickens' novels as superficial entertainment. Hardy valued for religious depth. Cult of Russian fiction in England after 1880. English inability to find resemblances between Dickens and Dostoevsky. Persistence of reputation as childhood classic. Lack of interest for adults because preoccupied with externals instead of "spiritual."

Other new developments by-pass Dickens. Invasion from France of aestheticism and naturalism. His discrediting when compared with more self-conscious novelists. Stevenson, James, Conrad, and Flaubert. Their concepts and attitudes towards Dickens' achievement. His influence on James and Conrad. James' reputation. High reputation of French novels after 1880. Moore, Bennett, and Wells as readers of Dickens. Continuing influence in twentieth-century novels an aid to Dickens' reputation. More recent breakdown of rigid aestheticism. Recognition of his art.

Dickens' present status. Conflicting evidence. Recurring examples of Lewes' estimate: Saintsbury, Graves, and others. Contrary examples from four groups of defenders. Shaw's praise of social criticism. His debt to Dickens' method. Marxist social critics. Appreciation of his range as creator of vivid characters. Priestley, Swinburne, Chesterton, Santayana. Chesterton's importance as debater. Limitations. Gissing's search for realistic Dickens. Impasse developed by critical preconceptions of nature of reality. The sober symbolist of

CONTENTS

Wilson, Lindsay, and Johnson. Their interpretation aided by counter-revolution in criticism. Recognition of poetic resources of the novel in Joyce, Lawrence, and Kafka. Dickens as twentieth-century novelist. Parallels to Kafka. Summary of variety of appeal. Variety a sign of greatness. Dickens and Shakespeare.

PART ONE

[1836-1848]

"Whether our great-grandchildren do or do not read Mr. Dickens, they will all have to recognize that their great-grandfathers certainly did."
—George Stott, in the *Contemporary Review*, 1869.

"With Coleridge . . . the very fact that any doctrine had been believed . . . by whole nations or generations of mankind, was part of the problem to be solved, was one of the phenomena to be accounted for. . . . [He] considered the long or extensive prevalence of any opinion as a presumption that it was not altogether a fallacy."—John Stuart Mill, in the *Westminster Review*, 1840.

CHAPTER 1

THE PROSPERING OF PICKWICK

"Write on, young sage! still o'er the page pour forth
    the flood of fancy;
Wax still more droll, wave o'er the soul Wit's wand of
    necromancy.
Behold! e'en now around your brow th'immortal laurel
    thickens;
Yea, Swift or Sterne might gladly learn a thing or two
    from Dickens."
              (*Poetical Epistle from Father Prout to Boz*,
              December 14, 1837)

TO the majority of nineteenth-century readers, *Pickwick Papers* was the most likeable book ever written by Dickens. In the twelve years following his death, for example, when over 4,000,000 copies of his novels were sold, the sale of *Pickwick* far outdistanced all the others.[1] Earlier, during the 1850's and 1860's, Dickens had been plagued by reviewers demanding a return to the manner of his first novel, and, as might be expected, he himself vainly wished that attention might be shifted away from *Pickwick* to the novels of his maturity.[2] His wish has been granted in the twentieth century, at least partially granted. *Pickwick* has continued to attract the antiquarians of literature, those who are interested in finding out which room was occupied by the Pickwickians during their visit to the Bull Inn at Rochester, and it remains an endless subject for the designers of Christmas cards, but it has not received so much adult critical attention as it deserves. The word *adult* may provide a clue, for it is a book that can be enjoyed by the child or the adult, but rarely by the adolescent. The disappointment of reading it at the wrong age is apt to result in a persistent neglect in maturity. For books long unread, an algebraic symbol is filed away in the reader's mind as a substitute for the total experience, and often the symbol is not merely simplified but false.

A tendency to overlook *Pickwick Papers* is part of a general tendency at present to emphasize the great symbolist artist in Dickens, his bitter insight into the confused muddledom of life, at the expense of the equally great humorist artist. This present study will reflect the same tendency, but one should beware of its one-sidedness. If Dickens' work has more in common with the kind of writing represented by Kafka, Dostoevsky, or Faulkner than his Victorian critics recognized (had the comparison been possible), he has also more in common with Smollett and Surtees than some of his more humorless twentieth-century critics have recognized. The revival of Dickens, if it is to be firmly based, ought to be able to embrace his zestful humor as well as his more topical contemporaneousness.

In such circumstances, literary history may be of service to the literary critic by providing perspective. Its role is similar to Coleridge's (as described by John Stuart Mill): to remind us that the persistence of a literary work as a source of pleasure for successive generations is a fact not to be lightly overlooked by the critic. One-sided criticism seems to stem from a fear of stodginess. To stimulate the indifferent, the critic resorts to urtication and becomes, in the process, merely eccentric. Among the most distinguished practitioners of this shock treatment is Dr. F. R. Leavis. Throughout his essays, reputations are tumbled round like roulette balls— a very exciting display. In *The Great Tradition* (1949), Fielding's novels are solemnly banished together with ninety-five percent of Dickens' works, excepting only *Hard Times* which is briefly discussed in an appendix. One can imagine that such startling treatment, given as a lecture, would pack a hall with fascinated undergraduates (they love the sound of smashing marble), but in print it becomes disappointing. What gives edge to one's disappointment is that Dr. Leavis demonstrates brilliantly, in a few short passages, that he can analyze a chapter of Dickens with unusual skill, his analysis providing a model of one kind of criticism much needed for future studies.

These questions of the future direction of criticism must

be postponed, however, for later chapters. More immediately, our concern will be with the past and present. At first glance, the story of the reception of *Pickwick* seems familiar ground; every study of Dickens makes passing reference to it. Closer inspection shows that except for some reprintings of the early reviews, and some useful pages by Amy Cruse and Edgar Johnson, the ground has not been adequately explored. Because of the importance of the story here, some of its more familiar parts, as well as its less familiar ones, must be pieced together.

Before *Pickwick*, the *Sketches by Boz* had achieved a modest success and had earned their author the reputation of being what is conventionally called a "rising young writer." In England, fourteen notices and reviews (usually of a favorable sort) had greeted their publication, and, in Baltimore, Edgar Allan Poe had asserted that Boz was a "far more pungent, more witty, and better disciplined writer of sly sketches, than nine-tenths of the Magazine writers of Great Britain."[3] *Pickwick* began with a comparable small fanfare (Forster was certainly not exact in saying that it was launched without any advertisements whatever), but as is well known, the opening numbers fell strangely flat. When the publishers tried the desperate experiment of sending out 1500 copies of each number to some of the booksellers, the whole venture seemed on the verge of failure, for the booksellers returned almost all of the copies unsold. Credit for relieving the crisis at the time of the fourth number belongs, of course, to Dickens' creation of Sam Weller, but William Jerdan, the editor of the *Literary Gazette*, liked to believe that much of the credit belonged to him. Jerdan was delighted with Sam Weller, and on July 9 and August 13, he gave *Pickwick* the most useful kind of support by simply lifting large passages of the Weller monologues and printing them in his weekly magazine. For this gesture he does deserve credit. In later life, Jerdan wrote one of the dullest of autobiographies, but its dullness ought not to obscure his importance in the 1830's. His *Literary Gazette* was one of the most influential publications in England; it was relished by university undergraduates, and, incidentally, by Dickens himself.* The effects of Jerdan's noticing the Wellerian transfusion soon became marked. Purchasers flocked to the booksellers to buy back issues of *Pickwick*, and the sales soared from four hundred each number to forty thousand. By contrast, Scott's largest sale had been about thirteen thousand.[4] More than *Childe Harold* or *Waverley*, more than *Adam Bede* or *The Heir of Redclyffe* in later years, *Pickwick* was the most sensational triumph in nineteenth-century publishing. The *Quarterly* noted that Boz, like Byron, "awoke one morning and found himself famous, and for a similar reason: for, however dissimilar the men and their works, both were originals, and introduced a new style of writing."[5]

Many of the forty thousand purchasers have recorded the state of excitement that was aroused, each month, by the latest number. There were special reasons for their response, but over all was the thrill of a new planet swimming into the reader's ken, a sense of discovery never to be recaptured. Some there were, inevitably, who remained aloof. Sydney Smith was one; the name "Boz" seemed to him somewhat vulgar.[6] Poor Mrs. Frances Trollope was another. She was embarrassed because in the midst of the uproarious enthusiasm for *Pickwick* in her household, she herself did not find the book especially funny. One of her relatives used to arrive at her home vowing that each number had "out-Pickwicked Pickwick," and Mrs. Trollope was obliged to write to a friend asking her to explain the book's humor. She was afraid that age had made her obtuse to the "ecstasy" that other readers were finding.[7] The *Athenaeum* reviewer (Dec. 3, 1836) also refused to be contaminated and made some chilly observations about vulgarity in literature which were endorsed by the *Eclectic Review* a few months later.[8] An amusing satire of these anti-

---

* Six reviews or short notices of *Pickwick* appeared in the *Literary Gazette*: April 9, July 9, August 13, September 10, November 12, and, in 1837, March 7. S. C. Hall and others record that this magazine was so powerful that its adverse reviews could ruin the sale of any new book. See his *Book of Memories*, third edn., n.d., p. 285. See also the *Autobiography of William Jerdan* (1853), IV, 364-365; Leslie A. Marchand, *The Athenaeum* (Chapel Hill, 1941), p. 89n.; Nonesuch, I, 40.

Pickwickians is contained in Lady Bulwer's portrait of Miss Tymmons in her novel, *Cheveley* (1839):

> Miss Tymmons was . . . considered . . . a very genteel (!) girl; for she sat uprightly on her chair, never had a crease upon any of her clothes, scarcely ever spoke, and never laughed at anything that she heard or read, for fear it should not be proper, and had forbidden her brothers (with whom she was an oracle) to read the Pickwick papers, because, as she said, they were so "very low and ungenteel," and for her part she could not conceive why people thought them so clever.[9]

The anti-Pickwickians were the exceptions. Elsewhere the book was greeted with delight. What is most significant is that the forty thousand purchasers were drawn from all levels of society and from all ages. Miss Mitford's well-known letter of June 30, 1837 (to a friend in Ireland) stresses this diversity:

> So you have never heard of the "Pickwick Papers!" Well! They publish a number once a month. . . . It is fun—London life—but without anything unpleasant: a lady might read it all *aloud*; and it is so graphic, so individual, and so true, that you could curtsey to all the people as you met them in the streets. I did not think there had been a place where English was spoken to which "Boz" had not penetrated. All the boys and girls talk his fun . . . and yet they who are of the highest taste like it the most.

As examples of readers of the highest taste, Miss Mitford cites Sir Benjamin Brodie, a physician who took *Pickwick* to read in his carriage between calls on his patients, and (one of the most ardent of early Dickensians) Lord Denman, a judge who studied *Pickwick* on the bench while waiting for a jury to finish its deliberations.[10] Not having heard of Dickens, concludes Miss Mitford, "seems like not having heard of Hogarth, whom he resembles greatly, except that he takes a far more cheerful view, a Shakespearian view, of humanity."

Such warm acknowledgment from Miss Mitford does something to offset George Gissing's theory that female readers had virtually nothing to do with the book's success.*

More than any other novel by Dickens, *Pickwick* cut safely across party lines. The Duke of Wellington, an eminent Tory, was fond of reading the trial scenes aloud, and Dr. William Maginn, in an 1836 issue of *Fraser's*, hailed "Boz the magnificent" and paid him the high compliment of saying that he was no Whig.[11] In Holland House, too, there was enthusiasm at this time. Macaulay, who had revelled in *Pickwick* in India after encountering Alfred Jingle, returned to England knowing the novel "almost as intimately as his 'Grandison.' "[12]

In many middle-class homes, the arrival of a number was the signal for a family revel. In one home, the father's custom was to seclude himself for an hour or two studying each number in order to be able to read it aloud to his large family afterwards, with some control over his laughter. During this interval, the family's impatient anxiety to hear the new number was heightened by overhearing the father's "apoplectic struggles" to attain a "decent gravity" and by his "occasional shouts."[13] In a more subdued middle-class home, young John Ruskin and his father took turns reading the *Pickwick* numbers aloud. John afterwards learned most of *Pickwick* "by heart," but he had one typical complaint to make. "Dickens taught us nothing with which we were not familiar," he wrote; "we knew quite as much about coachmen and hostlers as he did."[14] Mr. Ruskin senior was to remain a constant admirer of Dickens' novels until death; his son's opinions, here as elsewhere, were more complex and must be discussed later at further length.

Other schoolboys of Ruskin's generation also paid tribute to *Pickwick*. Typical was Samuel Hole (1819-1904), later Dean of Rochester and still remembered for his book on rose gardening. In order to buy the monthly numbers, Hole paid

* Gissing considered, in fact, that all of Dickens' novels were written for masculine readers. "To-day the women must be very few who by deliberate choice open a volume of his works." Gissing, p. 132.

the highest of schoolboy tributes by spending half of his allowance upon them in spite of an "infinite appreciation of cheesecakes."[15] Connected with another clergyman is perhaps the best of all testimonials to Dickens' power over his first readers. Twenty years after its publication, a *Blackwood's* critic recalled with fondness his experiences as a young man during the time when he was being swept away by the "genial irresistible flood" of laughter provoked by *Pickwick*. He had gone to church and been put into a pew with two elderly ladies. In the midst of the service, he began to remember something about Tony Weller, about whom he had been reading the night before, and to his great consternation, he was seized with an unbearable urge to burst into laughter. Striving desperately to be quiet, purple in the face, he finally dived below the shelf on which the prayer books rested and laughed silently while his tears "dropped like rain upon the footstool." It seemed impossible to stop. "The choral symphonies of the anthem invested Mr. Weller's image with fifty-fold absurdity, blending him . . . in his top-boots and shawls, with angels ever bright and fair." Meanwhile the two ladies crowded off to the other end of the pew in amazement, and a verger and two churchwardens descended upon him as he helplessly tried to conceal his convulsions below the prayer book shelf. They marched him "down the centre aisle, between rows of faces fixed in devout horror," he with his eyes watering, and a handkerchief crammed down his throat. When his conductors got him out into the churchyard, he horrified them further by sitting on a tombstone and bursting into uninhibited cascades of mirth. The next day he called upon the dean to offer explanations, but the dean also being a Pickwickian, he obtained ready absolution. Afterwards he presented to the dean a morocco bound *Pickwick* with the inscription "from a penitent Sabbath-breaker" which is "to this day conspicuous on the shelf of the episcopal library, for he is now a bishop."[16]

Also retrospective is Mrs. Gaskell's account, in *Cranford*, of the reading of *Pickwick* in the country villages. More impressive, as a tribute to the variety of readers reached by the novel, is the following from a review of 1837: "Even the common people, both in town and country, are equally intense in their admiration. Frequently have we seen the butcher-boy, with his tray on his shoulder, reading with the greatest avidity the last 'Pickwick'; the footman (whose fopperies are so intimately laid bare), the maidservant, the chimney-sweep, all classes, in fact, read 'Boz.' "[17]

Other classes who studied *Pickwick* with a different kind of profit in mind were the merchants. Their selling of Pickwick hats and chinaware founded a trade that still persists in shops where tourists congregate. One reviewer, not much impressed with the book itself, was deeply impressed by its success: "Pickwick chintzes figured in linendrapers' windows, and Weller corduroys in breeches-makers' advertisements . . . and the portrait of the author of 'Pelham' or 'Crichton' was . . . pasted over to make room for that of the new popular favourite in the omnibusses."[18]

What were the reasons for this mighty vogue? To peep and botanize over the delight *Pickwick* provided may seem pointless—downright pointless as Dr. Slammer would say. It seems less pointless if we consider a sour judgment passed on the book in 1871 by a critic writing for the *London Quarterly Review*. In his opinion, if *Pickwick* had never been published until that later date, its success would have been only moderate at best. Although much of this judgment can be dismissed simply as an example of high Victorian smugness about the progress of taste, there is some truth in the contention that *Pickwick* was published "in the nick of time."[19] Part of its success is certainly attributable to its timely appropriateness for 1836-37. André Gide once warned a young novelist that the public only like novels "similar to the ones they already know." The triumph of *Pickwick Papers* illustrates this half truth.

Some of the early readers of *Pickwick* recognized that like most first novels it is a highly derivative work, and, in the twentieth century, German scholars have reminded us of this fact by carefully exploring its sources.* Several of the situa-

* See, e.g., Wilhelm Dibelius, "Zu den Pickwick Papers," *Anglia*, xxv

tions in which the Pickwickians become involved were adopted from the work of predecessors such as William Combe's satirical poems on the tours of Dr. Syntax and from R. S. Surtees' *Jorrocks*. The whole rambling structure of loosely connected episodes and stories stems from a tradition going back to Smollett (Dickens' favorite novelist) and beyond, as well as to the novels of high spirits such as Pierce Egan's *Adventures of Tom, Jerry, and Logic* and Theodore Hook's *Gilbert Gurney*—a tradition shared among Dickens' immediate contemporaries by the roaring novels of Charles Lever. According to the *Athenaeum's* analysis, *Pickwick's* ingredients consisted of "two pounds of Smollett, three ounces of Sterne, a handful of Hook, a dash of grammatical Pierce Egan."[20] Indeed Dickens' book often provokes the same reaction that Tom and Jerry's adventures provoke in the reader—an intoxicated sense of being on an endless spree. One anti-temperance statistician enthusiastically computed the number of references to alcoholic drinks in *Pickwick* to be two hundred and ninety-five "including the Inwariable."* The kind of novel-reader of 1837 who approved of boisterous high spirits in fiction welcomed *Pickwick* as another example of a familiar and well-loved *genre*.

All this evidence demonstrates Gide's thesis that popularity depends upon familiarity, but Gide really does not explain why one work rather than another can make such a surprising

---

(1912), 101-110. Dibelius' full-length study of Dickens (Leipzig, 1916), a very great book of its kind, summarizes the discoveries concerning Dickens' sources made by various German scholars. It is commonplace in the universities to study Wordsworth by a route which takes in his duller predecessors, and Dickens can be similarly studied. His more permanently interesting sources include Scott, Smollett, Fielding, Lamb, and Irving. Concerning his debt to Irving, a lively controversy can be followed in the articles by Ernest Boll and Christof Wegelin in *Modern Language Quarterly*, v (1944), 453-467, and vII (1946), 83-91.

* From an 1888 newspaper clipping (not identified) in the Dickens House collection. The article notes that brandy and water heads the list in *Pickwick*, whereas in *The Old Curiosity Shop*, with its more plebeian characters, beer and ale are most often mentioned. Some of the early reviewers of *Pickwick* objected to its bibulousness. "Why did he disfigure so excellent a picture by representing such frequent excesses?" asked one pious reviewer. (*Christian Remembrancer*, IV, 1842, 586.) At a later date, protest was made that its "pothouse flavour" made its popularity a "public misfortune." (*Dublin Review*, n.s., XVI, 1871, 349-350.)

impact. The success of Dickens' first novel owed more to its newness than to what it had in common with familiar recipes.[21] One way to indicate its newness is by falling back on the word "genius." As J. B. Priestley says, "it is simply our 1830 tale of high spirits raised and illuminated by genius."[22] To this overall explanation we can return in a moment. More immediately helpful is a specific comment by Thomas Hood. Hood confessed to Dickens that he had disliked *Pickwick* when he first read extracts from it, thinking it "only a new strain of Tom-and-Jerryism, which is my aversion." On second reading, however, Hood recognized its novelty, and " 'soul of goodness in things evil'—the goodness of Pickwickedness. I afterwards read it several times with increased delight."[23]

Hood's pun should not obscure the acuteness of his comment. What he says provides a clue to explain the book's extraordinary timeliness. *Pickwick* is a rare phenomenon in literary history. Published in the same year as Victoria came to the throne, it coincided exactly with a shift of taste traced by literary historians to the same convenient date. In fact the fit is almost too perfect, suspiciously so. Dickens somehow contrives, Janus-wise, to look back to Regency thoughtless high-spirits and forward to Victorian earnestness. Every decade of the nineteenth century can be described as a period of transition, but none so appropriately as the thirties. It is strange that this inter-regnum decade, much more fascinating than the 1890's, has received relatively little attention. Its central conflict between the old carefree bachelor way of life, the Bob Sawyer way, and the new Evangelical sense of earnest family responsibility, is abundantly reflected in Dickens' early writings. In 1828, Pierce Egan had boasted, in replying to the "venerable noodles" who complained because he and his imitators had "made this the age of Flash," that anything was better than the " 'Age of Cant.' "[24] Dickens, in his Preface to *Pickwick* (1838), boasted instead that "throughout this book, no incident or expression occurs which could call a blush into the most delicate cheek." In later life, he was to regret these words, but as a young man, he was satisfied to accept the new code that literature must be suitable reading for the family parlor. In one of his early sketches, "The Boarding-house," he had tottered on the edge of violating the restrictions, but in *Pickwick* he adapted himself to them with great skill.* Mr. Pickwick may blunder into a lady's bedroom in an Ipswich hotel, but all the offensiveness of this stock situation is transformed by Dickens into a charming and innocent scene. Only rarely did a reviewer find anything indelicate in the book of which to complain.[25] The novel of high spirits had been transformed into something as wholesome as Scott's work, and Dickens inherited much of Scott's public. Like Disraeli, Dickens dressed in the style of a dandy, but he did not write like one. In his hands, the novel of high spirits became the novel of good spirits. As the *Edinburgh Review* noted: "The tendency of his writings is to make us practically benevolent."[26] For the crucial modification Dickens made in the *genre* was not merely bowdlerization. More important was his introduction of a note of seriousness into the midst of the high jinks, most evident in the prison scenes but progressively marked throughout the book. Its opening chapter is merely flippant burlesque,[27] but the tone gradually changes as Mr. Pickwick develops into a tragicomic hero. "Old Pickwick is the Quixote of commonplace life," wrote Washington Irving, "and as with the Don, we begin by laughing at him and end by loving him."[28] *Fraser's* was less charitable and considered the change in Mr. Pickwick unnatural and clumsy.[29] Only recently, a highly ingenious defense of his transformation was presented by W. H. Auden who argued that Mr. Pickwick represents, in his early stages, a pagan god wandering imperviously through the world; later, through suffering, the god is transformed into a human creature.[30] Readers of 1837 may not have been able to be quite so ingenious as Mr. Auden, but, like Hood, many of them were aware of the novelty of Dickens' introducing a

* Dickens' early marriage and family responsibilities may have influenced his acceptance of the new code. By 1840, he was warning a contributor that writers should beware of saying anything in print that could not be said "anywhere." "Mrs. Scutfidge may have stripped in public—I have no doubt she did—but I should be sorry to have to tell young ladies so in the nineteenth century, for all that." Nonesuch, I, 285.

serious theme into what seemed to be a hilarious novel. The technique was chiaroscuro, with brightness predominant, but brightness accentuated by shadow. Although later novels by Dickens are much closer to Kafka, there are some scenes in this early one, such as Mr. Pickwick's visit to Serjeant Snubbin, which anticipate the mad comic-seriousness of *The Trial*.

Much of the newness of *Pickwick* then was its blending of the wine-colored stream of the Regency with the new dark brown current of the Victorian age. The newness of the blending prompted one reviewer to rate Dickens as a completely original writer: " 'Boz' should be compared to no one, since no one has ever written like him—no one has ever combined the nicety of observation, the fineness of tact, the exquisite humour, the wit, heartiness, sympathy with all things good and beautiful . . . the perception of character, the pathos . . . with the same force that he has done."* After defining the difference between fame and mere popularity, this same reviewer concluded that *Pickwick's* fame would be genuinely lasting. The *Edinburgh* reviewer followed suit,[31] and even the highbrow *Westminster* remarked that "the great and extensive popularity of Boz is the result, not of popular caprice, or of popular bad taste, but of great intrinsic powers of mind, from which we augur considerable future excellence."† This from the pen of Charles Buller deserves notice. Buller's review is otherwise mildly critical of Dickens' tech-

---

* *National Magazine* (December 1837), quoted by W. Miller and E. H. Strange, *A Centenary Bibliography of the Pickwick Papers* (1936), p. 169. The latter is a convenient reprinting of nine reviews of *Pickwick*. Excerpts from more than twenty other reviews, of less significance, are available in Walter Dexter's "How Press and Public Received 'The Pickwick Papers,' " *Nineteenth Century*, CXIX (1936), 318-329. A review omitted from both collections appeared in the *Court Magazine*, X (April 1837), 185-187. After praising Dickens' realistic pictures of London life, the reviewer notes: "What he gives you is literally true, but like a consummate artist, he does not give it to you literally." Cf. "Journalism Immortalized: the Endurance of Mr. Pickwick," *TLS*, March 28, 1936, pp. 249-250.

† *London and Westminster Review*, XXVII (1837), 285. Buller anticipates later critics in noting that Boz "shews no very peculiar skill in developing character in action." —Inspired by Buller's review, Carlyle read *Pickwick* but was not impressed. "Thinner wash . . . was never offered to the human palate." See *Letters of Thomas Carlyle to John Stuart Mill* (1923), p. 206.

nique, but not searchingly so. For significant criticism of Dickens' technique, we have to wait for the reviews of his subsequent work. Most of the early readers of *Pickwick* were too delighted to pause for much analysis.

The delight with which *Pickwick* was received brings us back to J. B. Priestley's easy explanation that the book was simply a tale of high spirits raised and illuminated by genius. The present chapter may have stressed unduly the book's appeal to the early Victorian reader on the basis of its strain of seriousness, for as the comments quoted from early readers reveal, its predominant appeal was certainly its sense of fun. The Victorian age, especially in its early phases, was more receptive to laughter, despite its growing puritanism, than some of its critics have recognized. Even in *Sartor Resartus*, which set the tone for the age, the earnest young Carlyle pictures with gusto and approval the great belly-laugh of his serious-minded hero, Herr Teufelsdröckh. *Pickwick's* appearance coincided with the vogue of such wits as Sydney Smith, Theodore Hook, Richard Barham with his *Ingoldsby Legends*, Douglas Jerrold, and the vogue of the popular Comic Annuals. In her *Fiction and the Reading Public* (1932), Mrs. Q. D. Leavis speaks with contempt of the Victorian fondness for laughter. Like Lord Chesterfield, who considered laughter to be vulgar, and like many twentieth-century critics, Mrs. Leavis advocates the unification of society by means of an aristocracy of taste. The Victorian reviewers wished to think they were performing a comparable aristocratic function, but in general, the Victorian age, like the Elizabethan, secured social unity by the more democratic and communal device of shared laughter. For readers during Dickens' lifetime at least, *Pickwick Papers* served this communal purpose better than any other of his works, and, for that matter, probably better than any other work of the century.

The humorous parts of this early novel show to best advantage the nature of Dickens' original genius, for his method was to take stock comic situations from his predecessors and then to transform them into something refreshingly new. Best of all, the most representative examples of his use of humor show how it served to hold together what is, structurally, a haphazardly organized work. The tone of humor reinforces the central theme of innocence confronting reality.

Two examples will serve. In the midst of the absurdities of the Eatanswill election, Sam Weller astonishes Mr. Pickwick with a tale about his father spilling some voters into a canal, a tale that was approvingly reprinted in some of the early reviews:

> "It's a werry bad road between this and London," says the gen'l'm'n.—"Here and there it *is* a heavy road," says my father—"Specially near the canal, I think," says the gen'l'm'n—"Nasty bit that 'ere," says my father—"Well, Mr. Weller," says the gen'l'm'n, "you're a werry good whip, and can do what you like with your horses, we know. We're all werry fond o'you, Mr. Weller, so in case you *should* have an accident when you're a bringing these here woters down, and *should* tip 'em into the canal vithout hurtin' of 'em, this is for yourself," says he.

Part of the appeal of such a passage was, no doubt, the fresh charm of its Cockney speech rhythms. According to the *Quarterly*: "The primary cause, then, of this author's success, we take to be his felicity in working up the genuine mother-wit and unadulterated vernacular idioms of the lower classes of London."[32] But there is something else. The *situation* here is comparable to endless numbers of situations in Combe, Egan, Hook, and Lever. Thomas Rowlandson could have illustrated it (as he illustrated Combe) by one of his magnificently savage caricatures showing great fat men, with brutal and tremendous faces, tumbling headlong into the canal. The amusement provided would be the same as that of any pie-throwing scene in a farce. What Dickens has done to this traditional scene by means of his style and tone is to raise it from the level of savage laughter onto a more genial plane. The most satisfactory comparison would be with James Thurber's celebrated sketch in which one swordsman, having sliced off his opponent's head, cries *"Touché!"* As Thurber explains in an essay, the scene had first been drawn by another artist who abandoned the subject because his version seemed too brutal to be amusing. In Thurber's version, we get the impression that the man who lost his head will soon pick it up and put it back on again, or that his opponent will return it to him "with profuse apologies."[33] Similarly, we do not feel that the canal-water actually penetrated the clothes of Tony Weller's passengers; they must have somehow emerged miraculously dry. There is an even closer parallel to Thurber's scene when Mr. Jingle warns the Pickwickians to beware of a low archway after their coach leaves from the Golden Cross: " '—mother—tall lady, eating sandwiches—forgot the arch—crash—knock—children look around—mother's head off—sandwich in her hand—no mouth to put it in—. . . shocking, shocking!' "

In some parts of *Pickwick*, of course, no modification is made of the traditional horse-play. Tony Weller's immersing of the Shepherd in the drinking trough could appear, unchanged, in the work of any of his creator's predecessors. The predominant tone, however, is usually different. Another example may confirm this point. Surtees' *Jorrocks's Jaunts and Jollities* (1834) was certainly one of the important sources of *Pickwick*. For his own purposes, Dickens selected from the saga of a grocer-sportsman its finest scene, the trial of Jorrocks. Bardell *vs*. Pickwick shows how his temerity was rewarded by this effort to surpass Surtees at his very best. At first glance, the speeches of Surtees' Serjeant Bumptious and Dickens' Serjeant Buzfuz seem identical in their humorous appeal, but if the two passages are read aloud in succession, we soon realize what Dickens has added, which is everything. Surtees' lawyer starts out on one level and remains there. Dickens' pace constantly shifts, and the fantasies are infinitely more daring. The whole scene pyramids, and the reader's imagination, stimulated by such flights of absurdity as Chops and Tomato sauce, warming-pans and slow coaches, takes wing. Hovering behind the clowning, too, is the real threat of the Fleet prison. Multiplicity of levels is also evident in the Kafka-like situation of the well-meaning individual enmeshed in the baffling nets of the law, a situation to be exploited more seriously later in the Chancery courts of *Bleak House* and in the Circumlocution Office. Here it is only incipient, and the vigorous fun is in the foreground.

One arrives at the obvious enough conclusion that humor was responsible for the great success of *Pickwick Papers*, but perhaps some of its distinctive qualities have been suggested. Humor was the most effective basis on which to build a reputation among a wide variety of the readers of 1837. All Dickens' subsequent novels were more ambitious in their appeal to the emotions of fear and pity and to the reader's sense of social justice; all were more ambitious in style and skillful structure. And because they were more ambitious, even though they gained him new readers, their reception was usually more mixed. His later reviewers set themselves to the task of analyzing his limitations according to their principles of novel criticism. For *Pickwick Papers*, principles could usually be set aside for the moment; the zestful humor was enough to sustain the book and to obscure its faults, especially its bumbling interspersed tales.* Some later readers have found these qualities are still enough to sustain it. "Parts of it are magnificent," said Flaubert, "but how faulty the construction is! All English writers are like that. Except for Walter Scott, they lack plan; which is intolerable to us Latins." In an un-Latinish rejoinder, Richard Aldington comments: "Art gives length of life to books, but abundance of life will do the same thing—and the *Pickwick Papers* had life abounding."[34]

This comment about vitality leads us back to Gide's observation that popularity depends upon the reader's familiarity with the *genre*. *Pickwick*'s early popularity can be partially accounted for in these terms, but not its sustained popularity. Even as early as the 1860's most of the predecessors from whom Dickens drew had become forgotten names, and *Pick-*

* Exception might be made for "A Madman's Manuscript," a tale much admired by Dickens himself. In 1937, it achieved fresh notoriety when an American bride applied for annulment of her marriage because her husband had forced her to read it on her honeymoon. "It'll frizzle anybody's hair," said her lawyer. *Dickensian*, XXXIII (1937), 227-228.

wick survived without its familiar counterparts. A critic of 1864, speaking of the way its "original genius" had revolutionized Victorian literature, remarked aptly: "*Pickwick* has been to us very much what the *Rape of the Lock* was to the poets of the last century."[35]

CHAPTER 2

POPULARITIES AND CONVENTIONS

I

IT can be plausibly argued that a conquest of the public made at the age of twenty-four was too easy and premature, and that Dickens never recovered from its intoxication. Evidence can be cited from his second novel to show an increase in his worst faults, a shrillness of tone or a maudlin rhetoric while addressing the reader:

> It was a solemn thing, to hear, in the darkened room, the feeble voice of the sick child recounting a weary catalogue of evils and calamities which hard men had wrought upon him. Oh! if when we oppress and grind our fellow-creatures, we bestowed but one thought on the dark evidences of human error, which, like dense and heavy clouds, are rising, slowly it is true, but not less surely, to Heaven, to pour their after-vengeance on our heads . . . where would be the injury and injustice, the suffering, misery, cruelty, and wrong, that each day's life brings with it!

Even a clergyman could soon protest that the young author had "assumed the tone of a public monitor and moral teacher, with somewhat too ostentatious and dictatorial an air."[1] Dickens' letters show that he could be modest enough about his success, but on some occasions he was exultant. After reading *The Chimes* aloud to a group of writers and painters in 1844, he wrote triumphantly to his wife: "If you had seen Macready last night, undisguisedly sobbing and crying on the sofa as I read, you would have felt, as I did, what a thing it is to have power."[2] That such power, tasted so early, would lead to its abuse was almost inevitable. Reviewers from 1837 to 1844 kept reminding him that he was writing too fast.

Probably the reason that this criticism galled him was its accuracy.

In quieter moments, Dickens might even have been prepared to admit that early popularity has certain disadvantages, but the larger question of whether popularity itself is something an artist ought to avoid would have seemed as ridiculous to him as Bishop Berkeley's question about the reality of matter seemed to Dr. Johnson. From the evils of patronage, he once said, "the people have set literature free."[3] That the public might become as tyrannical a master as the patron of earlier times does not seem to have occurred to him—except, in later years, with regard to bowdlerization.[4] This larger question seems less academic in the twentieth century. Studies such as *Fiction and the Reading Public* by Mrs. Leavis in England, and *The Great Audience* by Gilbert Seldes in America, have analyzed the cynical exploitation of public taste which has become increasingly dominant since 1900. The Victorian attempt to bring readers up to a better level of taste having been largely abandoned, it seems that the artist in the twentieth century must write for an exclusive and necessarily small group of the discriminating, and he can therefore never expect to be popular. "To be great is to be misunderstood," said Emerson. On such a premise, popularity is a sign of inferiority; success is failure.

Both of these studies make extremely depressing and disturbing reading. Perhaps there may be no way round the dilemma they present, yet it is helpful to turn back to the experience of George Eliot, who was concerned with a similar problem when her novels started to appear in the 1850's. As a book-reviewer, Eliot had been appalled by the trashy fiction which sometimes achieved popularity (however ephemeral) with the "multitude." She therefore wanted her *Scenes from Clerical Life* and *Adam Bede* to be savored by a "few appreciative natures," and not to be trumpeted by the "vulgar" and "ignorant." Yet she was overjoyed by their staggering popular success. Like Dickens, she followed the sales of her novels with keen interest, noting, incidentally, that *The Times* reviews had considerable effect upon the market.[5] Blackwood, her publisher, complimented her exquisitely when he said that she had proved herself "a popular author as well as a great author."[6] Thorough highbrow though she was, George Eliot found that popularity did not necessarily mean artistic inferiority. Robert Louis Stevenson's experience was similar. In an essay entitled "Popular Authors" (1888), Stevenson analyzed without acrimony the popular qualities of ephemeral favorites and remarked that the "literary author" writes instead for a small "family" of the discriminating.[7] As his letters show, however, he too was delighted when this family circle for his own books widened out to include a large audience.

Dickens was not oppressed by these distinctions. He wrote for the discriminating and the undiscriminating indiscriminatingly. In this he resembles Molière, who wanted his plays to be understood by his cook as well as by the court. The diversity of Dickens' reading public, illustrated in the previous chapter, is too often overlooked by those who assume that his readers consisted exclusively of the real-life equivalents of Kit Nubbles and Bob Cratchit. For Dickens, popularity meant that his novels gave pleasure to dons such as C. S. Calverley, whose *Pickwick* examination was a celebrated *jeu d'esprit* at Cambridge,[8] to statesmen such as Lord John Russell, the Prime Minister, who read *Copperfield* aloud with his wife after which "we cried . . . till we were ashamed,"[9] to astute critics such as Landor and Jeffrey, as well as to the lesser breeds of readers without the pale of educated tastes. Splits there were in his public, splits which widened markedly during his career, but especially during the period of his first five novels he succeeded admirably in fusing together the strata of various tastes. It was a rare feat. One twentieth-century novelist of quality, noting his own lack of a wide reading-public, observed wistfully: "For a good thing to be popular, there must be heart in it. I mean widely popular like Dickens or W. Scott."[10]

The relationship was to be a reciprocal one. Part of the warm-hearted zest of Dickens' early novels was generated by his feeling of oneness with his diverse public. If the audience was enjoying the show, so was he. To compare him to an actor or a public speaker seems unavoidable. J. B. Van Amerongen has demonstrated that Dickens' novels are less "dramatic" than has been commonly supposed,[11] but it would be difficult to rule out the importance of the actor's role in his relationship with the public. Periodical publication enabled him to get a sense of his audience's responses almost as a leading actor may do in a theatre, and to respond to them himself in turn. Addressing an audience of his readers in one of his last speeches, he said with evident feeling: "Let me assure you that . . . you have . . . brought to the consideration of me that quality in yourselves without which I should but have beaten the air. Your earnestness has stimulated mine, your laughter has made me laugh, and your tears have overflowed my eyes."[12] His temptations were the actor's temptations: the large voice and the obvious gesture will capture the gallery even though they may alienate some in the front row below. To a novelist such as Virginia Woolf, so intimate a relationship would have seemed impossibly irksome. Dickens revelled in it. To him, awareness of an audience did not make the actor any less of an artist than the type of writer who seems unaware of his public, only a different kind of artist. In this respect, his own work has been appropriately likened to that of the folk bard.[13] When he was producing a play and acting in it, he spoke of the "singular kind" of intense pleasure he felt, "a something that I suppose to belong to the labourer in art alone." And he added this revealing comparison: it is "like writing a book in company."[14]

That the popular novelist then, like the popular actor, might likewise be a great artist seemed to Dickens self-evident. He was distressed by the status of the novel and fully aware that it was the least respected of art forms. "If I have an object in life, it is to leave my calling (as I do believe I shall), much better than I found it."[15] To make the novel respected, he did not believe that it should be made exclusive (even had he been capable of doing so) but that it should be made great. In his view, the novelist, in turn, must be seriously dedicated to his art. Scott and Thackeray annoyed him by their occasional pose of being casual gentlemen dabbling with a not very important plaything. Thackeray's work suffered, Dickens said, because he "too much feigned a want of earnestness" and because "he made a pretence of undervaluing his art, which was not good for the art that he held in trust."[16] This view of the novel as an important work of art anticipates Henry James. In spite of the lapses of taste in his novels, and his concessions to his audience, Dickens' letters, prefaces, and speeches show a dedicated professionalism that is certainly Jamesian. In an address after the death of the painter, Maclise, he spoke warmly of his friend's having devoted himself "to the art goddess . . . whom he worshipped."[17]

I I

The lack of respect for prose fiction, against which Dickens tilted, is of considerable importance for an understanding of his public, especially of that most vocal section of his public: his reviewers. Its effect on the history of novel criticism is very marked, and it can still plague discussions concerning the status of fiction.

In Hugh Blair's *Rhetoric* (1783), widely known as an authoritative work even in the Victorian period, the novel is dismissed in three pages as a form of writing tending oftener "to dissipation and idleness, than to any good purpose." Blair apologizes for even introducing such an "insignificant class of writings" into a serious discussion.[18] During the first half of the nineteenth century, despite Scott's important contribution towards raising the status of the novel, Blair's attitude continued to be typical of many educated readers. In 1848, for example, De Quincey spoke with lofty scorn of the "story teller . . . a function of literature neither very noble in itself, nor, secondly, tending to permanence." In his opinion, "all novels . . . have faded with the generation that produced them. . . . How coarse are the ideals of Fielding!—his odious Squire Westerns, his odious Tom Jones."[19] It is therefore not surprising to encounter the airy tone with which John Wilson Croker introduces a discussion of *American Notes*: "Mr.

Dickens is, as everybody knows, the author of some popular stories, published originally in periodical parts."[20]

During the second half of the century, contempt for fiction seems less in evidence, but it died hard. It is very much alive in T. H. Green's clever essay on *The Value and Influence of Works of Fiction in Modern Times* (1862). Even today it lingers on in some quarters, especially in universities, and its influence may still be detected in *The Times Literary Supplement* in which the calibre of criticism accorded to novels usually falls considerably below that accorded to all other kinds of literature under review.

Historically considered, the complex origins of such an attitude may be traced back to the Puritans' distrust of fiction as something false and therefore trivial. To this cause we can return in a moment. Also important has been the indefinable dislike aroused in the well-read upon finding his haunts invaded by too many other readers:

> And saw the merry Grecian coaster come,
> > Freighted with amber grapes, and Chian wine,
> > Green bursting figs, and tunnies steep'd in brine;
> And knew the intruders on his ancient home. . . .

Most important of all, however, has been the predominance of what George Eliot called "silly novels." In poetry, surprisingly enough, the operation of Gresham's Law does not seem of much consequence. While the thousands of Mrs. Leo Hunters may compose their verses on the deaths of expiring frogs, the status of the occasional Wordsworth or Yeats remains unaffected and distinct. The status of the novel, however, has been persistently restricted by worthless fiction perhaps because, like the film, it lacks tradition. To Fielding, the word *novel* had become so tarnished by the debased coinage passing under its name that he valiantly sought new terms to describe his own works. Sometimes he referred to himself as one of the "historical writers who do not draw their material from records"—a phrase that seemed to have more respectable associations, and sometimes he tried to father off his orphaned progeny as lost members of Aristotle's family by calling them "comic epic poems." Fielding's effort failed, and the word *novel* continued in the nineteenth century to be so inclusive, so lacking in qualitative distinctions, that one has almost to summon a semanticist whenever the history of novel criticism is read.

In the twentieth century, there is less confusion. When Allen Tate writes, for example, that "the novel has at last caught up with poetry,"[21] we can safely assume that the word *novel* in this context connotes such works as *Emma, The Scarlet Letter,* or *Madame Bovary,* but that it does not connote the daily productions of contemporary fiction with their full-bosomed females leaning out from the dust-jackets. On the other hand, when John Chapman was recording in his diary for 1860 the chief faults of his wife, we can guess that the word *novel,* as he uses it, does not connote *Emma, The Scarlet Letter,* or *Madame Bovary;* but we cannot be sure. "Her chief reading is novels," Chapman notes. "Real study of any kind she has never applied herself to since her marriage. She . . . ought to have given them [the children] a good education. The chief thing she has done for Beatrice is to habituate her prematurely to read novels."[22] Failure to establish qualitative distinctions is especially noticeable in nineteenth-century criticism of the novel. The Victorian reviewer who describes the novel as contemptible may be referring merely to trash, or to such works as *Emma,* or (like De Quincey) to both, or sometimes to one and sometimes the other. In her eloquent defense of novels in *Northanger Abbey,* Jane Austen tried to be specific: " 'And what are you reading Miss—?' 'Oh! it is only a novel!' replies the young lady, while she lays down her book with affected indifference, or momentary shame. 'It is only *Cecilia,* or *Camilla,* or *Belinda*' or, in short, only some work in which the greatest powers of the mind are displayed." Here the literary type is endowed with concrete referents, yet a reviewer might readily substitute a different list of titles from Sheridan's *The Rivals* such as *The Fatal Connection, The Mistakes of the Heart,* or *The Memoirs of Lady Woodford.* The transposition may seem a mere semantic quibble, but it explains much of the inadequacy and confusion which are often to be encountered in the criticism of Dickens and other early novelists. Flaubert's awareness of this confusion between levels of quality adds to the ironies of *Madame Bovary*, for his great novel is itself devoted, in part, to exposing the effects upon his heroine of an obsessive reading of silly novels.

By the 1840's, Francis Jeffrey felt that the status of fiction had vastly improved: "It may be worth while to inform the present generation that, *in my youth*, writings of this sort were rated very low with us . . . and generally deemed altogether unworthy of any grave critical notice. . . . All this, however, has been . . . happily changed."[23] Jeffrey's optimism was perhaps premature. The "trash and rubbish" which, he said, had once passed as novels were still being passed as novels, and in increasing numbers. Some approximate statistics, in round figures, are interesting in this connection. In 1820, about 26 new novels were published in Great Britain; in 1850 about 100; in 1864 about 300; in 1950 about 2000. The increase in 130 years is from 1 novel every 2 weeks to 35 novels every week.[24] The proportion of spurious matter in this remarkable total is probably unchanged, but its pressure on the reputable novelist has been greatly reduced by some admission of qualitative distinctions in criticism. To damn *Nicholas Nickleby*, it is no longer possible merely to say that it belongs to the same form of literature as *The Mistakes of the Heart* or *The Memoirs of Lady Woodford*.

III

In considering the causes for the contemptuous attitude towards fiction, we have already indicated some of its effects. Most striking was an apparent critical anarchy, as Justin McCarthy explains in an excellent retrospective essay of 1864:

It is only of recent days that critics have begun seriously to occupy themselves in the consideration of prose fiction. It forced itself on them by its popularity and its influence. When it became utterly impossible to ignore it any longer, . . . it was then . . . too late to set about laying down laws, and forming schools, and prescribing this and proscribing that, and attempting all the freaks of pedantic power in which criticism delighted to indulge from the days of Zoilus to those of Rymer. . . . One result is that the novelist's art is by far the most fresh, vigorous, and flourishing of all the literary professions of the day. . . . Macaulay's influence over the average English mind was narrow compared with that of Dickens.[25]

It was in the aesthetic aspects of fiction that the anarchy of early Victorian criticism was most obvious. Reviewers of the thirties and forties spoke about "critical laws" for plot and character,[26] but they were groping their way with uncertainty. Good plotting, said an *Edinburgh* reviewer, was perhaps too much to hope for. "If the incidents be separately good, and tend to develop character, it seems all that we are . . . entitled to expect."[27.] The reception of *Pickwick* was certainly aided by such concessions. Later criticism was to be less liberal.

If anarchically minded about the craft of fiction, early Victorian critics were often in firm agreement about some of its other aspects. About purity of tone and language they were virtually unanimous. "The taste of the age has settled the point, that its proper office [the novel's] is to elevate and purify, as well as to amuse; and unless the writer keep this object constantly before him, he can never hope to win a lasting popularity."[28] Despite occasional grumblings from Thackeray, the point remained settled until the 1860's. Mrs. Grundy's standards of respectability were owing not to those of educated tastes in particular but to the middle classes in general, who, as they assumed economic and political control, imposed much of their code upon the nation. Like Plato (at least in *The Republic*), the middle classes paid literature the compliment of looking upon it as a force capable of moving a reader powerfully. It followed that either literature should be avoided altogether (as the extreme Nonconformists believed),[29] or that it should be restricted in such a way that the reader would be moved powerfully in the right direction only. As the previous chapter indicated, the basic consideration in finding this right direction was a respect for the sanctity of innocent maidenhood. Political considerations also played a part, as the reception of Dickens' novels in the 1850's indicates, but the sexual obsession was basic, and the reviewers' unanimity about purity of language stems from it. With unconscious humor, an *Athenaeum* reviewer noted that "the present century is the most decorous, *at least in speech*, of any of the nineteen."[30]

At best, the restrictions placed on language and subject can be regarded as a convention, and, like the convention of unity of time in neo-classical drama, they often led to an absurd deviousness in literature. In 1843, Dickens was complimented by Croker because "he manages his most *ticklish* situations with dexterous decency—his scenes, though low, are not immoral."[31] Croker's coy remark may be dismissed as merely silly. At worst, the restrictions can be regarded as having forced all early Victorian writing into an intolerable Evangelical strait jacket in which the free development of an adult literature became impossible. The following Podsnappian sample from *Blackwood's* has the full flavor of the worst sort of smug Victorianism:

> English novels have for a long time—from the days of Sir Walter Scott at least—held a very high reputation in the world, not so much perhaps for what critics would call the highest development of art, as for a certain sanity, wholesomeness, and cleanliness unknown to other literature of the same class. . . . The novel . . . has been kept . . . pure from all noxious topics. . . . Men did not snatch the guilty volume out of sight when any innocent creature drew nigh, or mature women lock up the book with which they condescended to amuse themselves, as they do in France. Our novels were family reading.

Writing in 1867, the reviewer here uses the past tense because he feels that feminine readers are becoming corrupted, and he reminds them that whereas the "wickedness of man" may not be disastrous to the "world in general," the "wickedness of women" is so. A woman, he adds, "has one duty of invaluable importance to her country and race . . . and that is the duty of being pure."[32]

Within the bounds of this convention Dickens' work was written. Nowhere is the reciprocal relationship with his audience more clearly demonstrated, and to less advantage. The diversity of his audience has been stressed, but Dickens thought of its members as having one thing in common: the family. His humor had to be household humor. His weekly magazine was given the appropriate title of *Household Words*. To one of its contributors he remarked (when asking her to revise the ending of her story so that it would be "less painful"): "You write to be read, of course."[33] Unless the story is revised, he said, "it will throw off numbers of persons who would otherwise read it, and who (as it stands) will be deterred by hearsay from so doing." In revising his own novels, Dickens reasoned in the same way. He accepted Jeffrey's advice not to allow Edith Dombey to become Carker's mistress; he accepted Bulwer-Lytton's advice to spoil the ending of *Great Expectations*; he obscured his fine study of Rosa Dartle's inhibitions and sadism.[34] He also obscured the strange Lesbian situation in *Little Dorrit*, to say nothing of poor Nancy, Sikes' mistress, and of Martha, the prostitute in *Copperfield*, who are obscured by sentiment. In the dialogue of his underworld characters, one can almost watch him wrestling with the dictates of the convention. In the original version of *Great Expectations*, the plumpness of Pip's cheeks prompts the convict to exclaim appropriately: "Damned if I couldn't eat 'em." While correcting proofs, probably with Forster's advice, Dickens revised the speech to read: "Darn me if I couldn't eat 'em."* In *Oliver Twist*, Sikes growls

* Forster collection of proof sheets in the Victoria and Albert Museum. Dickens was not the only author to rely on John Forster as a chief censor. Mrs. Browning noted that Forster would not allow one of Robert Lytton's poems to be printed because "of the improper flesh and blood in it." See *PMLA*, LXVI (1951), 603. —Reminders may be needed of how strong a

at his pursuers: "Wolves tear your throats!" It is one of the strongest oaths his creator allows him to utter, as well as a most unlikely one.

Attempts to be witty at the expense of Victorian prudery are, however, perhaps too easy to make. Nothing could be saner than Dickens' own comments, in *Copperfield*, that reading Smollett's novels will not harm children, because if the allusions are understood, the readers are no longer children. What is important is that from *Pickwick* onwards, he recognized that not merely popularity but publication itself depended upon his working within this unanimously accepted framework. And Dickens wrote to be read. In 1844, R. H. Horne summed up the significance of Dickens' efforts: "Three words—nay, three letters—would have lost him his tens of thousands of readers in nearly every class of society. . . . Upon such apparently slight filaments and conditions does popularity often hang!"[35] As Arnold Bennett remarked many years later, in *The Author's Craft*: "The sagacious artist, while respecting himself, will respect the idiosyncrasies of his public."

Other conventions were less rigidly agreed upon either by the reviewers or by Dickens himself. Many reviewers felt that freedom from indelicacy was not enough in itself: the novelist must somehow "teach." They would have applauded Carlyle's condemnation of Scott in 1838; the Waverley novels were suitable family fare, to be sure, but what lessons did they teach?[36] Lockhart had anticipated the attack by pointing out that they make "men and women better acquainted with human nature,"[37] but his defense was inadequate to meet the

---

word *damn* became in Victorian households. In his autobiography Frederic Harrison recalls the agony he suffered as a child, about 1840, "when my nurse told me I had committed the unforgivable 'sin against the Holy Ghost.' In a fit of passion I had uttered the word '*damn*.'" (*Autobiographic Memoirs*, 1911, I, 27.) The word appears in *Pickwick* in its unadorned state but only rarely thereafter (in *Hard Times*, for example) without such embellishments as *damme* or *demned*. In the 1870's, however, when Wilkie Collins was urged by his publishers to delete the word *damn* from a novel, he cited the example of Dickens, an "immaculate" writer who, said Collins, had used it whenever it was absolutely required. "I am damned if I take out damn!" he concluded. See Kenneth Robinson, *Wilkie Collins* (New York, 1952), pp. 232-233.

demands of some seekers after righteousness. Dickens and Thackeray were solemnly reminded by one reviewer that "their responsibilities are *enormous*. No two men are capable of exercising a wider influence for good or evil over their fellow-creatures."[38] What to teach was not so readily agreed upon. This same reviewer, for example, hoped that the two novelists would provide lessons showing the importance of the Established Church. There were at least two prongs to the fork. If the reviewer found no lesson, the novel was trivial, or if a congenial lesson, he applauded; if uncongenial, he warned the novelist to return to his task of entertainment and to avoid tiresome sermonizing, as Dickens was often warned by some conservative reviewers.

In general, it was increasingly agreed that useful fiction was better than "mere fiction." For a definition of the novel representative of mid-Victorian tastes it would be difficult to surpass one that appeared in the *Spectator* (July 4, 1857): "a series of probable events presented in the form of an interesting story, carried on by action dramatically developed, and containing broad views of life from which some lesson may be gathered." Earlier, a contributor to Horne's *New Spirit of the Age* noted that the novel had acquired a "more respectable status" by having "undergone a complete revolution" in the few years previous to 1844. "It is no longer a mere fantasy of the imagination, a dreamy pageant of unintelligible sentiments and impossible incidents; but a sensible book, insinuating in an exceedingly agreeable form—just as cunning physicians insinuate nauseous drugs in sweet disguises—a great deal of useful knowledge, historical, social, and moral."[39]

Dickens was not alone in participating willingly in this "revolution." Kingsley, Reade, Mrs. Gaskell, George Eliot, and others followed his lead. Thackeray's sense of overwhelming responsibility is most revealing. It was in the writing of *Vanity Fair*, he said, that he became aware of "a vast multitude of readers whom we not only amuse but teach." He confessed that a few years earlier he would have "sneered at the idea of setting up as a teacher at all," but that he had now come to believe in the role. "And our profession seems to me to be as serious as the Parson's own."[40]

A third convention, related to the others but distinct from them, was that a novel should be "elevating." Critics of the thirties and forties recommended the "noble style" and spoke of "sinking" or "rising" with the "subject."[41] F. T. Blanchard, while working his way through the criticism of these decades, was exasperated by constantly encountering the disdainful words "unrefined" or "low" applied to Fielding's realism, and he concluded that realism was frowned upon in favor of "romance." Exactly the opposite conclusion was reached by Miss Washburn. Her investigation shows that an insistence upon realism and probability together with a dislike of romance are very prominent features of early Victorian criticism. Both conclusions are legitimate, for a major disagreement about this aspect of art was typical of the period. The brilliance of Ruskin's early work in aesthetics was shaded by his floundering attempts, through five volumes of *Modern Painters*, to discover whether paintings that are "true" may likewise be "noble." Teniers, he decided, painted true representations, but his subjects were ignoble and he therefore belonged to a "lower" order of artists.

If, in other respects, Dickens adapted himself too readily to the wishes of his readers, he did show independence as far as the genteel conventions were concerned. He was prepared to take his stand with Teniers and Hogarth rather than with Raphael. If he avoided shocking his readers by impropriety of language, he did not hesitate to shock them by what many of them called his "low" subjects and "vulgar" characters. "All very well but damned low," said Lockhart of *Pickwick*, and *Oliver Twist* was much lower.[42] Dickens wanted to make the novel more respected but not by avoiding the world of St. Giles. Reviewers urged in vain that he should "paint something higher and better for our example and help."[43]

Dickens went his own way, yet it would also be a mistake to say that he merely moved in the opposite direction towards "realism" (as Blanchard uses the word) and a minute attention to probability. He himself fondly liked to think he had done so. He was most gratified when critics praised the verisimilitude of his novels, and most irritated when they spoke of his fantastic imagination or of some improbabilities. This important problem can be more appropriately discussed at length when we consider the attacks made on his novels by realist critics in the second half of the century. Suffice to say here that although Dickens paid little attention to the convention of the genteel, he was deeply concerned to make his novels satisfy those reviewers who recommended probability.

In *The Reinterpretation of Victorian Literature*, there is a vigorous and useful comment by Bradford Booth: "Dickens spoke *to* and even *for* a new public. In the story of the Victorian novel no fact is so important, and none has been so consistently disregarded. Virtually every feature of the novel of this period can be accounted for in terms of public taste, of which, as yet, no satisfactory study exists."[44] Before making haste to agree with these sentences, I must suggest two or three qualifying clauses: first, that in literature, one can never account for virtually everything. In addition, the term "new public" is too restrictive, especially as the comment is being made about *Pickwick Papers* which was admired by a diversity of readers with a considerable diversity of tastes. Furthermore, even if we confine attention to the "new public," it is apparent that Dickens did not always speak *for* them. One of the mysteries of his reputation is that it was sustained in spite of his biting satire of Victorian puritanism, and that readers who were under the influence of the real-life equivalents of Chadband and Mrs. Jellyby apparently admired the author who made these figures ridiculous.[45] In other respects, Booth's statement serves to sum up what the present enquiry has already suggested. Dickens' novels were certainly deeply affected in language, tone, structure, and story itself by the nature of his relationship with his assorted audience and by their standards of what to expect from a novel. Reciprocally, his popularity depended upon his accord, sometimes conscious and sometimes unconscious, with many of the predominant tastes of his age.

CHAPTER 3

SKYROCKET AND STICK

"The good author is he who contemplates without marked joy or excessive sorrow the adventures of his soul amongst criticisms."—(Joseph Conrad, *A Personal Record*)

I

UPON arriving in London in 1838, George Borrow found that "everybody was in raptures over a certain *Oliver Twist* that had just come out, and the *Memoirs of the Nickleby Family*." Although usually unimpressed by nineteenth-century literature, Borrow readily succumbed to the power of these early Dickens novels and confessed that he was, "like everybody else, delighted with them." A few months later, he reported to a friend in Spain that there had appeared in England "a second Fielding, a young writer, who, in certain novels founded on life in London and the provinces, as displayed in every grade of society, from the lowest to the highest, has evinced such talent, such humour, variety and profound knowledge of character, that he charms his readers, at least those who have the capacity to comprehend him. The true name of this new phenomenon is Charles Dickens."[1]

The response of the future author of *Lavengro* was typical of those readers who were aware of the new apprehension of experience provided by Dickens' novels. Others were impressed as well by his Scott-like productivity and by his variety. The *Athenaeum* noted, somewhat cynically, that "Boz has the town by the ear, and he is not so thorough-bred as we imagine if he lets go his hold in deference to the critics."[2] In five years (1836-1841), five long novels were tumbled onto the market, together with many other incidental publications. Charles Reade once asserted that writers should wait until the age of forty before attempting to write a novel, but he made an exception for Dickens because of the special circumstances of his early life.[3] Dickens' special circumstances seemed inexhaustible at first; the skyrocket of his reputation, sustained by a succession of rapid bursts, seemed to mount with scarcely a wobble until the time of *Martin Chuzzlewit.* Despite that important setback, however, he was established, by the time he was thirty-two, not only as "the true successor to Sir Walter Scott . . . the chief novel-writer of his time"[4] but also as the chief "spirit" of his age. The poet, R. H. Horne, aided by Elizabeth Barrett and other contributors, compiled his *New Spirit of the Age* in 1844. Of the forty figures discussed, Dickens is placed first, and Horne, in a seventy-six page essay, treats him virtually as a classic: "His best productions, such as 'Nicholas Nickleby,' the 'Old Curiosity Shop,' 'Oliver Twist,' and 'Martin Chuzzlewit,' will live as long as our literature endures, and take rank with the work of Cervantes, of Hogarth, and De Foe."* In 1902, Swinburne recognized that he had been living in the age not of Disraeli, Tennyson, Darwin, or Ruskin, but in the age of Dickens. Horne anticipated this apotheosis by many years.

Apotheosis at the age of thirty-two is certainly the general picture, yet it is well to consider the reception of some of these early novels more closely. Their variety is remarkable. Also remarkable is the idiosyncrasy of what might be called Dickens' formula. As an article in *The Times Literary Supplement* points out, most of the two thousand new novels

---

* Horne's discussion of the novels is sometimes erratic. He speaks, for example, of the "subtle delineation of young Martin Chuzzlewit" (I, 43). The faults of Dickens to which he draws attention include the lack of plan, lack of connection between some of the characters, and the general lack of discipline which are, he says, "not to be admired" (I, 29, 72). He is most suggestive in his defense of Dickens against the critics who complain that his creations are only caricatures. For this misconception, Horne argues, the illustrators must bear a large share of the responsibility. Dickens' best characters "have each the roundness of individual reality combined with generalization—most of them representing a class." Dickens' method is to show "how the nature of the individual has *been* developed externally by his whole life in the world. To this effect, he first paints his portrait at full-length," and then, says Horne, works from within; he "*feels in* the man, and the first words that man utters are the key-note of his character" (I, 24-25). Another influential early work in which Dickens was rated as the "greatest name in . . . contemporary literature" was Thomas B. Shaw's *Outlines of English Literature* (1849), pp. 484-490. Shaw devotes scarcely a sentence to Tennyson and Thackeray but treats Dickens, at some length, as a classic.

published in 1950 in Great Britain were based on a familiar formula which has existed unchanged for two hundred years. They typify fiction that is "as simple a narcotic as tobacco; and the need of a scullery maid to dream that she will some day marry the son of a duke is a basic pattern to it that hardly varies, even in an age when scullery maids are dying out and dukes transformed into mere turnstile attendants in their stately homes."[5] Reputable novelists such as Richardson and Charlotte Brontë have made use of this formula, yet Dickens, curiously enough, relies upon it very little. Here is a paradoxical feature of his popularity which seems to have been overlooked. Stevenson rightly noted that the scullery maid kind of readers "long, not to enter into the lives of others, but to behold themselves in changed situations, ardently . . . preconceived."[6] Consider *Pickwick Papers*. What sort of vicarious participation is available to such a reader here? She is forced, instead, to "enter into the lives of others." *A Tale of Two Cities* is closest to providing what the scullery maid asks for, but it is Dickens' least typical novel. In the novels told in the first person (*David Copperfield*, *Bleak House*, *Great Expectations*), there is also some opportunity for identification, yet *Great Expectations* is itself an ironic *exposé* of the Cinderella theme. With developing skill in handling point of view, Dickens' usual method is to provide the reader with a pair of eyes, the hero's, through which to watch his weird pageant. The hero or heroine may wander like Ulysses, but the reader's interest is more apt to be centered upon what is encountered than upon the hero's fortunes. As one late Victorian reader complained: "There is not one character perhaps in Dickens that a practical man could hope to take as an example. He has not created one hero or heroine."[7] The "practical man" and the day-dreaming scullery maid were alike in seeking a quality that is somewhat peripheral in the Dickens novel.

He had, of course, a formula of his own. "I think Dombey very strong—" he wrote to Forster, "with great capacity in its leading idea; plenty of character that is likely to tell; and some rollicking facetiousness, to say nothing of pathos."[8]

When reduced to the basic essentials—to make the reader laugh, shudder, and cry—the naked formula seems even more disconcertingly calculated than in his letter to Forster, but it describes *Macbeth* as well as it describes *Nicholas Nickleby*. To make the reader indignant, and to make him wait—these also Dickens sought, especially in his later novels:

> Timotheus, to his breathing flute,
>   And sounding lyre,
> Could swell the soul to rage, or kindle soft desire.

Mechanically considered, each Dickens novel contains all of the various ingredients, but in some, a particular ingredient predominates. In *Pickwick*, it is laughter; in *Oliver Twist*, it is fear; in *The Old Curiosity Shop*, it is tears. The early shift in emphasis from *Pickwick* to *Oliver Twist* was a significant one, as Dickens himself knew.

II

Readers of *Pickwick* who were expecting another double glass o' the inwariable were surprised by the somber flavor of the novel succeeding it. From the predominantly sunny atmosphere of *Pickwick*, it was startling to enter the dreary world of the dark workhouse and of the slime of Jacob's Island. Graham Greene (a writer ideally suited to discuss *Oliver Twist*) has pointed out that the comedy in Dickens' second novel is of minor consequence.[9] Mr. Bumble and Mrs. Corney, Fagin upon occasion, all provide comic relief, but this time it is relief rather than the center of the stage. In spite of the continued popularity of *Pickwick* and the demands by reviewers that he return to the Pickwickian vein, Dickens believed that the modification he had made was an essential one. During the writing of *Copperfield* in 1849, he remarked: "The world would not take another Pickwick from me now, but we can be cheerful and merry, I hope, notwithstanding, and with a little more purpose in us."[10]

In *Oliver Twist*, "a little more purpose" was noticeable in the unmasking of workhouse neglect and of police-magistrate Fang. Thomas Hood was pleased that Boz was moving "*along*

with the great human currents, and not against them . . .
recognizing good in low places, and evil in high ones."[11] Lord
Holland, who was reported to have spoken of *Pickwick* with
"discriminating discernment," was much more impressed by
Oliver Twist and mentioned it "almost with tears."[12] Elizabeth
Barrett was another reader who seems to have been pleased.
She became "quite cross" at her brothers who preferred
Charles Lever's novels to Dickens', and it is obvious that it
was the earnestness of his post-Pickwickian writing that attracted her. Lever, she said, made her "head ache as if I had
been sitting in the next room to an orgy . . . of gentlemen
topers, with their low gentility and 'hip hip hurrahs,' and
wine out of wine-coolers."[13] This was to be the voice of the
future. Unlike Dickens, Lever refused to heed it, and before
many years he was bitterly cursing the reading public. In
this respect, *Oliver Twist* can be called the first Victorian
novel.

Less unanimously admired was Dickens' demonstration
that he was a master of suspense and violent action. Once
again innocence was shown confronting realities, but this
time the realities were sensationally spine-chilling. Having
drawn upon one type of popular fiction in creating *Pickwick*,
the young writer had turned now to another: the Newgate
novel. Few readers today can yawn their way through Ainsworth's *Jack Sheppard* (1839) and *Rookwood* (1833),[14]
or Lytton's *Paul Clifford* (1830) and *Eugene Aram* (1832),
yet a knowledge of these works is helpful in understanding
the fortunes of *Oliver Twist*. Dickens liked to believe that
rather than imitating the Newgate novel he was showing up
its faults by presenting his criminals in no tender light, but
he failed to convince all of his readers. Thackeray protested,
with some cause, that Nancy is as sentimentally presented as
one of Lytton's criminal heroes,[15] a criticism that stung
Dickens into an angry reply in his Preface. And with Sikes,
although the sentiment is absent, Dickens unconsciously identified himself so intensely that the criminal sometimes seems
a kind of hero at odds with social convention.[16] In any event,
however different in intention, *Oliver Twist* was a story of

criminal violence and terror which could be damned by type, and was so damned. To Lord Melbourne, it was "just like the Beggar's Opera," the ultimate progenitor of Newgate fiction, and he added: "I don't like that low, debasing style. . . . I shouldn't think it would tend to raise morals."* Thackeray's biting parody of Newgate novels in *Catherine* (1840) likewise lumped together *Oliver Twist* with the others, for although the young Thackeray professed great respect for Dickens' humor and pathos, he disapproved of his sensationalism. In introducing his murder scene, Thackeray apologizes to the "discerning reader" who is "sick of the hideous scenes of brutal bloodshed which have of late come forth from the pens of certain eminent wits," and he explains, with contempt, that his scene is "for the public, which hath no such taste" and which "must have blood!"[17]

To show that to be moved by scenes of violence is a sign of the reader's bad taste has always been the approved way of attacking the literature of sensation, and it was often used against Dickens. In his authoritative study of sensation fiction, W. C. Phillips demonstrates that Dickens (together with his disciples, Collins and Reade) employed sensationalism to break through the thick crust of smug Victorian respectability,[18] but they achieved their end at the cost of alienating the kind of reader who cannot bear to be ruffled by violent emotions. Most literature can be classified as sensational or soporific, and in this sense, *Othello* and *The Turn of the Screw* differ in quality, but not in kind, from *Jack Sheppard* and *The Mysteries of Udolpho*. In much Victorian criticism, however, the epithet *sensational* was to be used not as a form of classification but as a value judgment.[19] Henry Fox found

* Melbourne's blunt remark may possibly have been reported to Dickens, for two paragraphs of the Preface to *Oliver Twist* are devoted to differentiating that novel from *The Beggar's Opera*. Another blunt remark by Melbourne was voiced in his stentorian tones after witnessing Dickens' production of *Every Man in his Humour* in 1845: "I knew this play would be dull, but that it would be so damnably dull as this I did not suppose!" See *The Greville Diary*, ed. P. W. Wilson (1927), I, 567. There is evidence to indicate that Melbourne's letters to Mrs. Norton, which were made public during a law suit in 1836, served as Dickens' model for the "evidence" presented by Serjeant Buzfuz against Mr. Pickwick. Whether the parallels contributed to Lord Melbourne's bluntness I do not know. See the *Cornhill Magazine*, n.s., XII (1889), 74-75.

Oliver Twist to be "painful and revolting." Like others with a distaste for the sensational, he had an equal distaste for what Tony Lumpkin's followers called the "low." "Oh damn anything that's low," as one of them exclaims. "I cannot bear it!" Fox affirmed that he agreed completely with Lady Carlisle who had said of *Oliver Twist*: "I know there are such unfortunate beings as pick-pockets and street walkers . . . but I own I do not much wish to hear what they say to one another." The conclusion of Fox's attack is especially interesting: "I know that the works are just now in such favour and popularity that few there are who venture to express an unfavourable opinion of them, and for the moment I am in a very small minority: but I suspect, when the novelty and the fashion of admiring them has worn off, they will sink to their proper level."[20]

For 1839, this minority report seems ominously prophetic, but it also indicates how royally Dickens' work was being greeted by the majority of readers. The *Quarterly* affirmed that this majority for *Oliver Twist* included both the ten-pounders and the ten-thousand-a-year men.[21] The latter, tired of "silly fashionable novels" set in Mayfair, welcomed the sensationalism of "Saffron Hill" as a change, because "silver forks had been paraded so continually that grim old Fagin, with his rusty toasting-fork and frying-pan, was considered as a relief."[22] Crabb Robinson, for example, was not so fastidious as to be upset by the sensationalism of *Oliver Twist*. He pronounced it to be a work "of pure genius" and "quite original":

> An excellent but not faultless book. Its merit lies in the truth of the picture of the condition and sufferings of the poor; its greatest fault that Oliver Twist has no character. . . . The unfortunate girl, Nancy, and her murderer Sikes are most admirably wrought—so is Bumble the Beadle; but Monks . . . is a failure. The Jew is also powerfully conceived, and the conclusion is wrought up with admirable power.[23]

Robinson disapproved of the serial publication of Dickens'

novels because he felt that it encouraged the writing of fragmentary sketches, but he also had a more personal reason that is very revealing. Sensation fiction, in serial form, was simply too exciting for him. Halfway through the numbers of *Barnaby Rudge*, he vowed not to read any more until the book was published in full: "I will not expose myself to further anxieties."[24] This vow was repeated in his diary on other occasions, but he seems to have been unable to keep it.

A similar kind of excitement is apparent in the most interesting of the reviews of *Oliver Twist*, which was written by Richard Ford for the *Quarterly*. Ford points out the many shortcomings of the book, especially its unfair satire of the Poor Law, its ridiculous plot tangles, its "unendurable" genteel females, its improbable hero, its slang, and its use of Newgate "low" characters.[25] In spite of this formidable indictment, he cannot conceal that he was deeply moved by the story of Sikes and Nancy, and that he found the fast-paced narrative of the pursuit of Sikes an exciting experience—even while disapproving of it! This mixed response to *Oliver Twist* is characteristic of other reviews as well. It is evident that of the elements constituting the Dickensian formula, his appeal to the sense of fear (however impressive as an indication of versatility) was less universally satisfying to his early readers than his humor and pathos. John Forster reports somewhat ambiguously that the novel "found a circle of admirers, not so wide in its range as those of others of his books, but of a character and mark that made their honest liking for it, and steady advocacy of it, important to his fame."[26] This is not to suggest that the book was a failure but that the extraordinary relationship between Dickens and his public was a more tempestuous affair than is always recognized. *Nicholas Nickleby*, with its more Pickwickian vein, helped to smooth out some of the differences, and then, after the brief setback of the opening numbers of *Master Humphrey's Clock*, came the most overwhelmingly triumphant reception of *The Old Curiosity Shop* (1840), a novel in which pathos predominates. No such celebrity greeted *Barnaby Rudge* (1841), but the numbers sold moderately well. Moreover, Dickens himself had little love for *Barnaby*, the unwanted child among his early novels, and its modest reception was therefore not especially crucial to him. The reception of *Martin Chuzzlewit* (1843-1844) was a different matter. Here, for the first time since the early numbers of *Pickwick*, Dickens encountered serious resistance from the novel-reading public and experienced his first real taste of failure. In 1837, Abraham Hayward had made a startling prediction: "Mr. Dickens writes too often and too fast; on the principle, we presume, of making hay whilst the sun shines. . . . If he persists much longer in this course, it requires no gift of prophecy to foretell his fate—he has risen like a rocket, and he will come down like the stick."[27] Such waspishness was annoying to Dickens but not seriously disturbing until *Martin Chuzzlewit* seemed to bear out the prediction. It was an important moment in his development, and, at some slight expense to chronology, it deserves to be discussed here before considering the reception of *The Old Curiosity Shop*, which can be reserved for the next chapter.

III

Most obvious proof for the failure of *Martin Chuzzlewit* was provided by the sales. *Nicholas Nickleby* had begun with a sale of almost 50,000 copies; *The Old Curiosity Shop* reached 100,000; *Barnaby Rudge* declined from 70,000 to 30,000. But *Chuzzlewit* began with only 20,000 and never rose beyond 23,000.[28] Forster notes that this novel eventually gained proper recognition when it appeared in book form,[29] a recognition substantiating Dickens' own conviction that it was one of his greatest works, but as a serial its failure appalled and alarmed its author. On June 28, 1843, after an interview with his anxious publishers, he admitted to Forster that he had been "rubbed in the tenderest part of my eyelids with bay-salt." Not only was his financial security threatened, but also his sense of artistic security. He began to wonder whether his gift of magic had been stolen from him.

In addition to the reports of poor sales, there was evidence of failure from other quarters. Even his faithful mentor, Lord

Jeffrey, considered most of the book to be in the wrong vein and told the author his opinion. So did another one of his faithful readers, Miss Burdett-Coutts, to whom the book was to be dedicated.[30] Jeffrey's reaction coincides with Crabb Robinson's who found it an "unpleasant" book, one that he never wanted to open again "so generally disgusting are the characters and incidents of the tale." Macready noted glumly in his diary after reading the fourth number: "It does not improve." Two months later, he added: "It will not do Dickens good, and I grieve over it."*

Further evidence of failure can be found in the cool response of the reviews. In several important periodicals, *Chuzzlewit* was greeted by a strange silence. Perhaps the editors felt that the extensive reviewing of *American Notes* had exhausted what might be said about a novel which, in part, covers the same ground. Of the few English reviews which appeared (I have located seven), most were adversely critical. *Ainsworth's Magazine* was unqualifiedly enthusiastic and praised the new "consistency of character" which Dickens had achieved, and the *Dublin University Magazine* considered it his most "masterly" book.† The other reviews were uniformly critical of the "bad temper and prejudice" of the American scenes,[31] the lack of "artistic craft" in the management of plot, and the lack of idealism and effective "good" characters.[32] The *North British Review* even found the pictures of Mr.

* *Henry Crabb Robinson on Books and Their Writers*, II, 646; *The Diaries of William Charles Macready* (1912), II, 206, 215. —In 1855, one reviewer made a penetrating suggestion on this point. He observed that by avoiding the "picturesque situations" of other novelists (that is, sexual situations), and by concentrating upon a world "where respectability and the strong grasp of appearances keep grosser sins away," Dickens had discovered a society in which "sometimes the meaner vices grow and flourish." *Blackwood's*, LXXVII (1855), 452.

† *Ainsworth's Magazine*, V (1844), 85; *Dublin University Magazine*, XXIII (1844), 520. For drawing my attention to the latter review and for other information in this section, I am indebted to Mr. Lawrence J. Hynes. —Others who shared Ainsworth's enthusiasm included Sydney Smith, who assured Dickens that even the American parts were "excellent," and Albany Fonblanque, the journalist, who was sustained through an illness by his enjoyment of Todgers's. See Lady Holland, *A Memoir of the Reverend Sydney Smith* (1855), II, 482-490, and E. B. Fonblanque, *The Life and Labours of Albany Fonblanque* (1874), p. 58.

Mould "uncalled for" and "an unfeeling attack on a respectable class of tradesmen."[33]

The criticism which irritated Dickens most was that the book's failure could be attributed to his having written too fast and carelessly. At Broadstairs in 1843, the half-senile old banker-poet, Samuel Rogers, added his quota of bay-salt by tactlessly observing to the author of *Martin Chuzzlewit*: "Everybody writes too fast." "It's the great pleasure of his life to think so," was Dickens' huffy comment afterwards.[33a] Charles Lever (himself one of the most slipshod of novelists) remarked to a correspondent in a somewhat buttery-mouthed letter: "I am emboldened to hope that I am improving as a writer. One thing I can answer for—no popularity I ever had . . . will make me trifle with the public by fast writing and careless composition. Dickens's last book [*Martin Chuzzlewit*] has set the gravestone on his fame, and the warning shall not be thrown away."[34] The funeral service was, we know, premature, but Lever's impression, current in some literary circles, seemed to confirm Hayward's prediction of 1837. The young novelist had risen like the skyrocket; now, apparently, he was coming down like the stick.

What were the reasons for the failure? Forster suggests that the change from weekly to monthly publication might be the cause, but most critics simply throw up their hands and exclaim that public caprice was responsible. "And who shall explain these caprices of the public?" asked Gissing.[35] His question was purely rhetorical, but the attempt to answer it is nevertheless worth making.

Only one scholar seems to have made the attempt. This is Miss Ada B. Nisbet whose excellent essay, "The Mystery of *Martin Chuzzlewit*," was published in 1950. Her premise is that there existed a fairly regular pattern of public reaction to Dickens' serial publications. "One of the obvious phenomena of public taste is that readers look for repeat performances and when disappointed tend to avoid repeat disappointments. The popularity of a writer's successive works, therefore, depends more upon the preceding publication than upon each work itself. This is especially true of serial publications."

Miss Nisbet suggests that readers "remembering their disappointment" with *Barnaby Rudge* did not hurry to buy copies of *Chuzzlewit*. Even more important, she suggests, was the damage done to Dickens' reputation by *American Notes* (1842), the first of his books to provoke a torrent of abuse against him. This abuse had a profound effect upon the sale, not of *American Notes*, it seems, but of the work which followed it.[36]

There is much to be said for the thesis that *American Notes* was Dickens' "Waterloo," or better, as Miss Nisbet says, his "Dunkirk." It was reviewed extensively on both sides of the Atlantic,[37] and although there is some evidence for Dickens' wistful assertion that the book had won "golden opinions from all sorts of men,"* its reception in England was predominantly hostile. *Blackwood's*, the *Quarterly*, *Fraser's*, and the *Edinburgh* pounced upon the book and gave the author a kind of drubbing to which he had never before been exposed. American readers like to think that the punishment was fit retribution for Dickens' slanderous account of American culture, or lack of it, but a study of the English reviews shows that hostility was provoked not entirely by Dickens' attack on America (although the sentiments of sportsmanship did play a part). It was provoked because Dickens had ventured to talk authoritatively about something of which he was plainly ignorant. Without the shield of fiction for protection, his superficial tourist's picture of American life was fair game for English reviewers. *Pictures from Italy*, another colorful sample of the journalist abroad, was similarly pounced upon by *The Times* (June 1, 1846), and its absurdities were savagely exposed. In reviewing *American Notes* for the *Edinburgh*, James Spedding, who had himself visited America, was easily able to show the limitations of Dickens' perspective.[38] His tone of cool contempt goaded Dickens into

---

* See Nonesuch, I, 497. The "golden opinions" might refer to Thomas Hood's review in *The New Monthly Magazine* (1842), pp. 396-406 which was enthusiastic because Dickens' "heart was in the right place." Two other reviews were at least beige colored, if not golden: the *Westminster*, XXXIX (1843), 146-160; and the *Athenaeum* (October 22, 1842), pp. 899-902, (October 29, 1842), pp. 927-929.

replying in a letter to the editor.[39] Even more contemptuous were the reviews in *Blackwood's* and *Fraser's*. The former was written by the novelist, Samuel Warren, who described himself modestly as an "honourable yet fearless rival" of Dickens.* Under the cloak of anonymity, he could be fearless enough and could agree with Croker's comment that the book was "an entire failure" and with Croker's prediction that for such writers as Dickens "an ephemeral popularity will be followed by early oblivion."[40]

It is obvious that Dickens' experiment in writing a book of travels did damage to his reputation, and Miss Nisbet's contention that this damage explains the failure of *Chuzzlewit* is especially useful in showing why the book had such a poor sale from the very outset. For the continued failure of *Chuzzlewit*, as a serial, other explanations (besides caprice) can be offered. The ineffective opening chapter might account for much. A reviewer rightly described it as "one of the very worst things Mr. Dickens has ever written."[41] Dickens, incidentally, seems to have profited from this mistake. The opening chapters of his later novels are usually superb. As a Trollope character said maliciously of the opening number of *The Almshouse*: "It's very well done, as you'll see: his first numbers always are."[42]

After the opening chapter, there was further cause for readers to be disappointed because the book neglected to provide what *The Old Curiosity Shop* had provided so abundantly. There was no little Nell. Ainsworth, in praising *Chuzzlewit*, inadvertently suggested one of the main reasons for its failure: "In brilliant delineation of life . . . in humour, in terror, and, *though not in the same degree*, in pity . . . this story bears the marks of the old masterly hand."[43] Dickens'

---

* See Mrs. Oliphant, *William Blackwood and his Sons* (1897), II, 231. The secret of Warren's authorship of the *Blackwood's* review (LII, 1842, 783-801) was learned by Dickens. See Ada B. Nisbet, "New Light on the Dickens-Poe Relationship," *Nineteenth-Century Fiction*, V (1951), 295-296. Warren's animus against Dickens reappeared in 1846 when he published a heavy-handed satire entitled "Advice to an Intending Serialist," in *Blackwood's*, LX (1846), 590-605. In ironic vein, he advised young novelists: "Do not fear to repeat yourself over and over again . . . and to harp upon the same string of pathos so long as it will vibrate pleasantly to the public ear. What we want, after all, is sale."

modification of what I called earlier his "formula" was more than disappointing to many of his readers. It was shocking. For not only had he reduced his emphasis upon sentimental pictures of innocent goodness, he had also shifted his satire away from remote institutions such as the Yorkshire schools and directed it upon the Victorian sanctuary: the home and family. The scenes of Mr. Pecksniff in the bosom of his family, sighing his beatific blessings upon home sweet home, are amiable in tone by comparison with later satirical pictures of Mr. Podsnap's dinner table. Yet, as Forster recognized, the motto proposed for the title page had to be rejected only because it was too apt: "Your homes the scene, yourselves the actors, here!"[44] Crabb Robinson was one of the readers who was shocked by the "predominant meanness" of the characters. Despite a fondness for Ruth Pinch, he reached the remarkable conclusion that in *Martin Chuzzlewit* Dickens "makes goodness contemptible."[45] In earlier novels, Robinson had enjoyed Dickens' tone, which he accurately described as a "combination of quiet imperturbable ease and good humour with utter heartlessness."[46] In *Chuzzlewit*, however, the heartlessness seemed to him oppressive.

On behalf of Robinson's impression there is something to be said. Biographers have noted the Quilpish streak in Dickens' own character, and in this novel he seems to be impishly inverting the world of *The Old Curiosity Shop* by presenting as his central character a man whose mouth is full of pious sentiments, but whose unspoken code is the same as Jonas Chuzzlewit's: "Do other men, for they would do you." The most disconcerting aspect of his impish inversion is (as one reviewer had the perception to note) that when Dickens himself makes sentimental authorial comments about Tom Pinch or Mary Graham, the reader hears the voice of Pecksniff.[47] The shocked disappointment experienced by such readers was effectively summarized by the *Westminster Review*: "We can scarcely believe that we are reading the work of a writer once remarkable for a keen perception of the poetry of human life; one who has shown us God's image reflected back from the haunts of poverty, and to whom belongs the rare merit of such creations as Little Nell."[48]

IV

So far we have been concerned primarily with the effect of *Martin Chuzzlewit* upon its first readers and the reasons for its failure. It is also interesting to consider how its reception affected Dickens himself. The most striking effect, as indicated earlier, was that the failure damaged the author's sense of artistic security as well as his sense of financial security. Between the opening number of *Chuzzlewit* and the opening number of his next novel stretched a remarkable gap of three and three-quarter years.* During the interval, he even considered abandoning serial publication altogether, and he toyed with a plan to bring out his next novel "all at once" in Paris.[49] It is also significant that as he began to write *Dombey and Son* Dickens experienced, for the first time, a real loss of nerve. His letters of 1846 speak not merely of the painful toil of composition, but of fear and worry about his "fading popularity," and of his "dread for the Dombey."[50] Self-confidence had been somewhat restored by the popular acclaim (if not the profits) of the Christmas books, but it was not until he learned of *Dombey's* opening number having sold 32,000 copies that the wound opened by the reception of *Chuzzlewit* began to heal over. For the rest of his life, although sometimes moody and depressed by feeling that he had exhausted his resources, Dickens never again was tormented with a sense of having lost contact with a large reading public. After the success of *Dombey*, his financial anxieties also came to an end.[51]

The *Chuzzlewit-Dombey* episode is an especially revealing example of Dickens' relationship with his public. Two aspects of it require discussion. The first (to be examined in the next chapter) is the effect of *Chuzzlewit's* failure upon the

---

* Writing to Forster in November 1843, he explained: "I am afraid of putting myself before the town as writing tooth and nail for bread, headlong, after the close of a book taking so much out of one as Chuzzlewit." See Nonesuch, I, 544.

kind of novel Dickens tried to write in *Dombey*. The second is the problem of his general attitude towards reviews.

Dickens' relationship to reviews seems never to have been adequately examined. His biographers have accepted without question his oft-repeated assertion that after 1838 he never read reviews of his books. A hoary unanimity among biographers seems to be so complete here that one hesitates to question it, especially because Dickens himself spoke so strongly on this point. In a letter of 1843, he consoled another writer by remarking: "When I first began to write, too, I suffered intensely, from reading reviews, and I made a solemn compact with myself, that I would only know them, for the future, from such general report as might reach my ears. For five years I have never broken this rule once, I am unquestionably the happier for it,—and certainly lose no wisdom."[52] Yet it does seem odd that an author who was so obviously concerned with the reception of his books by readers would entirely overlook those readers who happened to put their opinions into print.

Moreover, if Dickens did try to ignore reviews it was not because he considered them to be powerless or unimportant (at least until his later years). To what extent reviewers are responsible for the success or failure of a book was to the Victorians, as to us, a lively question. Bulwer-Lytton boasted in 1840 that a novelist could make his way in the teeth of opposition from "the dispensers of reputation."[53] Charles Lever noted, on the contrary, that the " 'Press-gang' take care that no man shall have success independent of them." The sale of *Henry Esmond*, according to Thackeray, had been "absolutely stopped by a Times article,"[54] (only 2500 copies were printed in 1852). Another Victorian novelist, the voluminous G. P. R. James, was even more emphatic in one of his letters:

> I will not talk to you the usual cant about not caring what reviewers say of you. It is all very fine but all very false; and I despise the man . . . who pretends not to feel what actually takes money out or puts money into his pocket, or who is stupid enough to believe that re-

views have not . . . that effect. They *do* work harm or good to every book, and harm or good to every author's reputation.[55]

Although Dickens might talk such "cant" himself, he found from experience that Lever and Thackeray and James were closer to the facts of the situation than was Lytton. His own explanation of the failure of *Chuzzlewit* was that what the reviewers had said about his work (presumably *American Notes* as well as *Chuzzlewit*) was responsible:

I think *Chuzzlewit* in a hundred points immeasurably the best of my stories. . . . If I have health, I could sustain my place in the minds of thinking men, though fifty writers started up tomorrow. But how many readers do *not* think! How many take it upon trust from knaves and idiots, that one writes too fast, or runs a thing to death! How coldly did this very book go on for months, until it forced itself up in people's opinion, without forcing itself up in sale.[56]

Dickens' attempt to ignore the reviews seems, then, to have been caused not by contempt for their power but by dislike of the pain they inflicted. Trollope acquired the erroneous notion that Dickens had the hide of an elephant and that reviews never wounded him.[57] His letters give a different picture. Although he did not have Tennyson's almost hysterical sensitivity and could occasionally make jokes about *The Times'* attacks upon his Christmas books, Dickens was easily upset by unkind criticism. As Hesketh Pearson suggests, he was a vain rather than a conceited writer and hence one for whom hostile criticism was especially threatening.[58] His intense dislike of literary parody is notable. When Albert Smith was elected to the Garrick Club, Dickens resigned. He did so because Smith had published two parodies of *Dombey and Son* in his magazine, *The Man in the Moon*. One of the parodies pictures the funeral of Paul Dombey at which a Requiem to Paul is sung by a chorus of Circulating Library Keepers:

Thou art gone from our counter
Thou art lost to our pocket,
Thou hast fallen, brief mounter,
Like stick from a rocket.*

The recurrence of the figurative skyrocket and stick may have added to Dickens' irritation.

Whatever Dickens' motives, his attempt to ignore reviews does not seem to have been carried out to the letter. A number of reviews, often highly critical, fell into his hands from 1838 to 1870. An appendix lists as many of these as I have been able to locate, and it is likely that he read more. In most instances, he read the review himself; in others, he may have learned its contents at second hand. In 1842, for example, he speaks in a letter of the attacks made upon *American Notes* by *Blackwood's* and by *Fraser's*, and it is possible that instead of reading them, he had received their gist in a "general report" from Forster or some other lieutenant, especially if the reviews were attacks. In 1857, he reminded Forster of his "twenty years" resolution never to read "any attack upon myself."[59] It should be noted that he speaks of *attacks* rather than of reviews in general.

The most telling indication of Dickens' awareness of reviews is to be found in his prefaces. Almost unfailingly, each preface consists of a rebuttal of points made against the particular novel by its reviewers: the exaggerated picture of Cheerybles, for example, or the spontaneous combustion of Krook. As bridge players say, Dickens' method was to lead to the weak suits, and he always seemed to know which they were.

It has been too easily assumed, then, that after 1838 Dickens' novels were produced in a reviewless vacuum. A parallel assumption about George Eliot's novels has also been shown to be erroneous.[60] Both novelists, even after resolving to avoid reviews, were yet aware of the critical reception of

* "Inquest on the Late Master Paul Dombey," *The Man in the Moon*, I (1847), 159. See also vol. III (1848), 59-67. For Dickens' comments on Thackeray's parodies, see Nonesuch, II, 29. In *Nicholas Nickleby* (ch. XXVIII), Dickens himself resorted to parody of the Silver Fork Novels, but it is a mild one.

their books as well as of their sales. What Dickens abandoned, after 1838, was the constant pulse-taking of the literary novice. In 1836, for example, he had sought out reviews of *The Village Coquettes* in the *Examiner*, the *Sunday Times*, the *Dispatch*, and the *Satirist*.[61]

Although such an ardent pursuit of clippings was abandoned in the 1840's, much criticism still continued to filter through to him. *The Times* (with a daily circulation approaching 40,000) was difficult to avoid, and the kind of attention his books received from that quarter was, at this period, not reassuring. After having loftily ignored his successful early novels, *The Times* reviewers noted that *Chuzzlewit* represented a decline because of its "crude, exaggerated, and unsettled visions."[62] Afterwards, their heavy artillery was trained on such targets as *The Cricket on the Hearth*, *Pictures from Italy*, and *The Battle of Life*. Later readers would agree that these three books (together with *A Child's History of England*) are the worst ever written by Dickens, but *The Times* did not mince words. Such phrases as "intrinsically puerile and stupid," "a twaddling manifestation of silliness," and "simply ridiculous" were combined with refrains that must have been maddening to Dickens: "Mr. Dickens repeats himself again and again"; he is "more eager to reap the fruits of a profitable and unheard-of popularity than to extend the horizon of his knowledge."[63] Solemnly posing as the guardian of public taste, *The Times* reviewer concluded one disclosure of Dickens' theatrical language with a thunderous question: "Shades of Fielding and Scott! is it for such jargon as this we have given your throne to one who cannot estimate his eminence?"[64] After reading some of this abuse himself, which he described as "another touch of a blunt razor on B.'s nervous system," Dickens concealed his discomfort under a cloak of humor. "Inimitable very mouldy and dull," he wrote. "Hardly able to work. Dreamed of *Timeses* all night. Disposed to go to New Zealand and to start a magazine."*

* Nonesuch, II, 3. One wonders whether financial profits were responsible for Dickens' lightness of tone here. Wilkie Collins heard that Dickens had made 4,000 guineas for *The Battle of Life*, a book "which everybody abused, and which, nevertheless, everybody read." See Kenneth Robinson, *Wilkie*

In the perspective of later years, Dickens sometimes felt that he had fared well at the hands of his critics. In conversation with Paul Féval he remarked: "Balzac and many other authors are marked as if criticism had upon them the effect of an attack of smallpox. They become gloomy and dispirited like jaded horses. They are too egotistical; the prickings of the flies of journalism make them nervous and ill-natured. For myself I have been spoilt in a contrary sense."[65] Perhaps when the overall picture of Dickens' reception is considered, there is much truth in his modest remark, but there were periods of his life during which he exhibited the same symptoms as those he noted in such jaded horses as Balzac. In the 1850's, the prickings of the flies of journalism were to be especially vicious, but it was during the period between *American Notes* and *Dombey* that he was most allergic to such attacks. The epoch-making successes of *Pickwick*, *Oliver Twist*, *Nickleby*, and *The Old Curiosity Shop* were followed by a period of comparative coolness, indifference, and disfavor, which left their mark upon Dickens and affected the direction he was to follow in *Dombey and Son*. After the slashing review of *The Battle of Life* had appeared in *The Times*, Francis Jeffrey wrote consolingly to the victim: "The general voice, I fancy, persists in refusing it a place among your best pieces. This Dombey, however, will set all right, and make even the envious and jealous ashamed of saying anything against you."[66]

Collins (New York, 1952), p. 50. Edward Fitzgerald was such a reader. Prepared, as a rule, to revel in anything by Dickens except his "melodrama," Fitzgerald warned Thackeray (January 1847) that *The Battle of Life* was a "wretched affair," but he did buy a copy. This Christmas book sold 23,000 copies in twenty-four hours when it appeared in 1845. By contrast, only 3,000 copies were printed of Thackeray's Christmas book for 1850, *The Kickleburys on the Rhine*. See *The Letters of Thackeray*, ed. Gordon Ray, II, 867. *The Cricket on the Hearth* also sold extremely well, better than *A Christmas Carol* or *The Chimes*. See *The Heart of Charles Dickens*, ed. Edgar Johnson, (New York, 1952), p. 75n.

CHAPTER 4

LITTLE NELL:
THE LIMITS OF EXPLANATORY
CRITICISM

I

ACCORDING to Oscar Wilde, one must have a heart of stone to read the death of Little Nell without laughing.[1] Wilde's quip was meant to be shocking as well as amusing, but for most readers of a later generation, the shock has been deadened. In the midst of the marked revival of critical interest aroused by Dickens' writings, well disposed readers may feel that it is a necessary kindness to assume that Nell, like Wordsworth's Lucy, is in her grave and ought not to be disturbed from there. Nell is nevertheless worthy of resurrection not because a fresh appreciation is required, but because of the problems which are suggested by her chequered relationship with the reading public from 1840 to the present. It is notable that we can read with pleasure what Dickens' contemporaries said of *David Copperfield*, but what they said of Little Nell fills us with astonishment or even a kind of embarrassment.

In *The Old Curiosity Shop* (which shared with *Pickwick* the most triumphant reception of any of his works), Dickens was once more modifying the eighteenth-century tradition from which his novels stem, but more radically this time. He was aware that with the exception of Goldsmith, and of Sterne's indulgent lachrymosity, his favorite novelists appealed only rarely to the reader's sense of pity. *Peregrine Pickle* and *Roderick Random* were, he said, "extraordinarily good in their way, which is a way without tenderness."[2] *Robinson Crusoe*, "a book I read very much," seemed "curious" as "the only instance of an universally popular book that could make no one laugh and could make no one cry. . . . I will venture to say that there is not in literature a more surprising instance of an utter want of tenderness and sentiment, than the death of Friday. It is as heartless as Gil Blas."[3]

This letter, written in 1856, shows an awareness of the shift of sensibility which had left a gap between his own age and that of Defoe. His awareness did not, however, foresee the possibility of a reversal in which there would develop a comparable gap between parts of his own work and the tastes of later readers. To judge from the response of his contemporaries, Dickens would have found it incredible to imagine a future decline of interest in Little Nell. As one of his fellow-novelists noted, she became Dickens' trademark.[4] A few readers did protest that the pathos was overdone, including his good friend Daniel Maclise who admitted: "I'm never up to his young girls—he is so very fond of the age of 'Nell,' when they are most insipid."[5] Such complaints were drowned out by the roar of applause with which the final scenes of *The Old Curiosity Shop* were greeted all over the English-speaking world. In one of his speeches in America, Dickens alluded with a flourish to letters he had received "from the dwellers in log-houses among the morasses, and swamps, and densest forests, and deepest solitudes of the Far West."[6] From a correspondent less attached to the backwoods, Washington Irving, he received a long letter praising the "exquisite pathos" and "moral sublimity" of the story of Nell.[7] That the author of the sentimental stories in *The Sketch Book* would respond to Nell is not unexpected. More surprising is the list of critical readers in England who were equally responsive. Edward Fitzgerald was so moved that he copied out all the parts of the novel in which Nell appears so that he would have "a kind of Nelly-ad or Homeric narration."[8] More violent was Daniel O'Connell who was so upset by the death scene that he burst into tears and threw the book out the window.* Sydney Smith,[9] Thomas Hood,[10] Landor, Carlyle, and Jeffrey were likewise overwhelmed. Landor, one of the most

---

* See J. A. Hammerton, *The Dickens Companion* (New York, 1910), p. 298. —Edgar Allan Poe also felt that although Nell was a great creation, her death was "excessively painful" to the reader and should have been avoided. *Graham's Magazine*, XVIII (1841), 250.

learned of critics, remarked emphatically that Dickens had now shown that he was "with Shakespeare the greatest of English writers, though indeed his women are superior to Shakespeare's. No one of our poets comes near him."[11] Jeffrey followed up the comparison to Shakespeare by declaring that there had been "nothing so good as Nell since Cordelia."[12] The death scene itself affected him so powerfully that a visitor, who discovered the grief-stricken critic with his head on the table and eyes filled with tears, concluded that Jeffrey was mourning the death of some intimate friend or relative.[13] In a sense he was. Forty years before reading *The Old Curiosity Shop*, he had been deeply affected by the loss of an infant son, and like the praise of the nameless readers who wrote to thank Dickens, Jeffrey's can be partially attributed to his personal identification with the situation.* Dickens defined his aim as an attempt to "do something which might be read by people about whom Death had been, with a softened feeling, and with consolation."[14] Jeffrey's tears were a measure of how successful the young author had been, and the sale, which reached 100,000 copies, was also a gratifying indication of success.[15]

I I

Although difficult to estimate, the effect of Nell's triumphant reception upon Dickens' own development as a novelist must have been profound. A capacity to rouse the reader's sense of tender compassion, tested earlier in *Oliver Twist* and in *Nickleby*, was here given full demonstration. Jeffrey, who addressed himself to Dickens as "your *Critic Laureate*,"[16] was thereafter at his elbow constantly requesting another Nell. Sometimes Dickens grew tired of this flood of advice,[17] but on the whole he was flattered that the dean of English critics had become deeply interested in the direction his novels should take. By the time of his discovery of Dickens, Jeffrey had of course been retired from his critical role for

---

* "His underlying tenderness of character made the memory of this loss ever afterwards a cause of nervous anxiety about children's complaints in the households of his friends." Henry Morley, *English Literature in the Reign of Victoria* (New York, 1882), p. 138.

many years, but his prestige was still very high.* His preferences as a reader of Dickens were of an unexpected kind. A
product of the hard-headed school of common sense, referred
to by Leslie Stephen as the despiser of sentimentalism,[18] Jeffrey had mellowed into a representative early Victorian reader
of the school of feeling. By 1840, what he admired was sentiment; for the other ingredients in Dickens' formula, he had
little real interest. He consistently preferred the "soft and
tender characters, to the humorous and grotesque,"[19] Nell,
Paul Dombey, Agnes Wickfield, and Tom Pinch being among
his favorites. "Little Tiny Tim," he wrote, is "almost as
sweet and as touching as Nelly."

> And is not this better than caricaturing American knav-
> eries, or lavishing your great gifts of fancy and observa-
> tion on Pecksniffs, Dodgers, Bailleys, and Moulds. Nor
> is this a mere crotchet of mine, for nine-tenths of your
> readers, I am convinced, are of the same opinion; and
> accordingly, I prophesy that you will sell three times
> as many of this moral and pathetic Carol as of your
> grotesque and fantastical Chuzzlewits.[20]

What must have made this reiterated advice impressive to
Dickens was that both the reviews and the sale of his books
seemed to confirm what the old man told him: many of his
readers were not yet ready for the Gothic fantasy and domestic
satire of *Chuzzlewit*. In his next novel he seems to have
sought to recapture such readers by following Jeffrey's advice. The opening number of *Dombey* contains a death scene,
and the fifth number was virtually what the judge had
ordered.† The death of Paul, which overwhelmed even

* See Lewis Gates, *Three Studies in Literature* (New York, 1899).
Lord Cockburn referred to Jeffrey in 1852 as "the greatest of British critics."
The subsequent decline of his status is traced in James A. Greig's *Francis
Jeffrey* (Edinburgh, 1948). Greig, unfortunately, does not discuss Jeffrey's
opinion of Dickens.

† On January 31, 1847, Jeffrey wrote: "Oh, my dear Dickens! what a
No. 5 you have now given us! I . . . cried and sobbed over it last
night. . . . Since that divine Nelly was found dead on her humble couch
. . . there has been nothing like the actual dying of that sweet Paul."
Similar applause can be found in the reviews. In an article concerning
Bulwer and Dickens, a reviewer described Nell as "the most perfect"
of Dickens' characters and her death as a "tragedy of the true sort." Its

Thackeray,[21] was a scene worthy to succeed that describing the last hours of Nell, and the relationship between Florence Dombey and her father was parallel to the relationship between Nell and her grandfather. Florence, as Jeffrey wrote with delight, gave promise of being "another Nelly!"[22] What Dickens called his "dread of the Dombey"[23] before publication was found to be groundless; the opening numbers proved that he had won back his public. When the book was finished, he wrote confidently to Miss Burdett-Coutts: "I hope you liked the little loves of Florence and Walter? If you had seen Jeffrey crying over them the other night, you would have been charmed with *him* at all events."[24]

It may be argued that artists (unlike rhetoricians) do not write books in such a manner, and that when Dickens sat down at his desk, he always forgot his audience as he did in writing of Little Nell. His letters about his plans for the death of Paul Dombey give a different impression; indeed fastidious readers have found them shockingly calculating in tone. Although he was once again emotionally involved in his story, he was attempting, this time, a repeat performance, and against the background of the failure of *Chuzzlewit* and the repeated advice of friends and reviewers, his apparently calculating tone is understandable. It might be more appropriate to argue that when an artist makes such a deliberate bid for the attention of his readers, he may be overtaken by other dangers. Even on Dickens' own terms, there was an ironical aftermath to his bid for favor. As Wilkie Collins noted, the scheme backfired.[25] After the death of Paul, the later numbers of *Dombey* seemed anti-climactic, and the disappointment of readers was reflected in the comparatively low sales of *David Copperfield* (less than twenty-five thousand) in spite of its being, as Collins remarked, "incomparably superior to 'Dombey.' "[26]

III

More important than the temporary loss of a few thousand

"counterpart" is the death of Paul. See the *Westminster Review*, XLVII (1847), 6.

readers caused by the backfiring of *Dombey* was the effect upon Dickens' later reputation of his fondness for sentimental scenes which he shared with his contemporaries. It would be difficult to find in literary history a more dramatic example of tides of taste than the story of the vogue and decline of Little Nell and Paul Dombey. For this reason, it has seemed appropriate to isolate the whole development from other aspects of Dickens' reputation, which are usually discussed over shorter segments of the time-span.

During Dickens' lifetime, the superlatives continued to be lavished upon Nell and her successors. Dean Ramsay considered that "nothing in the field of fiction is to be found in English literature surpassing the death of Jo."[27] The Spasmodic poet, Alexander Smith, talked of Nell in *Dreamthorp* (1863) in terms of praise anticipating Bret Harte's well-known "Dickens in Camp."* Another poet, Edward Heavisides, published an essay on Nell in 1850, remarking: "It must be a hard heart indeed that can read with indifference the history of the life and death of this promising child."[28]

Before Dickens' death, there were a few hard-hearted readers who refused to accept the prevailing verdict. Reviewers sometimes grumbled about the excessive pathos[29] or the tedious goodness of the young females. Of Esther Summerson, a *Spectator* reviewer admitted feeling "a wicked wish . . . that she either do something very 'spicy,' or confine herself to superintending the jam-pots at Bleak House."[30] Young Henry James, reviewing *Our Mutual Friend* in 1865, commented caustically on Jenny Wren: "Like all Mr. Dickens's pathetic characters, she is a little monster; . . . she belongs to the troop of hunchbacks, imbeciles, and precocious children, who have carried on the sentimental business in all Mr. Dickens's novels; the little Nells, the Smikes, the Paul Dombeys."[31] Another young and irreverent critic, Fitzjames Stephen, referred to the death-bed scenes as "luscious." In Dickens'

---

* *Dreamthorp* (Boston, 1907), p. 22. Bret Harte's tribute to Nell should be contrasted with his parody of Dickens called *The Haunted Man* which makes fun of Paul Dombey and sentimentality. See his *Condensed Novels* (1903), and Walter Hamilton's *Parodies* (n.d.), part 69, pp. 215-228.

novels, he wrote, "an interesting child runs as much risk . . . as any of the troops who stormed the Redan." Of Nell's death, "over which so many foolish tears have been shed," Stephen adds: "He gloats over the girl's death as if it delighted him; he looks at it . . . touches, tastes, smells and handles as if it was some savoury dainty which could not be too fully appreciated."[32] Augustus de Morgan's doggerel verses of 1861 sum up this minority report:

> A splendid muse of fiction hath Charles Dickens,
> But now and then just as the interest thickens
> He stilts his pathos, and the reader sickens.[33]

After Dickens' death, the vogue of Nell began gradually to decline. The novelist, Mrs. Oliphant, dismissed her as a "white smear,"[34] and G. H. Lewes noted that "most critical readers" now found her "maudlin and unreal."[35] Even Swinburne, who idolized Dickens' writings, asserted that Nell was about as real as a child with two heads. In the eighties, the gap between the "critical readers" and others grew wider. A discriminating critic, Matthew Browne, noted in 1880: "We have grown over-fastidious and too self-conscious in these matters. But if we cannot cry over Paul Dombey or Little Nell as Landor and Jeffrey did, we can find plenty of other things in Dickens to stir the fountains of tenderness and pity."[36] In reality, however, many readers still existed who *could* cry over Little Nell. The program in 1886 for a public "Dickens Birthday Celebration" contained such items as the recitation of a poem called "The Death of Little Nell," and the singing of a song about the death of Jo in *Bleak House* as well as another song about the death of Paul Dombey, these performances to be followed by a ball.[37] After such preliminaries, one suspects that the ball must have been what the immortal Mantalini would call "demd dismal."

In the nineties, Andrew Lang's analyses of the sentimentality of Nell prompted a protest from Henley, but, on the whole, there were few critical readers who were still susceptible to her.* George Gissing did try to say a few kind words

* In 1895, George Saintsbury, who despised Little Nell, was apoplectic

on her behalf, and G. K. Chesterton also tried, but failed. "It is not the death of Little Nell, but the life of Little Nell, that I object to," said Chesterton.[38] The last critic of any repute to have taken her altogether seriously seems to have been the American, Paul Elmer More. There are few, he writes, who will withhold their tears from this "picture of perfect meekness and gentleness fading flower-like in the breath of adversity. . . . We seem to hear . . . the cry of the Greek stage, '*Alas, oh generations of men!*' and of all great literature; and the reader is softened and broadened by association with the ancient pity of human life."[39] More's essay, published in 1908, must have given encouragement to those less cultivated readers who still clung to a belief in the greatness of Nell, but he seems to have had no successors of note in the twentieth century,* and the admirers of Nell, deprived of all critical support, have themselves diminished rapidly in number. Even eminent members of the Dickensian societies are prepared to abandon Nell to the maw of such critics as Aldous Huxley whose *Vulgarity in Literature* (1930) includes a discussion of the "pathological" sentimentality of the scene of Nell's death-bed and contrasts it with the death of Ilusha by Dickens' disciple, Dostoevsky. Dickens' heart overflowed with "rather repellant secretions," says Huxley.[40] Perhaps the kindest judgment that has been passed upon Nell in later decades is Sir Osbert Sitwell's: "For the appeal to sentimentality is . . . clumsily direct, . . . never morbidly insinuating or wistfully graceful, as are those passages in which Sir James Barrie, for example, stifles his understanding sobs. And which man of taste . . . who would not prefer the most ostentatiously dying . . . of Dickens' doomed children to that

---

when he read, in a "respectable book of reference," that Agnes was "the most charming character in the whole range of fiction." "*Agnes!*" he wailed, "no decent violence of expletive . . . could express the depths of my feelings at such a suggestion." (*Corrected Impressions*, 1895, p. 124.) Saintsbury's judgments in fiction were not always so infallible. He considered *Middlemarch* a "dead" book (*ibid.*, p. 166).

* But see, as an exception, Edgar Johnson's *Charles Dickens* (New York, 1952), I, 322-324, and also Stephen Spender's *World Within World* (New York, 1951), p. 254. Mr. Spender does not refer to sentimentality but to the existence, in real life, of the "unaccountably good and pure characters" who appear in the writings of Dickens and Balzac.

sexless, but elfin whimsy, Peter Pan?"[41] Sir Osbert's compliment is only a left-handed one at best, like Henry Miller's reference to "the harmless rose water vaporings of the back pages of Charles Dickens."[42] From Cordelia to harmless rose water vaporings is the history of Nell's progress in one hundred years.

I V

To account for the fact that Nell seemed a Cordelia to one generation and a Little Orphan Annie to another, one can try the resources of explanatory criticism. For this enquiry, the term explanatory criticism will mean any attempt to discuss some phase of a work of literature not by evaluating it or by impressionistic accounts of it, but by explanations of how it came to be what it is. Explanatory criticism includes biography, psychological analysis of the author, the history of ideas, and the history of taste and technique.

An axiom of many readers is that great scenes depend upon what is called the author's "sincerity" and "experience of life." Dickens himself believed in the axiom. In an article attacking *The Heir of Redclyffe*, he and Wilkie Collins condemned the death of Sir Guy as an "absurd" scene because of the author's lack of "experience of human nature."[*] Almost the same words were later applied to Dickens' own "exaggerated" death scenes by W. J. Dawson, who attacked him for relying upon "imagination rather than experience."[43]

One can reply to this charge of insincerity, regarding the creation of Nell, with the battery of facts assembled by biography. It is obvious that she was inspired by one of the most profound emotional experiences of her creator's life, and that not even the warehouse incident in *David Copperfield* was more like salt in a wound to him. Of *The Old Curiosity Shop* he confessed: "I am breaking my heart over this story, and

---

[*] "Doctor Dulcamara, MP," *Household Words*, Dec. 18, 1858, p. 51. —Amusingly enough, in *The Heir of Redclyffe* (1853) there are satirical references to Dickens' death scenes. As one character comments: "I found Amy in a state that alarmed me, crying in the green-house, and I was very glad to find it nothing worse than little Paul." A baronet protests against any further discussion of *Dombey* "when there is so much of higher grade" in fiction such as *I Promessi Sposi*.

cannot bear to finish it."[44] The grief and shock produced on Dickens by the death, in 1837, of Mary Hogarth were extraordinary not only because of their intensity but because, like Victoria's feelings after Albert's death, they were prolonged for years. During the first year after her death, he had dreams of her every night. They ceased, significantly, only after he had mentioned them to his wife.* In later years, as dozens of references in his letters testify, the dreams came back. Until his dying day, thirty-three years later, he wore her ring—an experience which reappears in the use of the ring in *Edwin Drood*. "I solemnly believe that so perfect a creature never breathed," he wrote.[45] In the year he was writing *The Old Curiosity Shop*, he was deeply disturbed by the news that the Hogarth family proposed to bury the body of Mary's brother beside her grave. Like Heathcliff, he passionately wanted that place for himself: "The desire to be buried next her is as strong upon me now, as it was five years ago; and I *know* (for I don't think there ever was love like that I bear her) that it will never diminish. . . . I cannot bear the thought of being excluded from her dust."[46]

The story of Mary Hogarth is fascinating in its own right, and, for the biographer, it is probably the best documented account we have of what Dickens himself called "the desperate intensity" of his nature.[47] For the critic, the story is a useful explanation of the artist's state of mind during the period when Nell was being created. It also provides conclusive evidence against those who think Dickens was insincere and lacked experience. "He overstates," says Lord David Cecil of the death of Nell. "He tries to wring an extra tear from the situation. . . . No Hollywood film-director, expert in sob-stuff, could more thoroughly vulgarise the simple and the tender."[48] Implicit in this condemnation seems to lurk the charge of insincerity, yet all evidence shows that the scene was written, as romantic critics would say, from the heart. As a man,

---

* See Nonesuch, I, 518-519; 624-625. It should also be noted that the unifying device of *The Old Curiosity Shop* is the dream. Concerning Dickens' methods of using dreams in his fiction, see Warrington Winters, "Dickens and the Psychology of Dreams," *PMLA*, LXIII (1948), 984-1007.

Dickens was deeply sincere about his subject, deeply moved by it.

But does biographical explanation really answer Cecil's criticism? Does it have any effect upon our judgment of *The Old Curiosity Shop*? Popular axioms to the contrary, it seems possible that a man may be intensely moved by some personal situation, and yet produce a work which strikes us as stagey, faked, "insincere" even. Perhaps the word *sincerity* belongs properly to ethics and to biography rather than to literary criticism, or, at least, it may have different connotations in each field. To push this doubt a little further, the danger of literary biography lies in the assumption that a moving experience on the part of the man will lead to a moving work of art. When Dickens portrayed the shocking experiences of his childhood in *Copperfield*, he somehow achieved the necessary perspective upon them. In portraying the equally poignant experience of Mary Hogarth's death, he was overwhelmed.

A second type of explanatory criticism, provided by psychology, is essentially a twentieth-century extension of the first. According to Jack Lindsay, for example, Dickens' feelings about Mary Hogarth were conditioned by the sister-complex which had affected him from childhood. "When alone with her [Mary], he felt himself returned to his own innocent childhood, before the forces of alienation had spoiled his life . . . and with her he could . . . retreat into a romping sweetness."[49] The creation of Nell was therefore, for Dickens, partly a form of wish-fulfillment, but her death was also partly what Lionel Trilling calls "mithridatic"—the symbolic representation of a painful experience, a catharsis for the artist of a situation which had become oppressive. Both explanations are interesting, yet, except for a change of vocabulary, the problem remains the same as it did for the biographical explanations.

A third type of explanatory criticism avoids the personal problems of the author and seeks to account for the nature of the work itself in terms of the predominant ideas, or the predominant tastes, of the age in which it was produced. For

Nell, a history of taste is especially helpful in enabling us to appreciate why her story made such an impact upon Dickens' contemporaries.

The cult of sensibility among the early Victorians had its roots in the late eighteenth century. J. M. S. Tompkins notes that after 1770, " 'sensibility' was a significant, an almost sacred word, for it enshrined the idea of the progress of the human race." Sensibility was a quality not found among the ancients; it was "the product of modern conditions; the heroic and tremendous virtues might be dying out . . . but modern security, leisure and education had evolved a delicacy of sensation, a refinement of virtue, which the age found even more beautiful."[50] The persistence of this attitude towards sensibility into the nineteenth century certainly affected the reaction of Dickens' readers to Nell. Throughout the early decades, its presence was deceptively obscured by masculine boisterousness,[51] but during the 1830's and 1840's, it came to full flower. Macaulay, one of the most devoted readers of Jane Austen, did not share her opinion of sensibility. Florence Dombey, he reported, "made me cry as if my heart would break."[52] After reading *The Chimes*, the Countess of Blessington (1789-1849) was embarrassed to encounter the eyes of her servants because her own were so red with tears. Her testimony is interesting because it indicates an early disagreement about Dickens' role:

> I have made many persons buy 'The Chimes' who were afraid it was not amusing, and [I] made them ashamed of expecting nothing better, nothing greater, from such a writer. They can laugh until their sides ache over Mrs. Gamp, but they dread weeping over dear good Trotty, that personification of goodness; sweet Meg, the *beau ideal* of female excellence; poor Lilian, and the touching but stern reality of Bill Fern, which beguiled me of so many tears. . . . I have read 'The Chimes' a third time, and found it . . . impossible to repress my tears.*

* R. R. Madden, *Life and Correspondence of the Countess of Blessington* (1855), II, 400-401. Perhaps the most tearful of Dickens' tearful

Although in fashionable drawing rooms the melting mood was especially prevalent, it was nursed at all levels. Dickens discovered on his reading tours that the death of Paul Dombey was "our greatest triumph everywhere."[53] From Ireland, he wrote: "I have never seen *men* go in to cry so undisguisedly as they did at that reading."[54]

Perhaps too much emphasis has been placed, in this discussion, upon the scene of Nell's last hours, for Dickens' early readers were moved not only by her death but by her situation throughout the novel. Dickens shared with them a delight in stories of renunciation in which one character gives up happiness for the sake of another. This literary convention is represented best by Sydney Carton's role or Eugene Wrayburn's (in *Our Mutual Friend*), for both men were unworthy, and their renunciation is therefore more moving.* It underlies the account of Nell's patient devotion to her selfishly obsessed grandfather. It reappears in variations of the role as played by Mary Graham, Florence Dombey, Agnes Wickfield, Little Dorrit and other heroines endowed with a patience beyond the reach of angels. For later readers, the antics of these heroines seem to have stimulated the most excruciating pages in all Dickens' work.[55] Because Nell embodied this renunciatory role as well as because of her death, it is appropriate to consider her the most representative figure in Dickens' sentimental gallery.

Some twentieth-century critics have argued that this early Victorian sentimentalism was a reflection of a general guilt-complex ("no one weeps more copiously than the hardened scoundrel") and that to cry over Little Nell was a form of penance for such crimes as child labor and Negro slavery in America.[56] The theory is ingenious, but it fails to explain why when the cult of the stiff upper lip replaced the cult of the tearful, there was no significant change in the economic conditions which are supposed (according to the theory) to be

---

contemporaries was Hans Christian Andersen, a great lover of *The Old Curiosity Shop* for which he had his own title. He called it *Nelly*. See *TLS*, May 2, 1952, p. 289.

* Dickens' most effective part as an actor was that of Wardour, in *The Frozen Deep*, a role which provided another example of renunciation.

responsible for the guilt-complex. Taste, like the Deity, moves in mysterious ways, and sociological criticism has not yet fully mastered the science of charting them. The decline of Nell's vogue did not coincide with any vast social ameliora- tion but with a shift of sensibility, sensed first by critical readers, in which the unabashed expression of sentimentality became anathema. One suspects that such a novelist as Ernest Hemingway is afflicted with a sentimental potential not re- mote from that of Dickens, but the later novelist fights it down with all his hairy strength. Even in E. M. Forster there seems to be a faint sentimental streak which is suppressed by irony and by the device of making death scenes into casual and inconsequential incidents. The latter device has led to a protest from at least one of Forster's admirers who points out that from the frenzy of Dickens' death scenes Forster has merely taken us to an opposite extreme which is equally unreal.[57] Whether unreal or not, it seems to be typical.

For a discussion of Little Nell, this kind of explanatory criticism, which is concerned with the conventions and states of mind which affected the kind of novel written in a given period, seems more useful than biography. Together with a fourth kind (already exploited in this chapter) in which a history of the different reactions of readers is traced, it helps us to understand part of the appeal that Dickens' heroine had for readers. If the scene of her death is, to us, a failure, we can shift part of the responsibility from Dickens to the age itself. Yet if these kinds of criticism are extenuating, it is because they use the past tense. The blot, as we see it, is still there.

The important clause, as *we* see it, leads to one further problem. By surveying the vogue of Nell and her decline, one seems to be driven, inevitably, into the camp of Frederick A. Pottle and the extreme relativists of criticism. In *The Idiom of Poetry*, Professor Pottle contends that there is no such thing as absolute good taste. Each age is equipped, figura- tively, with a certain wave-length, or band, of receptivity.[58] Little Nell came in clearly on the early Victorian radio sets. Now, however, she is drowned out by the static from other twentieth-century stations, or rather, she is no longer on our wave-length. Ingenious as the analogy is, and appealing to our twentieth-century love of gadgets, it leads to a suspension of all judgment. It makes explanation not a tool of criticism but the sole end of criticism. To follow the figure further, one wonders whether or not there may be a permanent wavelength, at the center of the dial, which is not entirely subject to the variations of frequency occasioned by time. William Ernest Henley, one of the first to overlook this possibility, protested that it was unfair of Andrew Lang to compare the death of Nell with comparable scenes in Sophocles: "The point is that, when Dickens wrote, the Romantic Movement was in full swing."[59]

Henley provides an early example (1899) of the relativistic argument. His point is important, but it does not answer Lang. Good explanatory criticism should have the function of providing a valuable perspective for judgment, of bringing to light fresh insights, and of correcting the fantastic mistakes made by the impressionist or romantic critic. As such it is a useful tool, but must it be an end in itself? In considering Nell's death scene, for example, a reader can bear in mind all the qualifying facts that the biographers, psychologists, scholars, and historians have brought to bear on it, and yet conclude that it may appropriately be described as inexcusably dreadful.

The death scene which Dickens most admired in all literature was that of *King Lear*, as acted by Macready.[60] In *The Old Curiosity Shop*, a reader senses again and again that the author was making a bid to write another *Lear*—which incidentally may account for some of the intensity of Macready's own emotions in reading the novel.* The parallel is especially marked in the scenes describing the old grandfather's grief after Nell's death, and a comparison therefore seems eminently fair.[61] The end of *King Lear* has remained profoundly moving and the other has become profoundly embarrassing.

* "I never have read printed words that gave me so much pain. I could not weep for some time. . . . I cannot criticize it." *The Diaries of W. C. Macready* (1912), II, 116.

One difference may be that of situation. In *Lear*, the strong are defeated; in *The Old Curiosity Shop*, it is the weak who suffer. One situation is potentially tragic and the other potentially pathetic. More important are differences of style. Dickens' preliminary description of the snowstorm is effective and vivid, but as our attention is directed from the background towards the child's bed, the false notes begin; the author steps forward to comment in his own person. In such passages of comment, Dickens is almost always at a disadvantage.[62] Here virtually the entire passage (as R. H. Horne pointed out to Dickens' chagrin) is blank verse, into which he had unconsciously slipped:

> Oh! it is hard to take to heart
> The lesson that such deaths will teach, . . .
>   Of every tear
> That sorrowing mortals shed on such green graves,
> Some good is born, some gentler nature comes.*

"We hate poetry that has a palpable design upon us," said Keats. Dickens' blank verse seems to have just that. Of his personal sincerity there is not a shred of doubt. Of what might be called his artistic sincerity, there is. Oscar Wilde's laughter can be accounted for in terms of one of Conrad's observations:

> In order to move others deeply we must deliberately allow ourselves to be carried away beyond the bounds of our normal sensibility . . . like an actor who raises his voice on the stage. . . . And surely this is no great sin. But the danger lies in the writer becoming the victim of his own exaggeration, losing the exact notion of sincerity. . . . From laughter and tears the descent is easy to snivelling and giggles.[63]

Dickens' stagey qualities, often a source of great strength in other parts of his novels, were, in such solemn scenes as these, a constant liability. As a late Victorian critic noted: "The death of a child is . . . too ready a way of harrowing the

* See Horne, *A New Spirit of the Age*, I, 67. —Dickens admitted: "I *cannot* help it, when I am very much in earnest." Nonesuch, I, 808.

feelings" and such scenes, as Dickens arranges them, require "the gaslight to subdue [their] garishness."[64] Explanatory criticism is useful in helping us to understand why
Dickens' contemporaries were so little aware of the garishness
that they encouraged him to continue in the same vein, and
why Nell (together with *Pickwick Papers*) made Dickens
the most popular and admired novelist in the language. These
would seem to be its limits, and beyond them, the present-day
admirer of the rest of Dickens' work has to grope for other
ways of dealing with his sentimentality. One solution might
be simply to circumvent Nell, as Edmund Wilson does with
great skill in his excellent essays. It might be possible to
reverse what Edward Fitzgerald did to *The Old Curiosity
Shop*, an otherwise excellent novel, and, by extracting from it
a Quilpiad or a Swiveleriad, pretend that Nell did not exist.
The surgery would be difficult at best, and Nell remains the
inevitable whipping-girl of the anti-Dickensians, the principal
drag upon the full critical acceptance of his art, or, as Charles
Lamb might have embellished it:

> A fixed figure for the time of scorn
> To point his slow unmoving finger at.

PART TWO

[1848-1872]

"Here is the vast importance of the novel, properly handled. . . . It can inform and lead into new places the flow of our sympathetic consciousness, and it can lead our sympathy away in recoil from thoughts gone dead."—D. H. Lawrence

CHAPTER 5

THE CRITIC OF SOCIETY

I

THE reception of the seven novels which succeeded *David Copperfield* differed in various respects from the reception of the seven novels which preceded it. The components of Dickens' reading public, which had been hitherto relatively unified, began to split apart; his sales, which had been hitherto erratic, became steady. In the present chapter and in the two which follow, this splitting apart of the mid-Victorian public will be discussed, with reference especially to the reactions of readers towards his social criticism, his artistic methods, and his handling of probability. Also to be discussed is the establishment of his steady following of loyal readers.

In 1857, Charles Lever summed up in a letter the general outline of Dickens' position after *Copperfield*: "Dickens is hourly going down in estimation but his sale continues so 'Il se moque de ses critiques.' "[1] Of *Bleak House*, Dickens himself reported happily: "It is a most enormous success; all the prestige of Copperfield (which was very great) falling upon it, and raising its circulation above all my other books."[2] That is, the sale of *Bleak House* followed the pattern already traced for his novels of the 1840's. Disappointment in *Dombey* after the death of Paul had reduced the sale of *David Copperfield*, but the "prestige" of the latter shot up the sale of the next novel, *Bleak House*, to over 35,000 copies (10,000 more than *Copperfield*). Thereafter, with or without prestige, sales continued to rise up towards the level of *Edwin Drood's* 50,000.[3] Of some of the later Christmas books, more than a quarter of a million copies were sold.[4] Meanwhile, cheap reprintings of the earlier novels (issued in three-halfpenny weekly numbers) also helped to swell the volume of sales. By 1870, according to Anthony Trollope (a shrewd commentator upon the commerce of literature), the English-speaking public numbered one hundred millions, and in England, at least, Dickens' novels were to be found "in every house in which books are kept." "It is very strange that such a demand of an author's works should have grown up during his own life, . . . that it should have continued with unbated force,— and that it should exceed, as I believe it does exceed, the demand for the works of any other writer in the language."*

If during the second phase of Dickens' career he lost a powerful and highly vocal section of his readers, he acquired a reliable following of book-buyers who were now relatively immune from criticism. Among many of them he was a kind of Bourbon monarch who could do no wrong. "Darling Dickens" was the phrase applied to him by the Cowden Clarkes even before they had made his acquaintance.[5] At Oxford and Cambridge, in the fifties, were undergraduates who soaked themselves in his work to such an extent that their detailed knowledge was enough to stagger Dickens himself.[6] Games of quotations were played which demanded an intimate understanding of even the plot of *Oliver Twist*,[7] and the games were resumed whenever the friends came together in later life.

Typical of this early generation of Dickensians was the painter, Edward Burne-Jones, who bore his enthusiasm from Oxford to his studio where his wife was obliged to read the works of Dickens aloud to him while he worked over his canvases. After reading the Mrs. Gamp scenes to him a countless number of times, Lady Burne-Jones began to be somewhat aweary of them, but her husband's zest was insatiable.† Her

---

* *St. Paul's Magazine*, VI (1870), 372. See also Trollope's letter to Chapman, September 25, 1871, concerning a new edition of Dickens reaching a sale of 200,000 copies. According to Edgar Johnson's estimate, Dickens' readers in the British Isles numbered 1,500,000, or 1 out of every 10 persons in the population. He bases these figures upon sales of *The Old Curiosity Shop* (100,000) multiplied by the probable number of readers for each copy (15). Because accurate statistics are lacking for later sales, however, such overall estimates must remain very rough guesses at best. For comparisons with twentieth-century sales, see Albert Guérard, *Literature and Society* (Boston, 1935), p. 238.

† G B-J, *Memorials of Edward Burne-Jones* (New York, 1906), I, 142 and II, 56, 161. Scott was another favorite; *The Antiquary* was read twenty-seven times. It should be added that Burne-Jones' wife was not the only Pre-Raphaelite lady who found Dickens to be exhausting. William Morris'

fate could have suggested to Evelyn Waugh the grotesque situation used in *A Handful of Dust*. The hero of Waugh's novel is confined to the jungle for life so that he can read aloud the works of Dickens to his illiterate and half-mad host. With this kind of assistance from his wife, Burne-Jones freshened his knowledge of minutiae, astonishing one hostess, for example, by questioning her about "Mr. Pip," who, as it turned out, was an extremely minor character mentioned briefly in a scene from *Martin Chuzzlewit*.[8]

I I

Perhaps the largest group among these loyal early Dickensians was one about which it is most difficult to obtain information. Dickens himself credited the extensive sales of Macaulay's history and Tennyson's poems to working-class readers,[9] and it is likely that his own sales were similarly assisted. Below certain economic or social levels, however, the evidence becomes scarce. Diaries, letters, autobiographies, and essays—even if written—rarely survive. One gets a glimpse of such loyal readers in W. D. Howells' charming sketch of a workman from England who settled in his Ohio village in the fifties, a man who knew his Dickens as thoroughly and indiscriminately as some sectarians know their Bible.[10] One catches another glimpse of his working-class audience at the Birmingham Polytechnic Institute, where he was thanked because his writings had "so loyally inculcated the lessons of benevolence and virtue,"[11] and in a series entitled *Penny Books for the People* he was described in an epitaph in 1870 as "the fearless denouncer of meanness, tyranny, and wrong. The eloquent advocate of gentleness, justice, and right, who could unite with genial mirth the deepest lessons of wisdom and truth."[12] Dickens' letters also provide oc-

---

"interminable reading" aloud of *Barnaby Rudge* to his "bored companion," Jane Morris, did not add to the happiness of their menage. See Oswald Doughty, *Dante Gabriel Rossetti* (1949), p. 239. Among the younger generation, Clara Watts-Dunton was similarly bored when she had to witness Swinburne's insatiable delight in Sara Gamp, Micawber, and Bill Barley. See her recollections of Swinburne in *The Nineteenth Century*, September 1921.

casional accounts of the warm-hearted affection felt for his books by the newly literate among the underprivileged, an affection summed up best by the Irishman who stopped him on the street, after a reading, to thank him "not ounly for the light you've been to me this night, but for the light you've been in mee house, sir (and God love your face!) this many a year."[13] What Whitman, the chanter of democracy, longed for in vain, Dickens received in lavish measure.*

Some sobering evidence must be inserted here in order to tone down our dithyramb. One of the commonest errors in any discussion of Dickens is the unqualified assumption that because some butcher boys and workingmen and domestics were observed to be reading *Pickwick*, therefore all butcher boys and workingmen and domestics were readers of *Pickwick*. The measure which Dickens received was an extremely lavish one but not a full one. There must have been many thousands of his contemporaries who did not know his writings and some to whom he was entirely unknown. As late as 1857, a visitor to Hawthornden was horrified to discover that no one on the estate, neither servant nor inmates, had ever so much as heard the name of Dickens.[14]

Among those who would be similarly ignorant were the 8,000,000 persons in England and Wales who, in 1850, could neither read nor write—that is, almost a quarter of the population.[15] What is more important, among certain classes of the literate, Dickens was by no means the most popular author. A Manchester bookseller of the same period, breaking down his weekly sales among working-class readers, noted that while cheaply priced volumes of Dickens were selling at a rate of 250 a week, there were thousands of penny weekly numbers by other novelists being sold. G. W. M. Reynolds' penny serial, *The Mysteries of London* (1845-1856), for example, was selling at the rate of 1,000 a week.[16] With a style almost as lush as Bulwer-Lytton's and with scenes of

---

* An essay by Whitman appeared in 1842 which has been overlooked by Dickens' bibliographers. "Boz and Democracy," which includes a eulogy of Little Nell, is primarily a warm defense of Dickens against critics who find his books vulgar, wicked, and diseased. See Whitman's *Rivulets of Prose* (New York, 1928), pp. 19-30.

violence, lust, and suspense on almost every other page, Reynolds was the Mickey Spillane of the Victorian age. The accompanying illustration (reproduction on opposite page) is part of a typical Reynolds sequence. The virtuous girl, Ellen, has been forced by poverty to support her ailing father by posing as a model first for a maker of plaster masks, next for a painter of shepherdesses, then for a sculptor who obliges her to pose half nude, and finally, in desperation, for a photographer (a Frenchman of course) before whom she must remove all her clothes. This elaborately drawn out strip-tease is dexterously managed by Reynolds so that each weekly number closes with the prospect of another item of the young woman's wardrobe being removed in the next number. The story of David Copperfield's pursuit of Dora would seem, by comparison, somewhat flat. It is no wonder that Dickens deplored the debasement of taste that Reynolds' writings exerted.

According to *The Times*, however, one of Dickens' great contributions to education was his capacity to lure away some working-class readers from their diet of Reynolds. *The Times* argued that although such a book as *Great Expectations* was "addressed to a much higher class of readers than any which the penny journals would reach," and although it satisfied "the better class of reader" by other qualities, its sensational story contained enough marvels to be able to compete successfully with Reynolds' serials on their own ground.*

In speaking of the sale of Reynolds, I am not attempting to banish the well-established notion that Dickens was a popular author among what he called the "People." I have tried to indicate merely that it was by no means an unchallenged reputation. That his works penetrated every stratum of the reading public is indisputable, but it seems evident that among

* *The Times*, October 17, 1861, p. 6. Dickens himself hoped that Charles Knight's proposal to publish inexpensive books would contribute towards "an end on which my heart is set—the liberal education of the people." See Nonesuch, I, 606. Sometimes his interest in "education" cost Dickens a group of his readers. Henry Mayhew reports that after an attack on begging letters in *Household Words*, the street-patterers, who had once ranked Dickens as a favorite (together with Marryat and Ainsworth), stopped reading him. Henry Mayhew, *London Labour and the London Poor* (1864), I, 268.

working-class readers, he gained *most* of his reputation in the stratum he addressed at the Mechanics' Institutes at Birmingham and Manchester: the more conscientious and ambitious operatives who were seeking further education. For these readers, throughout the period aptly labelled by the Hammonds *The Bleak Age*, his works provided some of the imaginative stuff desperately needed by those whose leisure was as fractional as their daily wage, stuff which a generation of Gradgrinds and Mrs. Pardiggles and Mrs. Clennams considered to be wasteful and ungodly. There was, in addition, the more direct and obvious appeal of his social criticism: the cheerful championing of the underprivileged in the earlier novels and stories, the contemptuous satire of abused privilege in the later. Here again, Dickens was able to compete successfully with Reynolds, part of whose stock in trade consisted of rumbling invectives against the selfish rich. Working-class readers could value Dickens' books for similar reasons. As one minor radical publication observed, Dickens "was not only a romancer"; he was a "mighty preacher."[17] *The People's Journal* praised his writings as "a continual preaching from the text of Burns—

'A man's a man for a' that!' "[18]

It is easy for Marxians to show that Dickens erred by failing to treat the industrial workman as a special case, and it is apparent in *Barnaby Rudge* and *Hard Times* that he was suspicious even of trade unionism itself.* Yet because the limits of his social criticism were not rigidly definable, its scope could be extended to take in a variety of classes. The satiric vein in which he presents Lady Bowley's song for the villagers (in *The Chimes*) could be appreciated equally by the Coketown workman and by the clerk, Bob Cratchit:

* Cf. Edgar Johnson, *Charles Dickens* (New York, 1952), II, 811-812. Evidence from *Household Words* is cited to demonstrate that Dickens gave his "personal support" to the labor movement. In general, for a suggestive explanation of why Dickens' social criticism was often misinformed and least effective when conditions of workmen in northen industry are being described, see Louis Cazamian, *Le roman social en Angleterre* (Paris, 1904), pp. 216-217, 245, 294-312.

O let us love our occupations,
Bless the squire and his relations,
Live upon our daily rations,
And always know our proper stations.

Rightly or wrongly, he acquired a magic reputation as one who had only to raise his trumpet and the walls of folly would fall. "Ah, sir!" said a cabby at the time of the novelist's death, "Mr. Dickens was the gentleman who looked after the poor man. We cabmen were hoping he would give us a turn next."[19]

Gratitude from working-class readers was undoubtedly an incentive to Dickens' didacticism, yet it would be a mistake to consider that his popular audience was alone responsible in this respect. There was also pressure from those more solid reviewers, previously discussed, who similarly praised him because he was "not a mere novelist." According to a reviewer in the *Westminster*: "In all his tales there is a latent desire to improve and strengthen the charities of life, raise the trampled upon, soften intolerance, diffuse knowledge, promote happiness."* Oddly enough, twenty-two years later, in 1864, the *Westminster* reversed its verdict. "We believe him to have been the main instrument in the change which has perverted the novel from a work of art to a platform for discussion and argument."[20] Aestheticism might help to account for this reversal, but one suspects that the real cause was the exposure of Benthamism in *Hard Times*.[21] During Dickens' lifetime, there were not many readers who objected to the didactic as such.† What aroused opposition was not that he was considered a "mighty preacher," but that what he preached was distasteful. Especially distasteful was the preaching in the novels following *Copperfield*, and the *Westminster's*

* *Westminster Review*, XXXIX (1843), 74. G. M. Young cites similar praise from a Nonconformist sermon of the forties: "There have been at work among us three great social agencies: the London City Mission; the novels of Mr. Dickens; the cholera." *Early Victorian England* (1934), II, 460.

† Macready was an exception. "I hold it to be the business of the novelist to narrate, without any interruption whatever of personal feeling: animus on the part of the writer begets resistance in the reader." See Lady Pollock, *Macready as I Knew Him* (1884), pp. 59-60.

suggestion that he ought to return to the task of art was typical in being motivated by political considerations.

Religious considerations also played a part in this later criticism. A review of *Bleak House* in the *Rambler* (1854) makes the kind of complaint which was to reappear subsequently when Dickens was contrasted with Dostoevsky. Dickens (according to this reviewer) is "the prophet of an age which loves benevolence without religion, the domestic virtues more than the heroic."

> The product of a restlessly observant but shallow era, his great intellectual characteristic is a most unusual power of observing the external peculiarities of men and women, as distinguished from all insight into that hidden nature whence flow the springs of their conduct. And morally there is probably not another living writer, of equal decency of thought, to whom the supernatural and eternal world simply is *not*.[22]

All too readily one slips into using such clumsy words as *teach* and *preach*. Dickens' social criticism embraces a wide variety of techniques all the way from the crude, direct sermon of personal indignation lamenting the death of Jo to the masterful channeling of a comparable indignation into symbolical devices including the dust heap in *Our Mutual Friend*, the fog in *Bleak House*, the marshes of *Great Expectations*, or symbolical characterizations such as the Murdstones or Gradgrinds. From the point of view of his popular reputation, however, the question was not always whether the technique of his social criticism was clumsy or artful, but whether the criticism itself was palatable (as it was for many working-class readers) or infuriating (as it was for the contributors to the *Saturday Review*). And because the tone of his satire became much more obviously astringent after 1850, the evaluation of his later novels was more and more affected by the political and social predilections of his readers and critics.

III

The complexities of Dickens' role as a critic of society

can only be skimmed over here, but even a brief summary may indicate why the role has been so variously interpreted. In part the *bon bourgeois* with the characteristic reactions of the householder and father of ten, Dickens was also in larger part an anarchist, the unpredictable foe of institutions and established social order. In his attitude towards industrialism, for example, one encounters the typical ambivalence which makes it impossible to pin party labels upon him, as one can with Disraeli. The portrait of a heroic, self-made industrialist in *Bleak House* is succeeded by the contrasting portrait of Mr. Bounderby in *Hard Times*. As a public speaker, and often as a novelist, Dickens appears to be on the side of Macaulay, chanting the praises of industrial progress. In one speech, he made fun of an elderly gentleman he had encountered during a railway journey. Whenever the train left a station "with a shock and a shriek as if it had had a double-tooth drawn," his fellow passenger bewailed the "new fangled notions" and longed for the return of stage coaches. Yet, whenever the train was delayed, he had his watch out and waxed indignant about the lack of speed.[23] What Dickens neglected to add was that the story applied equally well to his own position. As a novelist, he often deserts Macaulay and sides with Ruskin in evoking a happier, more picturesque past. For railway engines, even before his accident in 1865, he had a kind of horror.[24] Of machines in general, he shared something of the dread more passionately expressed by heroic vitalists such as Carlyle and D. H. Lawrence. Industrialism appalled him whenever it became associated in his mind with human hardness—as in Coketown. Here one does arrive at a consistent reference point in Dickens' position. It was the heartless hardness of both Utilitarianism and Victorian puritanism that stimulated his typical criticism: M'Choakumchild with his facts, and Miss Murdstone with her "uncompromising hard black boxes, with her initials on the lids in hard brass nails." And David Copperfield added that he had never seen "such a metallic lady altogether as Miss Murdstone was." In a sentence, the unnecessarily heartless inhumanity of puritanism is equated with the necessarily heartless machine. If the days of the stage coaches seemed romantic, it was because the men associated with them seemed more completely human and uncommitted to a mechanical code of economics and social relationships.

From this central position, the human comedy of Dickens' novels is developed. If Bergson's theory of the mechanical basis of laughter is true, the position would seem to be an ideal starting point from which to expose the mechanical behavior of beings incompletely human. It was a position that could lend itself to sermons on the "Carol Philosophy," or, more effectively, to novels of manners, a sphere more appropriate for his purposes.*

IV

Dickens' attack on the hundred-headed monster began with cheerful good humor and confidence. There were even concrete manifestations of success following the earlier attacks. A heartless police magistrate was discharged after the publication of *Oliver Twist*, a heartless Yorkshire schoolmaster was shamed into retirement after *Nickleby*.[25] Even a bumpy road in Maryland was repaired after it had been described in *American Notes*.[26] An air of breezy confidence continues to blow throughout *Martin Chuzzlewit* even though the comic antagonist this time was more formidable and unlikely to be dislodged, but in *Dombey* the breeze has lost much of its force. The world of commerce leads to a somber book. In what Lionel Stevenson aptly calls the "Dark Period" novels,†

---

* An effective summary of the theme of *Our Mutual Friend* occurs in a letter from Paris, written after Dickens had seen an exhibition of English Victorian paintings. "There is a horrid respectability about most of the best of them—a little, finite, systematic routine in them, strangely expressive to me of the state of England itself." In Arnoldian vein, he contrasted these paintings with "the passion and action" of the French exhibit. "Don't think it a part of my despondency about public affairs . . . when I say that mere form and conventionalities usurp, in English art, as in English government and social relations, the place of living force and truth." Nonesuch, II, 700.

† "Dickens's Dark Novels, 1851-1857," *Sewanee Review*, LI (1943), 398-409. It might be more accurate to refer to this as his *darkest* period, for his earlier novels have their share of darkness also. Even the *Sketches by Boz* contain somber anticipations of the novels of the 1850's. What occurred was a marked heightening of the shadowing. One reviewer detected

the tone has changed to something closer to gloom and even despair. The theme of the social criticism in these books is best expressed by Stephen Blackpool: "Ah, Rachael, aw a muddle! Fro' first to last, a muddle!" How often that word *muddle* appears in the later books! In *Bleak House*, old Krook likens his junk shop, with its "rust and must and cobwebs," to the Lord Chancellor's court. "There's no great odds betwixt us," he says. "We both grub on in a muddle."

Among the various causes for this loss of confidence was Dickens' recognition, as he approached the Dark Tower itself, of how strong and pervasive were the forces which his novels were exposing. In *Bleak House*, *Hard Times* (concerned with the philosophy of hardness itself), and *Little Dorrit*, he was confronting the very whips and scorns which, as Hamlet soliloquized, drive men to suicide. It is remarkable how many of Dickens' later themes are summed up in four lines from the bitter speech:

> Th'oppressor's wrong, the proud man's contumely,
> The pangs of despis'd love, the law's delay,
> The insolence of office, and the spurns
> That patient merit of th'unworthy takes.

In *Oliver Twist*, despite an atmosphere of gloom, the law was still dismissible with Mr. Bumble's celebrated blast: "If the law supposes that . . . the law is a ass—a idiot." In *Bleak House*, however, *the law's delay* is all powerful. It is a "monstrous maze" (as it is labelled when Mr. Vholes is introduced) in which even the well-intentioned become lost and broken, or are driven to madness and agonized death. Aunt Betsy Trotwood's cottage, a symbol for David Copperfield of the haven of security he longed for, reappears in the next novel, but the haven this time has been given a new name. It is called Bleak House. In *Edwin Drood*, the last book by a writer whose name is always linked with the genial cheerful-

---

the change as early as *The Chimes*. Its predominant "sadness" he contrasted with the note of *The Old Curiosity Shop* in which "pleasure won the victory over pain." "There is a gloom in the mind as we shut the book . . . a feeling of some frightful extent of wrong." The *Edinburgh Review*, LXXXI (1845), 183.

ness of Christmas, there occur a violent quarrel and a sordid murder scene on Christmas eve, and the Cloisterham setting, with its Christmas pantomime, its Wax-Work, and its clown who performs "miserably" seems almost a parody of Christmas at Dingley Dell. If the great Christmas dinner scene in Joyce's *Portrait of the Artist* strikes us as an early Dickensian scene turned upside down, it is well to be reminded that Dickens himself had performed the same reversal. In *Great Expectations*, a Christmas feast is interrupted by a search-party, and the festive banter of Uncle Pumblechook is punctuated by sounds of the blacksmith's hammer repairing the manacles which are to restrain an escaped convict.

The effect of this change of tone and increased scope of Dickens' social criticism upon the reception of his novels after 1852 was a mixed one. Often it was obscured by the conditioned reflexes of readers who were familiar with his early writings. His reputation for cheerfulness was summed up in some satirical verses of 1849:

> Crickets, whose chirping says our wives are true,
> And tuneful kettles sing long chapters through,
> These are the elements of modern fame,
> And still uphold the vulgar Boz's name.[27]

Even after the cricket on the hearth had begun to sing sour notes, Dickens' reputation for cheerfulness persisted among less perceptive readers who had been conditioned to expect no change. In 1872, one historian commented: "His sense of fun is visible through his mask of dolefulness, and the effect he produces on the reader is certainly not that which he appears to desire."[28] Other readers such as Ruskin, who detected the new notes, applauded them, while still others, such as Trollope, found them excruciating and especially inappropriate because they coincided with the transition from the hungry 1840's to the prosperous 1850's.

Before we turn to these readers, however, there is the problem of whether Dickens himself was aware of the change. Once again the clue to his conflict seems to reside in his peculiar sense of responsibility towards his public. He was aware that the reputation for cheerfulness he had acquired had to be sustained. In 1860, he was obliged to assure Miss Coutts that he was as "cheerful" as ever:

> As to my art, I have as great a delight in it as the most enthusiastic of my readers; and the sense of my trust and responsibility in that wise, is always upon me when I take pen in hand. If *I* were soured, I should still try to sweeten the lives and fancies of others, but I am not —not at all.[29]

Four years earlier, a perceptive visitor had observed the somberness of his conversation, a quality which had thrust its way into his novels in spite of his determination to subdue it for public occasions. "The mind of Dickens, which most of his readers picture to themselves as revelling in sunshine, was in fact more attracted to the darker side of life, though there was far too much of geniality in him to permit it to become morbid."[30] The acuteness of this impression can be tested by comparing two of Dickens' letters from this period. The first was to a stranger who was suffering from depression. In bouncing Victorian fashion, he urged her to stop "brooding over mysteries" and, instead, to "be earnest" about realities and duties. At a later date, he was writing to Forster about his own "dishevelled state of mind," his "miseries of older growth" and his "crushing" sense of having missed the happiness of life.[31]

In view of Dickens' virtually suicidal behavior in his last years, a biting comment in the *Saturday Review* seems especially telling. The comment refers to the preface to *Little Dorrit* in which Dickens had spoken of its large sales:

> Apart from the question of taste . . . the very prominent announcement of a large sale looks a little like latent suspicion that it was not quite deserved. "Oh, I am very well," replied Mr. Merdle, after deliberating about it; "I am as well as I usually am!" and the man went and cut his throat forthwith. This may serve to remind Mr. Dickens that uncalled-for asseverations of well-doing do not prove the heart to be quite at ease.[32]

Twelve years later, in one of his last essays before his death, Dickens admitted that there had been a time when "in the general mind," his temporary unhappiness of spirit had been identified with the case of Mr. Merdle.[33] Characteristically, he made fun of the "remarkable coincidence," but once again the asseveration of well-doing did not prove the heart to be quite at ease.

V

Another reader who finally recognized that Dickens' heart was not at ease was Thomas Carlyle. The recognition came very late. In 1874, after praising Dickens' cheerfulness as usual, he made a more penetrating observation:

> and, deeper than all, if one has the eye to see deep enough, dark, fateful, silent elements, tragical to look upon, and hiding, amid dazzling radiances as of the sun, the elements of death itself. Those two American journeys especially transcend in tragic interest, to a thinking reader, most things one has seen in writing![34]

This observation anticipates much of the most recent interpretation of Dickens' work, but it was based, significantly, upon reading Forster's biography rather than upon reading Dickens' novels. Although Carlyle had some admiration for Dickens as a living man, his real attitude seems to have resembled Miss Emily's in William Faulkner's story. Full love came only after death. Carlyle's reading of Dickens requires, however, more than passing attention. His influence upon Dickens was profound, and the effect of Dickens' writings upon him was, to say the least, interesting.

It is ironical that the writer who had probably the most potent influence upon Victorian literature himself affected to despise literature. Carlyle's best literary criticism, written before 1832,[35] shows an awareness of the flexible potentialities of the novel, but as he became thereafter progressively obsessed with the Condition of England Question, he began to despise the novel as well as to despise poetry. Unsuccessful himself as novelist and poet, he had made his way as an historian and had come to the conventional conclusion that fiction was false and hence worthless. "I believe the world will soon discover that some practical work done is worth innumerable 'Oliver Twists' and 'Harry Lorrequers,' and any amount of other ingenious dancing on the slack rope."* Before a commission investigating conditions in the British Museum, Carlyle testified in his usual vein that novel readers and the insane ought to be separated from serious readers.[36] Combined with his instincts as an historian was an ancestral puritanism which simply disapproved of the novel as a waste of time. His comments thus develop to the point of absurdity an attitude which, as we have seen, crops up frequently in Victorian reviews.

During the period after the publication of *Pickwick*, Carlyle retained some affection for a few of his early favorites among novelists. These included Cervantes and his fellow countryman, Smollett, but for most later novelists he displayed only contempt. Jane Austen's novels were "dish-washings";[37] George Eliot's *Middlemarch* was "neither amusing nor instructive, but just dull."[38] His essay attacking Scott's lack of edification is considered to have seriously damaged that novelist's fame.[39] Except for *Henry Esmond*, he did not admire Thackeray's novels. According to Allingham, he had "not read most of them."[40] If what Carlyle says about Dickens' novels seems harsh, one should hardly be surprised. At least he preferred them to Thackeray's because, as he said (when *Dombey* and *Vanity Fair* were appearing simultaneously) Dickens' were more cheerful.[41] The reason given is revealing. Carlyle wanted Dickens to be a prophet, but, failing that, he was prepared to accept cheerful humor as a low kind of substitute. As he said in 1849: "Dickens has not written anything which will be found of much use in solving the problems of life. But he is worth something; worth a penny to

* D. A. Wilson, *Carlyle to Threescore-and-Ten* (1929), p. 573. Carlyle believed that he was paying Meredith a high compliment when he said: "Man, ye suld write heestory! Ye hae a heestorian in ye!" Opposite to complimentary was his advice to an invalid to read "the last volume of Macaulay's History or any other new novel." See J. A. Hammerton, *George Meredith* (1909), p. 108, and H. Morley, *English Literature* (New York, 1882), p. 291.

read of an evening before going to bed."[42] As light reading he enjoyed *Great Expectations*, "that Pip nonsense,"[43] which sent him into roars of laughter. But laughter was not enough for Carlyle in these later years, and he was sometimes ashamed for having succumbed to it.* He went so far as to tell one visitor, in 1860, that he never read Dickens' books![44] As might be expected, the novels which came closest to pleasing his captious tastes were *Hard Times*, *A Tale of Two Cities*, and *Little Dorrit*.[45]

How much of this scorn for the novel was passed on to Dickens we do not know. Carlyle's frankness was proverbial, and it would have been unusual if he had spared Dickens his opinions. Dickens seems to have been able to ignore his tiresome limitations as a literary critic and to recognize that in this strange and angry man was the embodiment of the explosive forces of dissatisfaction underlying the complacent exterior of Victorian life, forces of which Dickens' novels were also the embodiment. After the mid 1840's, while Forster remained the permanent advisor, Carlyle took over from Jeffrey, another Scot, the role of "Critic Laureate" for Dickens.† His influence on the later style of Dickens' novels is easily seen, and likewise his influence upon Dickens' ideas. A *Fraser's* reviewer drew attention, in 1851, to the parallels between the satirical sketch of model prisons in *Copperfield* and in Carlyle's *Latter-Day Pamphlets*.[46] Mrs. Jellyby and Mr. Honeythunder, who were deeply offensive to liberal readers, likewise represent one of the main themes of *Latter-Day Pamphlets* and of *Past and Present*: that charity must begin at home.

Writing about *Hard Times* to Carlyle, to whom the novel is dedicated, Dickens said: "I know it contains nothing in

* Concerning Dickens' public readings, see D. A. Wilson, *op.cit.*, p. 505. "Dickens does it capitally, such as *it* is; acts better than any Macready in the world . . . and keeping us laughing—in a sorry way, some of us thought—the whole night. He is a good creature, too, and makes fifty or sixty pounds by each of these readings."

† In 1844, Dickens requested Forster to have the Carlyles hear his reading of *The Chimes*. Carlyle's verdict, he felt, was "indispensable." (Forster, p. 356.) Again, in 1863, he wrote to Carlyle: "I am always reading you faithfully and trying to go your way." Nonesuch, III, 348.

which you do not think with me, for no man knows your books better than I."[47] One result of such discipleship was that Dickens' social criticism became widened in its scope and his tendency to be unpredictable became accentuated. To liberals, an especially offensive example of Carlyle's influence was the support that this supposed radical gave to Carlyle and his reactionary followers during the Governor Eyre Case.*

Of course the difference between the political positions of the two writers are endless, and part of Carlyle's contemptuous attitude towards his disciple can be explained by these differences.† Carlyle's importance, however, does not depend upon whether or not Dickens always agreed with him, but upon his general insistence that social criticism was more important than entertainment. After Jeffrey had been at Dickens' elbow urging him to emphasize his vein of sentiment came Carlyle urging him to emphasize his attacks upon the "vast blockheadism"[48] of Victorian society. If the death of Paul Dombey was exactly what Jeffrey had wanted, the Circumlocution Office was almost what Carlyle had wanted, and he was delighted by it—at least for a time.[49] His influence on the novels after *Copperfield* is, in this respect, incalculable. One gets a revealing glimpse into their relationship in one of Dickens' letters urging him to attend a reading of *Pickwick*. Almost apologetically, to assure the stern Master that it would not be entirely a waste of time, Dickens said: "You would find a healthy suggestion of an abuse or two, that sets people thinking in the right direction."[50] It is curious that

---

* Carlyle's influence in changing Dickens' attitude towards Negroes and slavery has been traced by Arthur Adrian in *PMLA*, LXVII (1952), 315-329. See also the present writer's article on "The Governor Eyre Case in England," *University of Toronto Quarterly*, XVII (1948), 227-228. The portrait of Mr. Honeythunder reflects Dickens' dislike for the philanthropists who had been attacking Governor Eyre: "You were to abolish military force, but you were first to bring all commanding officers who had done their duty, to trial by court-martial for that offence, and shoot them." *Edwin Drood*, ch. VI.

† "He [Dickens] thinks men ought to be buttered up, and the world made soft and accommodating for them, and all sorts of fellows have turkey for their Christmas dinner." (D. A. Wilson, *Carlyle at his Zenith*, p. 126.) These words evoke Mr. Bounderby's speeches about the workmen who "expect to be fed on turtle soup and venison with a gold spoon." See also Mildred G. Christian, "Carlyle's Influence on the Social Theories of Dickens," *The Trollopian*, I and II (1947), 27-35 and 11-26.

the conservative attacks on *Bleak House* and *Little Dorrit* took the line that Dickens was hoping to please the mob, whereas Dickens himself hoped that he was pleasing a man who, in many respects, was more conservative than Colonel Sibthorp. That his attempts really failed to impress the sage very deeply was not Dickens' fault.* It was primarily that this important and influential reader, gifted with perhaps the most vivid imagination in a century of vivid imaginations, had become so soured in his maturity that he was almost ashamed of the faculty in himself and scorned it in others.

VI

Carlyle's disciple, John Ruskin, also wrestled with the problem of truth and the imagination, yet by comparison with his master, as a reader of novels, he was relatively uninhibited. More than any other major Victorian prophet and social critic, Ruskin recognized the importance of the novel. His discussions of art and society are crammed with allusions to his favorite novelists such as Scott, Dickens, and Richardson, whose work he read and reread with zest throughout his long life. In fact his characteristic complaint in later years was that he knew *Pickwick* and some of Scott's novels so thoroughly (virtually "by heart") that rereading was superfluous.

One of Ruskin's early works was his "Essay on Literature" (1836), a defense of fiction against puritan criticism. His subject was the moral effect upon the reader of "the perusal of works of fiction," and he plunged into the defense of Scott and Bulwer with the same kind of ardor he later displayed in the defense of Turner in *Modern Painters*.† Banishing the

* Except for Hesketh Pearson, Dickens' biographers seem to have been misled by Carlyle's eulogy of Dickens in 1870. In old age he continued to speak unkindly of the novels. See *Life and Memoirs of John Churton Collins* (1912), p. 44. In 1874, Edward Fitzgerald used a significant phrase when writing to a friend: "I, for one, worship Dickens, in spite of Carlyle and the Critics: and wish to see his Gadshill as I wished to see Shakespeare's Stratford and Scott's Abbotsford." *Letters* (1910), II, 172.

† Ruskin's taste for Turner may account for his admiring the storm scene in *David Copperfield*. See the *Works of Ruskin*, III, 570.

puritan arguments about "falsehood and imagination" as mere nonsense, he contended that the novel could "humanize" the mind and therefore improve the moral feelings.[51] Forty-five years later, in a second essay, "Fiction, Fair and Foul," he was less cocksure about the moral benefits. In this fantastically rambling lecture he includes an elaborate comparison of the novel to a Greek vase: "A feigned, fictitious, artificial, supernatural, put-together-out-of-one's head, thing. All this it must be, to begin with."[52]

Whether *Nicholas Nickleby* resembles a Greek vase Ruskin does not say. His extensive references to Dickens' novels, based on a thorough knowledge surpassed only by his knowledge of Scott's, are not concerned with structure. Most of the references are general evaluations, especially of Dickens' role as a social critic, and it is evident that his estimate veered from praise to blame. The humorist, the "word-wit,"[53] consistently won his admiration. Writing to his father in 1863 he said: "I know no writer so voluminous and unceasingly entertaining, or with such a store of laughter . . . at things inherently grotesque."[54] More interesting was his recognition that Dickensian humor had serious overtones, as in the trial scene in *Pickwick*.[55] "I believe Dickens to be as little understood as Cervantes, and almost as mischievous."[56] This is the kind of *aperçu* that gives Ruskin stature as a critic. Crotchety, garrulous, full of whims and absurdities, Ruskin's talk about books may be all these, yet it often astonishes us with its insights.

During the 1850's, as Ruskin developed from a critic of art into a critic of society, he was happy to welcome Dickens as an ally. The Carlylean slant of the later novels delighted him, and *Hard Times*, especially, seemed a welcome blast against the hard, *laissez-faire* code which had become his obsession. Even the architecture of Coketown is seen as Ruskin tried to make his contemporaries see it. The typical Coketown church, "a pious warehouse of red brick," and the jail which "might have been the infirmary," the infirmary which "might have been the jail," and the town-hall which "might have been either" all anticipate Ruskin's lecture entitled *Traf-*

fic (1864) in which he addressed a group of Yorkshire business men about the building of an Exchange. In *Unto this Last*, the book which infuriated the same kind of readers who were infuriated by *Hard Times*, there is eloquent praise of Dickens' social criticism:

> The essential value and truth of Dickens's writings have been unwisely lost sight of by many thoughtful persons, merely because he presents his truth with some colour of caricature. . . . But let us not lose the use of Dickens's wit and insight, because he chooses to speak in a circle of stage fire. He is entirely right in his main drift and purpose in every book he has written; and all of them, but especially *Hard Times*, should be studied with close and earnest care by persons interested in social questions.[57]

In the same passage, Ruskin expressed a wish that Dickens would use "more accurate analysis" when taking up subjects of "high national importance." Having sloughed off the gorgeousness of his own *Stones of Venice* style, and having struggled to develop a clear, Swiftian prose, he was apt to find Dickens' "exaggeration" troublesome. So long as he considered Dickens a political ally, he was prepared to overlook the defect, but when he sensed that Dickens had somehow fallen into the camp of Macaulay, he considered the exaggeration unforgivable. "Dickens's delight in grotesque and rich exaggeration . . . has made him, I think, nearly useless in the present day."[58]

From the lover of gargoyles these words may sound strange, but by 1870 Ruskin had developed a keen sense of whether or not allies were truly loyal. He repudiated the suggestion that he had anything in common with Charles Kingsley. "Kingsley stepped westward—Yankee way. I step eastward, thinking the old star stands where it used to."[59] The same criticism was applied to Dickens in a letter which roused the wrath of Charles Norton:

> Dickens was a pure modernist—a leader of the steam-whistle party *par excellence*—and he had no understand-

ing of any power of antiquity except a sort of jackdaw sentiment for cathedral towers. He knew nothing of the nobler power of superstition. . . . His hero is essentially the ironmaster; in spite of *Hard Times*, he has advanced by his influence every principle that makes them harder— the love of excitement . . . the distrust both of nobility and clergy.[60]

The ambivalence of Dickens' attitude towards industrialism could hardly be more clearly demonstrated than by the diversity of Ruskin's impressions of that attitude.

In these later complaints against the steam-whistle side of Dickens, Ruskin was using the Toryism of Scott as his measuring stick. Scott was not religious—it saddened Ruskin to admit it—but he was indubitably no modernist. And Scott was also used as a measuring stick in one other aspect of Ruskin's evaluation of Dickens. Scott's novels were healthy; Dickens' were morbid. "Fiction, Fair and Foul" is oddly deterministic in its premise that modern industrial society must inevitably produce morbid literature, and to the extent that Dickens reflected that morbidity rather than caused it, he might be exonerated. According to this thesis, readers of all classes in modern urban communities are driven to seek stronger and stronger stimulants in literature. Hugo, Gautier, Balzac, and George Sand provide such stimulants by their portrayal of "animal passion";[61] Dickens by his portrayal of death. When *The Old Curiosity Shop* was published, Ruskin had been among the small minority who found the death of Nell "a diseased extravagance,"[62] and, in this later essay, he declared flatly that "Nell was simply killed for the market, as a butcher kills a lamb."[63] In *Bleak House*—a story which is neither "tragic, adventurous, or military"—there are nine deaths.[64] Ruskin's reasoning may be crotchety again, but he did have a perception that Dickens was not always the bouncing optimist he seemed to some other Victorian readers.

From this conflicting evidence, it is difficult to determine what values Ruskin found in Dickens' novels throughout the long period of his persistent reading of them. Although for an interval he recognized that in the later novels Dickens was engaged on the same side of the battle as he was, his more permanent verdict was that Dickens "never became an educational element of my life, but only one of its chief comforts and restoratives."[65]

VII

Matthew Arnold was another critic who sought restoratives and allies in his reading, but unlike Ruskin he rarely found either in prose fiction. Although considering himself much more awake to the main literary and social currents of his age than Ruskin, he remained relatively obtuse to the important role that the novel had assumed in his own age.* A conscientious and ardent reader, he hoarded the small quantity of time left to him from his own writing and school inspecting to concentrate attention upon Bishop Wilson, Sophocles, Goethe, Dante, and the *Pall Mall Gazette* rather than upon the time-consuming, sprawling narratives that Ruskin enjoyed. As a poet obliged to support himself by work in the civil service, he resented the success of "the undeniably powerful but most un-heaven-born productions" of popular novelists.[66] After telling one young writer that he did not rate novels as a high form of literature, he quoted Coleridge's remark that "novel reading spares the reader the trouble of thinking, it saves him from the boredom of vacancy, and establishes a habit of indolence."† The remark may remind us of Dr. Thomas Arnold's complaining that *Pickwick* and *Nickleby* were responsible for a "decrease of manly thoughtfulness" at Rugby.[67]

Despite this fastidiousness, Arnold did, of course, explore the writings of a number of novelists. George Sand, an Oxford discovery, remained one of his favorites, and two of his three essays on novelists are devoted to her books. His

* The essay on Tolstoy, written a year before his death, does show that Arnold in his last years was taking the novel more seriously. Had he lived longer, it is probable that he might have had much more to say on the subject.

† Stephen Coleridge, *Famous Victorians I Have Known* (1928), p. 33. The author reports that Arnold told him he had been offered £10,000 for writing a novel, but he had refused to attempt it.

letters make occasional references to Fielding, Scott, Thackeray, and Charlotte Brontë, and his notebooks show that he read (or tried to read) a few novels by Trollope, George Eliot, and Balzac, as well as an occasional novel by Reade, Bulwer, Hawthorne, Flaubert, Cooper, and Harriet Beecher Stowe.[68] For Wilkie Collins' novel about a reformed prostitute, *The New Magdalen*, he had a strange admiration.[69] After retirement, he had free time enough to spare for all six of Jane Austen's novels, and the year before his death he was planning to read Hardy's *Hand of Ethelberta*.

The list itself is not unimpressive, but one never senses, in Arnold's letters or essays, that these books left the kind of firm imprint upon him that Ruskin retained.

Of Dickens, we know that Arnold read *David Copperfield* in 1880 and *Our Mutual Friend* in 1881, and that he resolved, several times during his last years, to read *A Tale of Two Cities*. It is possible that others were read at Rugby and Oxford, but no reference is made to them. In fact, Arnold is a useful corrective for the literary historian who assumes that celebrated books are invariably read hot from the presses by all educated readers. When *Little Dorrit* was published, Disraeli declined comment upon it saying that he had never read anything of Dickens except an extract in a newspaper.[70] Others, like Arnold and T. L. Peacock and J. R. Lowell, seem to have discovered his novels late in life. In 1887, after commencing *David Copperfield*, Lowell wrote to C. E. Norton: "I had never read it, I find, though Mr. Micawber has become so proverbial that, finding his name in it, I thought I had. . . . It is amazingly well done so far as I have got."[71] Peacock is a more striking example. It was in ripe old age, when he had resolved to confine his reading to Greek, that he discovered Dickens for the first time. *Pickwick* sent him into frequent fits of laughter, "although, on the whole, he preferred *Our Mutual Friend*." Lizzie Hexam he declared to be his ideal of womanhood.[72]

In "The Incompatibles" (1881), Arnold made what he admitted was his first "comment in print" concerning Dickens:

What a pleasure to have the opportunity of praising a work so sound, a work so rich in merit, as *David Copperfield!* . . . But to contemporary work so good as *David Copperfield*, we are in danger of perhaps not paying respect enough, of reading it (for who could help reading it?) too hastily. . . . What treasures of gaiety, invention, life, are in that book! what alertness and resource![73]

The exclamation points from Arnold are high praise, but as E. K. Brown notes with amusement, there appears to be some exaggeration in Arnold's saying of *Copperfield* that he had been "reading it again" when, in a letter of 1880, he stated that he was reading it for the first time.* Actually, Arnold had read *Copperfield*, in some fashion, almost thirty years earlier,[74] and must have forgotten having done so.

The delight of his rediscovery is conveyed again and again throughout twenty pages of the essay. What Arnold rejoiced to have found (as Ruskin did in *Hard Times*) was an ally. That Dickens' social criticism, beginning with *Sunday Under Three Heads*, has much in common with Arnold's, ought to be evident enough to later readers, but apparently had not been so evident to Arnold himself. After twenty years of battle with the Philistines, Arnold was delighted "to take the words of anybody rather than myself for showing the impression which this class is likely to make."[75] Dickens, he says, knew the middle classes intimately, as he himself, on his inspection tours, painfully got to know them. "With the hand of a master he has drawn for us a type of the teachers and trainers of its youth, a type of its places of education. Mr. Creakle and Salem House are immortal."[76] With its Murdstones, Creakles, and Quinions, *David Copperfield*, Arnold finds, is an "all-containing treasure-house" of English Philistinism.[77] And it

---

* See E. K. Brown, *Matthew Arnold* (Chicago, 1948), pp. 199-200. Although evidence is lacking, I myself have had the impudent impression that there may be a similar sleight of hand at work in the essay on Tolstoy. When Arnold deftly avoids discussing *War and Peace*, one may wonder whether he had read that novel. For a discussion of the importance of Arnold's essay on Tolstoy, see Marion Mainwaring's article in *Nineteenth-Century Fiction*, vi (1952), 269-274.

is true that each of these characters might have appeared, with little modification, in Arnold's satirical narrative, *Friendship's Garland*, just as Mrs. Rachael in *Bleak House* and Brother Hawkyard in *George Silverman's Explanation* could be transposed to *Culture and Anarchy*, *St. Paul and Protestantism*, or even the essay on Wordsworth. The mutual target of their satire was the intolerable dullness and hardness of middle-class life rather than its wickedness. All this is not to ignore equally obvious differences. At the core of Dickens' didactic purposes is an ideal that all classes might simply enjoy life with kindness. Arnold hoped that all classes, but especially the middle classes (whom he tried to cajole with every persuasive device) might enjoy life intelligently and provide intelligent leadership.

In "The Incompatibles" Arnold was unconcerned with such important differences and hailed Dickens as a fellow David-in-arms. It is characteristic that what roused his enthusiasm was the social criticism. In his essays on Tolstoy and George Sand, it is not so much their narratives that interest him as their search for "la vie idéale."[78] In 1884 he observed that "the work of humanitarians and idealists like George Sand and her master Rousseau" had gone out of fashion. In their place were the realists and naturalists such as Balzac and Flaubert, fortified by the theories of Taine and his concept of detached objectivity.[79] Ardent Francophile that he was, Arnold felt, nevertheless, that the new direction in France was a mistake and that a humanitarian purpose is essential in literature. The great writers, Shakespeare, Sophocles, Dante, Rabelais, George Sand, might take as their motto, he says, a line from the *Agamemnon*: "Let the good prevail." Such writers "deal with the life of all of us—the life of man in its fulness and greatness."[80] Dickens' name does not appear this time in the honor roll of Arnold's academy, but any defense of Dickens' kind of novel of social purpose, published during the 1880's, was of assistance in sustaining what had become, at that time, a somewhat clouded reputation.

Of different stature from Arnold today, but influential in his own generation, J. C. Jeaffreson (1831-1901) was an-

other critic whose discussion of Dickens was primarily concerned with his role as a commentator upon society. "It
would seem indeed that society was tired of being merely
amused, and thirsted for instruction even in its moments of
relaxation."[81] On this premise of "earnestness of purpose"
Jeaffreson sets out to show the superiority of Dickens to Scott.
His lengthy discussion in *Novels and Novelists* (1858) is an
unqualified panegyric of Dickens as a reformer, and he notes
with pride that most Victorian novelists, such as Reade,
Kingsley, Mrs. Stowe, and Charlotte Yonge, whether skilfully
or not, have followed the lead of "the greatest . . . living writer
of prose fiction":

> His benefits to mankind are as innumerable as the
> flowers that cover the earth. . . . There is not a human
> heart in these islands . . . which Dickens has not at some
> time or other influenced for the better. . . . Amongst us
> there is not a grinding task-master who would not have
> been more selfish, . . . had Dickens never lived to write.
> . . . We have been in his hands only plastic clay that
> he has fashioned. . . . We cannot . . . look out upon
> the world save through his eyes.[82]

VIII

Jeaffreson's paean anticipates the obituary notices, but before these are discussed, the swarm of hornets stirred up by
Bleak House and its successors must be examined. It was the
social criticism in the later novels that was primarily responsible for the splitting of Dickens' public. Although disgusted
reviewers often concentrated their attention upon his decline
as an artist, their attacks were usually motivated by an
animus against a wide-sweeping criticism of society that
alienated conservative and liberal alike. As E. P. Whipple
noted, such characters as Vholes and Sir Leicester Dedlock
delighted the liberals and angered the conservatives, whereas
Mrs. Jellyby delighted the conservatives and angered the
liberals.* Both agreed that the author of *Pickwick* had taken a

* Mrs. Jellyby provoked Lord Denman, formerly an ardent Dickensian,
into publishing a rancorous pamphlet attacking *Bleak House*, and she also

wrong turn and had listened to bad advice from such enthusiastic readers as Jeaffreson:

> As humourist we prefer Dickens to all living men. . . .
> But gradually his old characteristics have slipped from
> him. . . . All his inspiration now seems to come from
> without. . . . A booby . . . assures him that his great
> strength lies in "going to the heart of our deepest social
> problems"; and straightway Dickens, the genial Dickens,
> overflowing by nature with the most rampant hearty
> fun, addresses himself to the melancholy task, setting
> to work to illustrate some enigma which Thomas Car-
> lyle perhaps, or some such congenial dreary spirit . . .
> has left rather darker than before. Another luminary
> tells him that it is the duty of a great popular writer
> to be a great moral teacher, and straightway a piece of
> staring morality is embroidered into the motley pattern.
> . . . Lastly comes the worst tempter of all . . . at whose
> instigation are elaborated some plebian specimens of all
> the virtues. . . . The result of some such guidance . . .
> appears in *Bleak House* and *Little Dorrit*, as well as in
> great parts of both *Dombey* and *Copperfield*.[83]

This article called "Remonstrance with Dickens" is written in a "more in sorrow than in anger" spirit. In the wilderness of *Little Dorrit*, says the writer, "we sit down and weep when we remember thee, O *Pickwick!*"[84] With reference to *Little Dorrit*, the *Saturday Review* made a similar observation: "We admit that Mr. Dickens has a mission, but it is to make the world grin, not to recreate and rehabilitate society. Sam Weller, Dick Swiveller, and Sairey Gamp are his successes . . ."[85] When Lord Chief Justice Campbell complimented Dickens by saying that he would rather have written *Pickwick* than have become Lord Chief Justice, he would have been much more gracious if he had specified *Bleak House* instead of *Pickwick*.

Hitherto faithful admirers of Dickens began to abandon

---

aroused the feminist wrath of John Stuart Mill. See Sir Joseph Arnould, *Memoir of Lord Denman* (1873), II, 332-333, and *Dickensian*, XL, p. 141.

him after reading *Bleak House.* "Dickens all cant (Liberal cant, the worst sort)" wrote Miss Mitford in 1853.* The *Quarterly* damned him by calling him, of all things, a "Pre-Raphaelite." The term was apparently used to refer to any kind of mad radical,[86] yet it was mild enough coming from a magazine which had said *Jane Eyre* represented "a murmuring against the privations of the poor, which . . . is a murmuring against God's appointment."[87] In *Aurora Leigh* (1857), there is a passage which indicates how fully Dickens had built up a reputation as an *enfant terrible*:

> We talked modern books
> And daily papers. . . . Is London full? is trade
> Competitive? has Dickens turned his hinge
> A-pinch upon the fingers of the great?[88]

The fingers pinched most painfully by *Hard Times* were those of the Utilitarians, but other shades of believers in *laissez-faire* were likewise offended. Macaulay, a tireless novel-reader and an admirer of *Pickwick* and *Nickleby*, repudiated *Hard Times* because of its "sullen socialism,"[89] returning thereafter to his less provocative favorites: Richardson, Austen, and Scott. *Blackwood's* found the book based on a "petulant theory" and spoiled by adherence to a "didactic principle."[90] Such reviews could be almost chastely aesthetic when necessary. It was an American critic, however, who provided the best analysis of why *Hard Times* seemed fatuous. E. P. Whipple stated that Dickens' readers were "vexed with an author who deviated from the course of amusing them, . . . only to emphasize *notions which were behind the knowledge of the time.*"[91] The criticism of Utilitarian hardness in *Hard Times* is childish, Whipple said, because it challenges the "laws" of political economy, which are as inexorable as the law of gravitation. "The time will come when it will be as intellectually discreditable for an educated person to engage

---

* *The Friendships of M. R. Mitford* (1882), ii, 249. See also *The Autobiography of Mrs. Oliphant* (1899), p. 186. "I think it would go against the grain to applaud him highly in his present phase." Henry Crabb Robinson was another reader who lost interest in Dickens' novels in the 1850's.

in a crusade against the established laws of political economy as in a crusade against the established laws of the physical universe."[92] This hardy assumption is still with us and makes an occasional public reappearance when the economic heresies of Lord Keynes are being discussed. In the secure prosperity of the 1850's, the assumption seemed so self-evident in many quarters that Dickens and Ruskin were regarded as either fools or madmen. Indeed, rumors began to circulate, especially in America, that Dickens had been "shut up in a madhouse."[93] One of the most prominent of these rumors was that after having read a slashing attack upon *A Tale of Two Cities* in the *Saturday Review*, he had fallen into a fit. It was said that he had been confined to bed for months, after having been restored to mere consciousness by "a dozen physicians" and "the constant application of warm flannels."[94]

The review in question, the most violently abusive to appear in Dickens' lifetime, was certainly enough to make any author fall into a fit. Sir William Robertson Nicoll, who describes it as "the most infamous, perhaps, in the whole record of English criticism," attributes it to the pen of Sir James Fitzjames Stephen,* the writer of a series of articles in the *Saturday Review* which were designed to demonstrate that the author of *Little Dorrit* was a "quack and an impostor." In 1861, the "worthy gentlemen who distil vinegar for the benefit of society" in the pages of the *Saturday Review* decided to call off their attacks temporarily.[95] It was said that they were obliged to do so after a reader had counted up the number of allusions to Dickens' writings in the very issues in which these writings were being assailed as "puppy pie and stewed cat."[96] Actually, *Great Expectations* itself seems to have been responsible for the temporary lulling of the

---

* Nicoll, *Dickens's Own Story* (New York, n.d.), p. 212. M. M. Bevington, in his study of *The Saturday Review* (New York, 1941), ch. VI, has assigned to Stephen five of the attacks on Dickens which appeared from 1857 to 1859. He also shows that all of the attacks were inspired by the "general policy" laid down by Stephen and that they followed in his identical vein. Although Mr. Bevington has not formally identified the reviewer who slashed *A Tale of Two Cities*, it would seem that Nicoll was probably correct in assigning it to Stephen himself.

assault; it was reviewed generously as a return to Dickens' "best vein," the vein of *Chuzzlewit* and *Copperfield*.*

The instigator of the abusive attacks preceding *Great Expectations*, Fitzjames Stephen, was a downright young barrister with two axes to grind as far as Dickens was concerned. At Cambridge he had written a readable essay on fiction which is virtually naturalistic in its insistence upon photographic exactness. *Robinson Crusoe* was Stephen's ideal novel because it is almost as "truthful" as biography.[97] With admirable common sense, but not much else, he argued that Jane Austen's "sequence of incidents" is a regrettable distortion of reality.[98] What his attitude towards Dickens' highly stylized creations would be is not difficult to imagine. "No popularity can disguise the fact that this is the very lowest of low styles of art."[99] *A Tale of Two Cities* is concocted, says Stephen, by "a system of cookery which procured for its ingenious inventor unparalleled popularity" and spread the "conviction that the principal results of a persistent devotion to literature are an incurable vulgarity of mind and of taste, and intolerable arrogance of temper."[100] *A Tale of Two Cities* is admittedly one of the most strained of Dickens' works, and Stephen has little trouble in exposing the mechanism of its grotesqueness, which he does with sadistic relish. The illustrations, he notes, "are thoroughly worthy of the text. It is impossible to imagine faces and figures more utterly unreal."[101]

The hatred inspiring this review did not stem entirely from the offense *A Tale of Two Cities* had given to Stephen's taste for naturalness of characterization. It stemmed even more from the offense which *Bleak House* and *Little Dorrit* had given by exposing the ineptitude and obtuse incompetence of the law courts and the civil service. These touched the young Benthamite on the raw. Moreover, his father, Sir James Stephen, one of the most powerful and prominent of

* *Saturday Review*, XII (July 1861), 69-70. Crabb Robinson reports that he was "seduced" by this praise to try reading Dickens again, but he found *Great Expectations* disappointing. (*Henry Crabb Robinson on Books*, II, 802.) There was also high praise for *Great Expectations* in *The Times*, October 17, 1861, p. 6, and in the *British Quarterly Review*, XXXV (1862), 135.

civil servants, had been under-secretary of state for the colonies. The son assumed, as Leslie Stephen tells us, that Tite Barnacle was a caricature of his father and of the sacred institutions to which his life and hard work had been devoted.[102] In 1857 Stephen had reviewed *Little Dorrit* itself in the *Edinburgh*, a review which goaded Dickens into the unusual act of making a direct reply in *Household Words*. Stephen's infuriated response to the Barnacles is the driving force behind his several notices and reviews of Dickens, and he makes one hit against the social criticism which was to persist among later critics: that Dickens was simply whipping dead horses. "He seems . . . to get his first notions of an abuse from the discussions which accompany its removal. . . . This was his course with respect both to imprisonment for debt and to Chancery reform."[103] With *Little Dorrit*, in this review, Stephen links Charles Reade's *It Is Never Too Late to Mend* and, of course, neglects to distinguish between Reade's pedestrian documentation and Dickens' imaginative projection of the maze and muddle of government.

It also seems evident that this hostility to Dickens was shared by Fitzjames Stephen's younger brother, who, in other respects, was a much more supple-minded critic of the novel. When Leslie Stephen was asked to contribute to a collection of essays on Dickens, he declined, saying that he feared that anything he might write would "strike a false note in a chorus of enthusiastic admirers."[104] A similar charitable withholding of judgment is evident throughout his *Hours in a Library*; in the midst of discussions of Charlotte Brontë, Disraeli, Kingsley, Balzac, Defoe, and other novelists, the name of Dickens is not even mentioned. His article on Dickens in the *Dictionary of National Biography* (1888) is especially cool towards the novels following *Copperfield*. "If literary fame could be safely measured by popularity with the half-educated, Dickens must claim the highest position among English novelists." It is interesting to speculate whether the influence of her father, Leslie Stephen, and of her uncle, Fitzjames, accounts for Virginia Woolf's distaste for Dickens. The impact of the Circumlocution Office, which Dickens himself felt to be his most provocative creation, seems to have been more far-reaching than even he had hoped.

Finally, in this connection, there is Anthony Trollope, who was also touched on the raw by the Circumlocution Office. As a novelist whose idols were Thackeray, and, to a lesser extent, George Eliot, Trollope considered that Dickens belonged to an inferior species in which sensation, exaggeration, and unnatural characterization were typical faults. "It has been the peculiarity and the marvel of this man's power, that he has invested his puppets with a charm that has enabled him to dispense with human nature."[105] In the three or four discussions of Dickens written by Trollope, it is always amusing to watch the struggle between his own distaste and his sturdy respect for the public taste which idolized Dickens. "It is fatuous to condemn that as deficient in art which has been so full of art as to captivate all men."[106] To solve his dilemma, Trollope looked to the future. "*Jane Eyre*, and *Esmond*, and *Adam Bede* will be in the hands of our grandchildren, when *Pickwick*, and *Pelham*, and *Harry Lorrequer* are forgotten," he wrote.[107] Meanwhile, he considered *Pickwick* to be admirably useful as a moral tale, especially for the young.[108]

Aside from Dickens' failure to create human character and human action, Trollope was offended by the mannered style of his prose, and like many critics, he warned his fellow novelists that Dickens was generally a bad model to follow.[109] If we consider the literary ancestry of Mr. Slope, it is evident that Trollope spoke from the experience of having himself been influenced by Dickens—usually, it may be said, to good advantage.[110]

As his letters show, Trollope's dislike of Dickens as a novelist was increased by his lack of admiration for the conceit of the man.[111] Strongest of all, however, was his irritation against the apparent irresponsibility of Dickens' social and political criticism. In the midst of his obituary essay is a key passage: "He thoroughly believed in literature; but in politics he seemed to have no belief at all. . . . To his feeling, all departmental work was the bungled, muddled routine of a Circumlocution Office. . . . If any man ever was so, he was a radical at heart, believing entirely in the people, writing for them, speaking for them. . . ."[112] From a conscientious civil servant who firmly believed in the importance of his work, this judgment is significant, and it explains the principal incentive which prompted the vigorous satire against "Mr. Popular Sentiment" in *The Warden*.* Trollope had learned in the Post Office that reform must develop from a slow and laborious weighing of alternatives. Dickens' fearless and explosive haste seemed to him as horrifying and as irresponsible as it seemed to Fitzjames Stephen. The effect on him of *Little Dorrit*, in particular, has been traced by some skillful detective work on the part of Bradford Booth who discovered that Trollope was provoked by the novel to write a review of its first three numbers. *Little Dorrit* was also responsible for Trollope's defense of the civil service in the first edition of *The Three Clerks*.[113]

The beef-and-potatoes reality of Trollope's dream world and the hearty common sense of his own character have often caused him to be labelled as the most representative Victorian. In the coolness of his attitude towards Dickens' novels, he himself felt that he was unrepresentative, and indeed, because of his own insecurity as a youth, he had chosen to cut himself off from what Carlyle called the great "daemonic" current of nineteenth-century life. His dissatisfaction is, however, of considerable importance. It is in line with a *Spectator* article in which an unusually curious judgment was passed on Dickens' "teaching." "It is not really English, and tends to modify English family feeling in the direction of theatric tenderness and an impulsiveness wholly wanting in self-control."† Whether a stiff upper lip is more "English" than a quivering humanitarianism, or even whether it is more Vic-

* Lionel Stevenson suggests that *The Warden* was projected after Trollope had read some articles in *Household Words* exposing conditions in the Charterhouse. See "Dickens and the Origin of 'The Warden,' " *The Trollopian*, II (1947), 83-89.

† "Charles Dickens's Moral Service to Literature," *The Spectator*, XLII (1869), 475. In his Introduction to *Bleak House* for the Waverley Edition, John Galsworthy also notes that Dickens' lack of reticence was most decidedly "un-English."

torian—here are questions which Sir Thomas Browne might classify as almost above antiquarism. Trollope's dissatisfaction is at least an important reminder of the pitfalls in any overly facile generalizations about Victorianism—into which the present study has no doubt often slipped—and is a further indication of the diversity of tastes which divided Dickens' public after 1850.[114] The *Athenaeum*, for example, which has been called a "mirror of Victorian culture," reacted in exactly the opposite way from Trollope. It had been harsh in its comments upon Dickens' early work and was won over by the social criticism of *Bleak House* and *Our Mutual Friend*.[115]

IX

Unanimity was temporarily restored on the occasion of Dickens' death. The important assessments of his role as an artist were not made on that occasion, most of the comment being centered upon his social criticism. From the perspective of 1870, the animosities stirred up by *Hard Times* and *Little Dorrit* could be overlooked for the moment. In the solemnly rolling prose of *The Times*, there was no reminder of earlier controversies:

> Fewer still, we believe, will be regarded with more honour as time passes and his greatness grows upon us. He has done as much as Addison, Johnson, or Goldsmith to "correct the vices," "ridicule the follies," and purify the sympathy of his generation. The Abbey, as the shrine of English genius, would be incomplete without him.[*]

The feeling that Dickens had served as England's conscience was typical of most of the obituaries. Queen Victoria herself spoke of "the great loss." "He had a large, loving mind and the strongest sympathy with the poorer classes. He felt sure that a . . . much greater union of classes would take place in

---

[*] *The Times*, June 13, 1870, p. 11. The obituary in *The Times* was inspired and perhaps written by Lord Houghton, at whose ancestral estate Dickens' grandmother had once served as a housekeeper. See James Pope-Hennessy, *Monckton-Milnes: The Flight of Youth* (1951), pp. 216-217.

time. And I pray earnestly it may."[116] To Lord Shaftesbury, Dickens seemed like the pagan Naaman, " 'by whom the Lord had given deliverance to Syria!' " Though Dickens' social criticism was not made "on Christian principle," yet, in rousing attention "to many evils and many woes," he was "a servant of the Most High."[117]

Biblical analogies also appear in the funeral sermon preached by the Dean of Westminster, who spoke of the novel as the modern equivalent of the parable.[118] Although it was recognized, even by Broad Churchmen, that Dickens' ecclesiastical affiliations were somewhat tenuous,* his social criticism had acquired a New Testament aura of considerable importance to its status. It was especially important in mollifying the feelings of Nonconformist and Evangelical readers which had been frayed by Stiggins and Chadband.[119]

In a less ambitious sermon than Dean Stanley's, Benjamin Jowett summed up most effectively and reasonably how much his contemporary readers valued Dickens' general achievement as a critic of society:

> Works of fiction would be intolerable if they attempted to be sermons directly to instruct us; but indirectly they are great instructors of this world, and we can hardly exaggerate the debt of gratitude which is due to a writer who has led us to sympathize with these good, true, sincere, honest English characters of ordinary life, and to laugh at the egotism, the hypocrisy, the false respectability of religious professors and others. . . . He whose loss we now mourn occupied a greater space than any other writer in the minds of Englishmen during the last thirty-five years.[120]

* Gladstone, a High Churchman, made a typical entry in his diary after reading *Nicholas Nickleby*: "No church in the book, and the motives are not those of religion." John Morley, *Life of W. E. Gladstone* (1903), I, 220.

CHAPTER 6

THE ARTIST

I

DICKENS' place in literature will be determined not by virtue of any moral purpose which animates his art, but in spite of it. . . . A novelist . . . is to be judged by his novels . . . not as they further this or that social propaganda."[1] This protest against the exploitation of Dickens as a humanitarian, written by W. A. Sibbald in 1907, reflects the influence of the aesthetic movement, but even during his lifetime there were some readers who were less concerned with his role as the goad of social consciences than with his success in creating a satisfying and unified world of probable actions and characters.

One of these readers was George Henry Lewes. His early novel, *Ranthorpe*, stuffed with learned quotations on every page in a manner he missed in Dickens' works and admired in his wife's, is a dull novel but an interesting document. In one passage, Lewes predicts that the growth of economic equality will lead to the development of an aristocracy of taste and intelligence—a thesis which anticipates the classification of readers into highbrow, middlebrow, and lowbrow, later to be developed by Virginia Woolf and others. " '*Si on annonçait M. de Montmorency et M. de Balzac dans un salon, . . . on regarderait M. de Balzac.*' "[2]

An important trait of Lewes and other highbrow readers is restlessness. Equipped to discover and encourage new talent or genius, the highbrow reader is likewise more easily dissatisfied, more ready to abandon the successfully established artist for pastures new than is the average reader. The fluctuation in the status of Ernest Hemingway or Aldous Huxley among critics in recent years is typical of a pattern which can be detected in the reception of *Bleak House* and *Little Dorrit*. Do what he will, the successful novelist reaches a point at which he is doomed to be damned. The crisp dialogue of

Hemingway, once so admirable, is regarded as a wearisome trick; the picturesque minor character of Dickens is regarded as a mere mechanism. What was characterization in Simon Tappertit becomes caricature in Mr. Pancks:

> Every character strikes an imposing attitude . . . and goes through all the scenes with . . . one fixed spasmodic intensity of exaggeration. His actors are never in repose, never relax the strong stare, never vary from the monotonous rigidity of matter or manner. Not one . . . ever subsides into the commonplace speech of real life.[3]

As David Masson said more politely in 1859: "the public have caught what is called his mannerism or trick; and hence a certain recoil from his later writings among the cultivated and fastidious."[4] Artistic as well as political considerations were responsible for the splitting apart of Dickens' public.

If critics such as Lewes were on the lookout for new talent, their wishes were suddenly rewarded in 1847 by the appearance of *Vanity Fair, Jane Eyre*, and (of less consequence at the time) *Wuthering Heights*. The next three years also saw the publication of the industrial novels of Charles Kingsley and Mrs. Gaskell, as well as of Hawthorne's *Scarlet Letter*. "Worth . . . fifty Dickenses and Bulwers" was Lockhart's verdict after reading *Jane Eyre*.[5] And Mrs. Carlyle, whose taste Dickens valued highly, was equally emphatic after spending a night reading *Vanity Fair*: "Very good, indeed, beats Dickens out of the world."[6] Lewes himself, reviewing *Vanity Fair* for the *Athenaeum*, praised its quietness "in a literary age which has a tendency to mistake spasm for force."[7]

This group of novels confronted Dickens with the first serious literary competition of his career. During the eleven years before 1847, the bareness of the field is remarkable. Half forgotten writers including Theodore Hook, Harrison Ainsworth, Charles Lever, G. P. R. James, and Samuel Warren, were said by his contemporaries to be his rivals,[8] and even Bulwer-Lytton and Disraeli, his chief living competitors, seem minor talents in the eyes of posterity. In the eyes of Bulwer-Lytton himself, the author of *Pickwick* was a genius and the only contemporary novelist worthy of his competition.[9] Lytton envied Dickens' capacity to please both critics and public, especially from 1836-1846,[10] his own reputation being almost exclusively a popular one which lasted into the twentieth century but which has wilted from lack of critical nourishment.*

Mention might also be made of French novelists such as Hugo, Eugène Sue, and Balzac, whose work received some attention (often of a horrified kind) during this period, but the real impact of French fiction upon English readers was not felt until later.[11] Browning's reverence for Balzac, whom he considered far superior to all English novelists,[12] was ahead of his time. It was a reverence which, incidentally, may account for his apparent lack of concern for Dickens' novels. Although an interesting study could be made of the abundant exuberance and the zest for the grotesque shared by the two writers, the author of *The Ring and the Book* apparently studied his craft of fiction in novels other than those of Dickens. One of his few recorded references to a work by Dickens is to *Pictures from Italy*, which he found, at best, "readable" but which his wife found vulgar.†

Whether or not Balzac himself might also be charged with vulgarity, there were no doubts, on this score, about Thackeray. After having been embarrassed by a novelist who referred to Michael Angelo as a humbug, highbrow readers were overjoyed to discover the gracious and civilized tone of *Vanity Fair*. How responsible this distinction was in causing

---

* According to Lewis Melville in 1906: "The public has never forsworn its allegiance, and his books, read by hundreds of thousands, rival those of Dickens in popularity." (*Victorian Novelists*, p. 4.) In *The Nigger of the Narcissus* Conrad mentions the friendship of Bulwer-Lytton among sailors as "a wonderful and bizarre phenomenon."

† *The Letters of Robert Browning and Elizabeth Barrett Browning* (New York, 1899), II, 167. Some of Elizabeth Barrett's enthusiasm for Dickens seems to have evaporated by 1845: "You have heard, I suppose, how Dickens's 'Cricket' sells by nineteen thousand copies at a time, though he takes Michael Angelo to be 'a humbug'—or for 'though' read 'because.'" (*Ibid.*, I, p. 354.) It would seem that J. W. T. Ley in *The Dickens Circle* has considerably exaggerated the friendship between Browning and Dickens. Percy Fitzgerald makes a similar error in saying that "Browning was a great Dickensian." See *The Book Monthly*, III (1905), 21. For an amusing account of the Brownings reading *Copperfield*, see *Elizabeth Barrett Browning: Letters to her Sister* (1932), p. 130.

"Lift me up!—Tie me in my chair!—Fill my glass!"
(from R. S. Surtees, *Jorrocks's Jaunts and Jollities*, 1838)

Little Nell
(from a painting by Emily Macirone)

A Scene from Reynolds' *Mysteries of London* (1845)

FAREWELL TO DICKENS

John Bull's Farewell to Dickens

'Twas not without a touch of pride
We sent, to greet our Yankee brother,
The man whose lessons, far and wide,
Instruct all men to love each other.

(from an issue of *Judy*, October 30, 1867)

readers to switch allegiance away from Dickens has been best indicated by W. D. Howells: "There is certainly a property in Thackeray that somehow flatters the reader into the belief that he [the reader] is better than other people. . . . I felt I must be of a finer porcelain than the earthen pots which were not aware of any particular difference in the various liquors poured into them." Dickens, by contrast, "never appeals to the principle which sniffs, in the reader. The base of his work is the whole breadth and depth of humanity itself."[13] Thus the diagnostician of snobbery came himself to exemplify what twentieth-century advertisers call *snob-appeal*.

The superiority of *Vanity Fair* to *Dombey and Son* was urged on two particular counts so often as to become commonplace. The first was the naturalness of style; the second was naturalness of characterization and narrative. Behind these judgments was a powerful trend in Victorian criticism towards a restoration of neo-classical standards, a trend related to the development of the Parnassian school in France, to Matthew Arnold's Preface for his poems of 1853, as well as to the emergence of more rigid conceptions of the nature of prose fiction.

To appreciate the Victorian critical attitude towards Dickens' style requires something of an effort of historical imagination. In the twentieth century, he has been described by A. C. Benson as "a supreme master of language; his vocabulary was enormous. . . . There never was such a craftsman."[14] And Graham Greene speaks of his mature style as a "secret prose" which gives us "that sense of a mind speaking to itself with no one there to listen." *Great Expectations* is written in "delicate and exact poetic cadences, the music of memory, that so influenced Proust."[15] What we have lost is a sense of how shockingly revolutionary Dickens' prose seemed to his contemporaries. His master, Carlyle, writing to John Sterling (June 4, 1835) was acutely aware that his own trombone-like prose was sounding a blast against the strongholds of decorum: "Do you reckon this really a time for Purism of Style. . . ? I do not: with whole ragged battalions of Scott's-Novel Scotch, with Irish, German, French, and even Newspaper Cockney . . . storming in on us, and the whole structure of our Johnsonian English breaking up from its foundations,—revolution *there* as visible as anywhere else!" It was a revolution that was to lead through Dickens to D. H. Lawrence, and, eventually, to the anarchy of Gertrude Stein and Henry Miller.

Carlyle's reference to Dr. Johnson is perceptive, for even in the 1850's Johnsonian style was still the yardstick for many reviewers. The scene in Mrs. Gaskell's *Cranford* when a quarrel breaks out in the village between the adherents of *Pickwick* and the adherents of *Rasselas* is almost symbolic. In the *Quarterly*, a reviewer of *Oliver Twist* grumbled that "these Dodgers and Sikes break into our Johnsons, rob the queen's lawful current English. . . ."[16] *Fraser's*, a magazine more at ease with the stylistic revolution, noted simply that "the old school" was disgusted because "instead of seeking the 'well of English undefiled' by Twickenham," Dickens had taught writers to "draw at haphazard from the muddy stream that has washed Mile End."[17]

Some of these complaints were simply against the lowness of the dialogue of Mrs. Gamp or Sam Weller. In 1860, it was even suggested, in a letter to the *Athenaeum*, that "an edition of Dickens' novels should be brought out in classical English. . . . I think the language of the lower orders ought never to appear in print."[18] More often, the lack of "classical English" was found in Dickens' own style rather than in his dialogue. As Fitzjames Stephen said in 1858: "Till our own days, almost every popular writer formed his style on the classical model." Even Coleridge and Lamb had been "taught to write." Dickens, however, seems to be unconsciously writing parodies of Johnsonian English by making fun of "that style of writing which demanded balanced sentences, double-barrelled epithets, and a proper conception of the office and authority of semicolons."[19] Such Dickensian expressions as "highly geological home-made cakes" or "undeniable chins" were lashed as "gross offences against the English language."[20] Especially offensive were such wildly hyperbolical comparisons as the account of Mr. Mell blowing his flute "until I almost thought he would gradually blow his whole being into the large hole at the top, and ooze away at the keys." As another example of stylistic eccentricity, Taine cited the following sentence concerning the disillusionment of Tom Pinch: "He had so long been used to steep the Pecksniff of his fancy in his tea, and spread him out upon his toast, and take him as a relish with his beer, that he made but a poor breakfast on the first morning after his expulsion."[21]

Implicit or explicit in all these outbursts was the assumption that so mannered a style implied a "want of literary education,"* an assumption fortified by the lack of allusions in his books to literature, music, or painting. After observing that Dickens rarely quotes from any works other than Shakespeare or the Bible, George Stott added: "For good breeding and refinement he exhibits a very decided contempt."†

It is hardly necessary to point out that Thackeray's style, for all its affinities with eighteenth-century urbanity and polish, is hardly Johnsonian. He could be racy and even slangy at times, but because the raciness was that of the Cambridge college or the London club, his fastidious readers were reassured. "And what delightful English he wrote!" exclaimed the editor of *Punch*. "He knew this and was proud and said that Dickens might be a greater 'moralist' but that he was the best [*sic*] grammarian, and 'anybody could be moral!' "[22] It was agreed by such readers that Thackeray wrote with the easy grace of a gentleman and Dickens with the "factitious adornment" and "constant straining for effect" of a journalist.[23] "His style was to the style of Dickens what marble is to clay."[24]

The most judicious comparison between the two styles and between the two novelists in general was written by Pro-

* Mrs. Oliphant, *William Blackwood and his Sons* (Edinburgh, 1898), II, 305-306. In view of all this, it is amusing to read Dickens' attack on Lord Londonderry for bad grammar and abuses of the language. See *Bulletin of the John Rylands Library*, XVIII (1935), 189.

† *Contemporary Review*, X (1869), 217-223. See also the *Dublin Review*, n.s., XVI (1871), 322-323: "The charm of association is entirely wanting in Mr. Dickens's works," whereas in Thackeray's "educated readers" can "appreciate the subtle . . . infusion of art, learning, and *savoir vivre*. . . . In the time to come, when the classes who are now ill-educated and who do read Mr. Dickens but do not read Mr. Thackeray, shall be well educated, they will read both, and reverse the popular verdict."

fessor David Masson. A long article, appearing in 1852, served as the basis for a chapter on Dickens and Thackeray in his later published *British Novelists and their Styles*—one of the best early histories of the novel. Sometimes Masson's critical standards seem conventional or even quaint. An eminent and learned Miltonist, he tends to speak airily of all novels as "light literature,"[25] but such lapses are of small consequence in view of his serious concern with organic unity in fiction, and in view of his various insights.

The central point of Masson's comparison is based on the difference between the "real" and the "ideal" in art. Recognizing that as applied to painting, the term "ideal" refers to "the more ambitious departments of landscape or figure painting,"[26] Masson extends it to include any form of imaginative heightening or distortion, whether the subjects be from Mount Olympus or St. Giles. Hence Dickens is classified with Raphael and Reynolds rather than with Hogarth. "Thackeray is essentially an artist of the real school. . . . All that he portrays—scenes as well as characters—is within the limits, and rigidly true to the features, of real existence. In this lies his particular merit. . . ."[27]

What differentiates Masson from most critics of the 1850's is that he was not so obsessed with the virtues of realism as to rule out Dickens' kind of art. Instead of insisting that realism is better, he indicates that it is different. In his view, both kinds are legitimate.[28] Dickens, he says, has an "essentially susceptible and poetic nature,"[29] and his style, while often exaggerated, reaches heights of which Thackeray is incapable. His characters are exaggerated because poetically conceived. "It is nonsense to say of his characters generally . . . that they are life-like." Instead they are "transcendental renderings of certain hints furnished by nature."[30] In Masson's opinion, this is likewise the method of Homer, Shakespeare, and Cervantes.[31]

> It does not follow that Mr. Dickens' method is wrong. The characters of Shakespeare are not, in any common sense, life-like. They are not portraits of existing men and women; . . . they are grand hyperbolic beings; . . .

they are humanity caught . . . and kept permanent in its highest and extremest mood. . . . Art is called Art, says Goethe, precisely because it is *not* Nature; and even such a department of art as the modern novel is entitled to the benefit of this maxim.[32]

Masson's emphasis upon the imaginative nature of Dickens' novels makes his essay one of the best to appear in the novelist's lifetime. Its value becomes especially apparent when it is compared with the more representative Victorian essays on realism and probability which are discussed in the next chapter. It is interesting that the comparison of Dickens to Shakespeare, which subsequently became commonplace enough, was first developed by Masson and Landor, the two critics who were also among the first to compare Keats to Shakespeare, although on grounds of language and "negative capability" rather than upon imaginative idealization of character and action.

In fairness to Masson, it should be added that he seems to have a slight preference for the everyday world of Thackeray. He insists, however, that the hyperbolical world of Dickens has its own laws of probability and can have its own proper harmony and unity. His critical principle is still cogent and applicable:

When the aspiration of the artist in this style is greater than his powers of harmonious conception, the result is the extravagant or the unnatural; perfect art is attained only when the objects as represented are elevated above objects as they appear, precisely to that degree in which a world constructed expressly in the mood of the artist's intention might be expected to exceed the common world.[33]

Masson's essay, which was read by both novelists,[34] prompted a revealing reply from Thackeray. After speaking of Dickens' "divine genius" and of the consistent charm of his novels, Thackeray stated his disagreement with Goethe's doctrine of ideal art. "In a tragedy or a poem or a lofty drama you aim at producing different emotions." But a novel, to

Thackeray, was not to be confused with other kinds of literature. This was the crucial point: "the Art of Novels *is* to represent Nature: to convey as strongly as possible the sentiment of reality." According to such a theory, Dickens' art is therefore not legitimate:

> I quarrel with his Art in many respects: w.^h I don't think represents Nature duly; for instance Micawber appears to me an exaggeration of a man, as his name is of a name. It is delightful and makes me laugh: but it is no more a real man than my friend Punch is.[35]

Thackeray's letter is representative of his central position as a reader of Dickens. Of the novels from *Pickwick* to *Bleak House* he was a devoted if not uncritical reader.[36] Such works as *Nicholas Nickleby* (which he reviewed in his essay "Dickens in France") were great favorites in his own household,* and his letters, as well as early reviews and sketches, reflects his own admiration of Dickens' humor and humanitarian sentiments.[37] Unlike David Masson, he looked for realism in Dickens' books and sometimes found it. He remarked that *Pickwick* "contains true character under false names; and . . . gives us a better idea of the state and ways of the people than one could gather from any more pompous or authentic histories."[38] On the other hand, Nancy, in *Oliver Twist*, seemed to him unrealistic, and he made fun of her relentlessly.[39]

After his own principles of realism had been embodied in *Vanity Fair* with immense success, Thackeray's attitude as a reader of Dickens was inevitably modified. Before 1847, it was only rarely that any reader considered him a potential competitor with Dickens.† After *Vanity Fair*, the evidence

---

* See Anne Thackeray Ritchie, *Chapters from some Unwritten Memoirs* (New York, 1895), p. 76, and *Thackeray and his Daughter*, ed. Hester Thackeray (New York, 1924), p. 62. Thackeray was requested by his ten-year-old daughter to write a novel like those of Dickens, but, as he added, "Who can?"

† In 1845, "Bon Gaultier," Thackeray's colleague on the staff of *Fraser's*, offered to back him against Dickens for a hundred pounds. See the *Eclectic Magazine*, XXII (1851), 80. Another early speculator was John Sterling whose preference, expressed in 1841, was tactlessly reported in Carlyle's biography of Sterling.

was obvious to everyone, not least to Thackeray himself. Abraham Hayward, who had predicted that the stick of Dickens' skyrocket was doomed to fall, wrote to the newly crowned novelist: "You have completely beaten Dickens out of the inner circle already."* Thackeray had too much mature self-knowledge to be wholly taken in by such compliments,[40] and he had the good sense to complain that an unpleasant kind of rivalry was being fostered (or "FO(R)STER'D" as John Chapman aptly punned) by partisans.[41] Moreover, he praised *Dombey* and especially *David Copperfield*[42] with disinterested generosity, and he was saddened by reports that Dickens "can't forgive me for my success with *Vanity Fair*; as if there were not room in the world for both of us!"[43]

At the same time, the role of Dickens' rival appealed to him strongly. On January 7, 1848, he admitted to his mother: "There is no use denying the matter or blinking it now. I am become a sort of great man in my way—all but at the top of the tree: indeed there if the truth were known and having a great fight up there with Dickens. I get such a deal of praise wherever I go that it is rather wearisome to hear." Perhaps as a result of the endless comparisons, which strained their personal relationship, both novelists virtually stopped reading the works of the other after 1850.† Urged on by his daughter, Thackeray did read snatches of *Little Dorrit* during his American tour, but if we can believe the doubtful authority of Edmund Yates, he pronounced the book to be "deed stupid."[44] He did, however, read enough extracts during this period to be astonished by Dickens' "fecundity of imagination."[45] There is something pathetic in a prophecy he made in 1840 after seeing Maclise's portrait of Dickens' face: "I think we may promise ourselves a brilliant future for this one. There seems no flagging as yet in it, no sense of fatigue, or

---

* *Letters of Thackeray*, II, 449n. In a letter from Mrs. Brookfield, there is an amusing account of the conversion to *Vanity Fair* of Arthur Elton, a "mild country gentleman" who had been hitherto exclusively one of the "absurd Dickensites." *Ibid.*, pp. 584-585.

† *Letters of Thackeray*, III, 409. Commenting in 1854 upon a review which had ranked Lytton above Dickens and himself, he wrote: "I think Dickens is (not that I have read him of late; but thinking back of him, I think he's the greatest *genius* of the three)."

consciousness of decaying power. Long mayest thou, O Boz! reign over thy comic kingdom."[46] Much as Thackeray might look down upon his rival's vulgarity or lack of realism, he could finally only marvel at Dickens' overwhelming energy. "What is the use of my trying to run before that man, or by his side? I can't touch him," he said. More than twenty years after his prediction about Dickens' portrait, he admitted to a visitor: "I am played out. All I can do now is to bring out my old puppets. . . . But, if he live to be ninety, Dickens will still be creating new characters. In his art that man is marvelous."[47] Wrung from an author whose writings fill a goodly shelf in the library, Thackeray's compliment may seem strange to us, but it is typical of an age of literature more energetically productive than any other.

If Thackeray himself usually displayed modesty and good sense when comparisons were made between his novels and Dickens', his admirers in the "inner circle" were less restrained, a circle that included some distinguished names in letters such as Charles Kingsley, Trollope, Charlotte Brontë, and George Eliot.[48] On June 11, 1855, during a visit to England, Hawthorne made a shrewd observation in his notebook: "Dickens evidently is not liked nor thought well of by his literary brethren—at least, the most eminent of them, whose reputation might interfere with his. Thackeray is much more to their taste. Perhaps it is for his moral benefit to have succeeded late."

One of the most eminent of these literary brethren seems to have been Tennyson. Tennyson's tastes in fiction were, in most respects, very similar to Macaulay's. Both were infatuated readers of Richardson, Scott, and Jane Austen, and both had an indiscriminate and "voracious appetite" for trashy fiction. Tennyson enjoyed reading even Marie Corelli and Ouida.[49] They seem to have differed, however, in their estimate of Dickens. Although Dickens was a loyal admirer of Tennyson's verse, and named one of his sons "Alfred D'Orsay Tennyson Dickens" (much to the amusement of Browning), there is no indication that Tennyson returned the compliments. The only surviving comment he made was a remark, in 1846, that he wished Dickens would "dismiss his sentimentality."[50] Thackeray's novels, on the other hand, he pronounced to be "delicious: they are so mature. But now the days are so full of false sentiment that, as Thackeray said, one cannot draw a man as he should be."[51] The story remains a tantalizing fragment, and there is an especially tantalizing glimpse of Tennyson attending Dickens' funeral service in Westminster Abbey. One wonders what his thoughts were during Stanley's sermon on the subject of his distinguished and popular contemporary whose facial features, he was startled to realize, bore a marked resemblance to his own.[52] Whatever thoughts passed through his mind were cut short at the end of the service. The Laureate's living presence had created a sensation, especially among the female mourners, and measures had to be taken to release him from the crowd of admirers pressing round him.[53]

Tennyson's enjoyment of Thackeray's novels was qualified by a dislike of their cynicism—"heart-withering" as Mrs. Tennyson called it.[54] These complaints, combined with a dislike of excessive authorial comment, were reiterated endlessly by Dickensites in reviews and discussions.[55] Even *The Times*, which had hailed the mature realism of *Vanity Fair* and contrasted its subtle characterization with Dickens' clumsy simplification,[56] later lost patience. One reviewer said acidly that "the aspirations toward sentimental perfection of another popular author are infinitely preferable to these sardonic divings."* As has already been indicated, Dickens' Pickwickian reputation for cheerful good feeling persisted in many circles during the fifties and sixties, despite the Dark Period novels. Most of the comparisons, on this score, were therefore to his advantage. Representative of such readers was Serjeant Ballantine whose autobiography includes a lively appreciation of Dickens which contrasts with the "disgust" felt for Becky Sharpe. Of *Esmond*, he adds: "When I read a novel

---

* Quoted by Lionel Stevenson, *The Showman of Vanity Fair* (New York, 1947), p. 225. The same criticism is made in a review of *The Newcomes* in *The Times* (August 29, 1855, p. 5); and the *Edinburgh Review* describes authorial comment as Thackeray's "greatest blemish" (XCIX, 1854, 202).

. . . I do not care for the anatomy of human nature, however skilfully it may be laid bare."[57]

In what an Oxford professor inadvertently called the Dickery-Thackins controversy,[58] there is one reader of whose opinions we know relatively little. This is Dickens himself. It was Thackeray's belief that Dickens' reading of "a certain yellow-covered book" had a profound effect on his art and accounted for the improvement of *David Copperfield* over his earlier novels in simplicity and in "foregoing the use of fine words."[59] One is inclined to dismiss the suggestion as fantastic, yet it is probable that at least the warm reception of *Vanity Fair* (if not a study of its prose style) did have a profound effect on Dickens' development. It was, however, only one of several factors affecting the direction taken by his later books.

I I

Although Edgar Johnson's biography has presented a detailed account of the changes in Dickens' attitude towards life, no full-length study has as yet been made of his development as an artist. The general outlines are clear enough such as the shift of tone from the bouncing humor of *Pickwick* to the somber uncertainty and acrid social criticism of *Our Mutual Friend*. There is likewise an increased versatility in a prose style which flows almost effortlessly in *Copperfield* and, in the succeeding novel, takes on a harsh, jabbing, Carlylean rhythm as broken-backed and discordant as the bleak London world it reflects. And, as the proverbial schoolboy knows, there is an increased concern with plot, a concern with contrived suspense that has been responsible for more than eighty years of Droodian debate.

The increased concern with plot, in its ramifications, will be of special concern here. The main development, towards an increasingly contrived suspense, is obvious enough. By the time of *Edwin Drood* Dickens was competing with his own disciple, Wilkie Collins, in what had become the disciple's own specialty. What has been less obvious is that contrived suspense was only one of the many ways in which Dickens was attempting to unify his novels.

In his letters and prefaces, the two aspects of fiction most often discussed by him are probability and unity. It is noteworthy of his awareness of his readers that these were the two aspects of his own art most often attacked by critics. As has been previously indicated, the reviewers of the 1830's were apt to be indulgent concerning his sprawling, episodic narratives, but their comments became progressively astringent in the 1840's and 1850's. Adding to the astringency was a growing dissatisfaction with serial publication itself. *David Copperfield* was described by the *Prospective Review* as "a signal triumph over the disadvantages of a bad form. . . . The serial tale . . . is probably the lowest artistic form yet invented . . . which affords the greatest excuse for unlimited departures from . . . consistency, completeness, and proportion."[60] According to Thomas Shaw, serial publication was responsible for Dickens' poor plots and other faults because it tempts any novelist "to neglect that gradation, that proportion, that subordination of the parts to the whole which is as necessary to the due effect of a novel as of a picture or as of a work of architecture."* A highly Aristotelian article in the *National Review* (1855) lectured both Dickens and Thackeray for relying upon "anecdote" instead of the "fusing power" of unified action. "The neglect of the plot until after the characters have been determined is . . . fatal."[61]

One of the main lines of Dickens' development as an artist was an attempt to meet such criticism. Instead of abandoning the serial form, he tried to superimpose on it an overall unity. By the time of *Our Mutual Friend*, he could write in almost a Jamesian fashion of "the most interesting and the most difficult part of my design."

> Its difficulty was much enhanced by the mode of publication; for, it would be very unreasonable to expect that many readers, pursuing a story in portions from

---

* Shaw, *Outlines of English Literature* (1849), p. 486. Shaw considered Fielding "a far superior artist" to Smollett because the adventures of his plots "grow together" instead of being "thrown together." *Ibid.*, p. 325.

month to month through nineteen months, will, until they have it before them complete, perceive the relations of its finer threads to the whole pattern which is always before the eyes of the story weaver at his loom.[62]

It was typical of him, during this period, that upon rereading Scott's *Bride of Lammermoor* he was appalled by what he called "the clumsy shifts and inartistic treatment of the machinery."[63]

In the early novel, *Oliver Twist*, he tried unsuccessfully to contrive an effective plot, but he seems to have realized, gradually, that unity in a novel does not depend exclusively upon a tidy narrative, but upon atmosphere, theme, recurring symbol (which may be aided by serial publication), and point of view. In *The Old Curiosity Shop*, the narrative is almost as rambling as in *Pickwick*. Nevertheless, as his Preface indicates, there is a groping attempt to unify the incidents by the dream-like (sometimes nightmare-like) atmosphere which pervades the book from the opening scene in Nell's gothic bedroom. *Chuzzlewit* and *Dombey*, as was previously suggested, are integrated, sometimes too strenuously, by themes, and in *Copperfield*, a first person point of view is handled with a skill exceptional enough to rouse the admiration of Percy Lubbock.[64] "Let us have no meandering," says the old woman, in the opening chapter, who bought David's caul. Meander the narrative does, but it is an artful flow, as Dickens himself discovered when he tried to make extracts from it for a reading: "There is still the huge difficulty that I constructed the whole with immense pains, and have so woven it up and blended it together, that I cannot yet so separate the parts as to tell the story of David's married life with Dora."[65] *Bleak House*, according to Lionel Stevenson, is "a marvel of structural unity" in which the "vast array of characters" are linked, by Chancery, into "one intricate pattern."[66] *Little Dorrit*, the most sprawling of his mature novels, sometimes seems a reversion to the episodic manner of *Nickleby*, but it is interesting to note how self-consciously artistic Dickens' intention had become. Concerning "The History of a Self-Tormentor," a separate tale inserted in *Little Dorrit*, he wrote to Forster defending the use of the "introduced story" by Fielding and Smollett as a necessary way of presenting the main "idea" of "a full book" in capsule form: "In Miss Wade I had an idea . . . of making the introduced story so fit into surroundings impossible of separation from the main story, as to make the blood of the book circulate through both."[67] An assertion made by a *Times* reviewer in 1852 was true in a sense different from that intended: "The longer Mr. Dickens lives, and the more he writes, the more prone he becomes to leave the broad field of nature for the narrower path of art."[68]

To what extent this artistic development was appreciated or even recognized from 1848 to 1870 is difficult to estimate. The shift of attention to new favorites and weariness itself may account for the blindness of some readers. George Brimley, a prominent *Spectator* critic, was fatuous enough to treat the Chancery suit in *Bleak House* as if it were "The Stroller's Tale" in *Pickwick*. According to him, *Bleak House* suffered more than any other novel of Dickens from an "absolute want of construction." The Chancery suit, he maintained, "has positively not the smallest influence on the character of any one person concerned."[69] Instead of improving his art as his critics had been urging him to do, Dickens had remained afraid of thinning his audience (in Brimley's view) and done nothing to secure "the quiet approval of the judicious."[70] Much of the criticism during the two decades is of this order. The critic shakes his head sadly because Dickens has ignored his advice, and he returns the verdict: "No improvement." In the revised edition of Chambers' *Cyclopaedia of English Literature* (1858) there is a characteristic example of this kind of censure. In 1844, Chambers had lavished praise upon Dickens, adding, paternally, that complete success would be his when he had checked "all disposition to exaggerate." Fourteen years later, the same authority was no longer friendly to Dickens and reminded him that he had neglected to do what he was told, and that hence his later writings were less skillful than ever.[71]

A friendly article which provides the most adequate explanation of such criticism appeared in the *Illustrated London News*—a very important publication of the mid-century with a circulation of 100,000, the largest in England. The writer of the article himself considered *Bleak House* a great novel, and he believed that if it had been the first work from Dickens' pen, it would have achieved an unqualified triumph. Instead, it disappointed many readers because, after the astonishing early successes of Dickens, they were expecting "impossibilities" from him in maturity, and, in their eyes, "even that reasonable amount of improvement which ought to have occurred has not shown itself."[72] A young reviewer (it must have been a young reviewer) stated patronizingly of *Little Dorrit* that these later novels were being read only out of kindness to "an old favourite," or out of curiosity "to see what farther ravages time might have yet in store for the mental frame of a novelist already past his prime."[73] If William Morris had encountered the young reviewer, he would probably have knocked him down, two of his favorite characters being creations of Dickens' declining powers: Joe Gargery and Mr. Boffin.[74]

On the other hand, it was generally recognized by most critics that *David Copperfield* and, to a lesser extent, *Great Expectations*, were improvements over what had gone before. The style of *Copperfield* "is more continuous and careful" said Masson. *Fraser's* considered that "the plot is better contrived. . . . The author's taste has become gradually more and more refined."[75] As Harriet Martineau said happily:

> The finest thing in Mr. Dickens's case is that he, from time to time, proves himself capable of progress. . . . In humour, he will hardly surpass "Pickwick", simply because "Pickwick" is scarcely surpassable in humour: but in several crises . . . of his fame, when everybody was disappointed, and his faults seemed running his graces down, there has appeared something so prodigiously fine as to make us all joyfully exclaim that Dickens can never permanently fail. It was so with "Copperfield."[76]

Great Expectations also seemed "prodigiously fine." To

a generation of readers not yet exposed to the strange inhabitants of Faulkner's Yoknapatawpha county, the significance of Miss Havisham was not yet clearly understood, nor was the full bitterness of its theme (obscured, of course, by Bulwer-Lytton's ending). But after the tortuousness of *Little Dorrit* and the popular yet somewhat mechanical *Tale of Two Cities*, this book seemed fresh and alive.*

One gets the general impression from the reviews of the 1850's and 1860's that just as Dickens himself was becoming progressively conscious of the techniques of novel-writing, so were many of his critics. Although because of political considerations and of a growing demand for realism there was an inadequate appreciation of Dickens' own development as an artist, there had occurred, nevertheless, a marked advance in the general level of novel-criticism. Some reviewers were at least treating the novel as a serious work of art.

As a representative example of mid-Victorian reviewing, a lengthy analysis of *Copperfield* and *Pendennis* in the *Prospective Review* may be considered. Characteristically, the first half of the review is a solemn discussion of whether or not works of fiction, especially serial publications, have a healthy moral effect, and the conclusion is reached that Thackeray's sneering tone and lack of "moral vigour" are debilitating. Although Dickens' novels contain "too much sentimentality," "Quixoticism," and "bombastic blank verse," his view of life is "by far the more complete and more healthy." In the second half of the review, the writer settles down to analyze the two novels themselves. Dickens' dialogue, he notes, is not so consistently effective as Thackeray's because his characters sometimes talk too much like the author. With good cause he cites as examples of this failing the words of Martha by the bank of the Thames, and the meeting between Rosa Dartle and Emily. He then turns his attention to the narration itself, discusses the autobiographical novel as a difficult form of art, and adds that Dickens "has secured a

* See above, ch. 5, p. 104n. See also Hammerton's *Dickens Companion*, p. 325; Nonesuch, III, 214-216. Some elaborate windmill-tilting against the neglect of *Great Expectations* by its first readers was performed by Ford Madox Ford. See the *Dickensian*, XXXVII (1940), 114.

unity and completeness which we have never seen equalled in a serial tale." As an example of skillful narration, and a capacity to carry out simultaneously all the tasks which a novelist must perform, he quotes at length the fine scene of David's return to Yarmouth for a visit with Peggotty and Barkis.

If one accepts T. S. Eliot's dictum that a good critic can be discerned by his choice of quotations, the writer for the *Prospective Review* was indeed a good critic. Moreover, his appreciation of the handling of point of view in *Copperfield*, which must be quoted at length, reads like a paragraph from Lubbock's *Craft of Fiction*:

> It is in truth a very fine specimen of constructive skill. Complicated as the story is, and numerous as are the characters, all flows naturally from the mouth of the narrator, never leaving us to wonder how he got his information, and scarcely ever encumbered with devices to supply the gaps in his personal knowledge. Wonderfully well has the author succeeded in identifying himself with his principal personage. Every line is coloured with the hues of memory, and the subdued tone of a distant view is given to the whole; while sufficient strength of outline and vividness of colour are preserved, to enable us to feel a powerful interest in the progress of the story.[77]

Such a passage is worth bearing in mind when one encounters the usual generalizations of literary historians concerning the total inadequacy of novel-criticism in mid-Victorian England. Political and moral considerations might come first, but during the last two decades of Dickens' lifetime, there was a growing awareness of the aesthetics of fiction. Because it was often associated with the development of realistic standards, however, this awareness generally tended to work to Dickens' disadvantage by making critical readers dissatisfied with what seemed to them to be the crudities of his later works. That this reaction coincided with Dickens' own struggles to improve his style, structure, and art in general, is one of the several ironies of his relationship with his readers.

CHAPTER 7

THE POET AND THE CRITICS
OF PROBABILITY

"Dickens's figures belong to poetry, like figures of
Dante or Shakespeare, in that a single phrase . . . may
be enough to set them wholly before us."—T. S. Eliot

I

ONE of the prerequisites for the recent increase of interest in Dickens' novels has been a decline in the status
of naturalism and of realism in its most rigid forms. Under
the harsh fluorescent lamp-light of naturalistic criticism, Dickensian vitality seems most readily to dissolve into an insubstantial pageant. Because his novels, like Balzac's, occupy a
middle ground between the romantic and realistic, the harsh-
ness is especially glaring. Naturalistic and realistic criticism
can regard the frankly admitted romanticism of Dumas or
of Hawthorne as somewhat childish but acceptable. As G. H.
Lewes said: "In a story of wild and startling incidents, such
as 'Monte Cristo,' it is absurd to demand a minute attention
to probabilities. . . . Monte Cristo may talk a language never
heard off the stage, but Major Pendennis must speak as they
speak in Pall Mall."[1] The same charity cannot be expected by
the romantic novelist who professes to give an accurate portrayal of contemporary life. Such a writer wanders in a No
Man's Land in which he will encounter constant misunderstanding of his intentions.

Whether or not Dickens himself understood his own inter-
mediate position and intentions is an interesting question. It
is usually assumed that he was like a glassblower who, when
asked how he created magic shapes with traditional tools,
replied: "How do I do it? I just blows."[2] Unlike Bulwer-
Lytton and Wilkie Collins, he had little use for prefaces. He
often said that a book should stand or fall without prefatory
buttressing,[3] and when goaded into writing one, his discussion

was always brief. His prefaces need to be compared with his letters before their value can be estimated. As for the letters themselves, a mountainous correspondence, a reader's first impression is indeed one of disappointment. Like the letters of Balzac, which depressed Flaubert acutely,* most of Dickens' letters deal with everyday matters and only occasionally mention his novel-writing. A German critic, after supposedly working through these documents, exclaimed that nowhere is to be seen a letter or even a preface in which there is a single critical remark or a statement of aesthetic convictions.[4] A more careful sifting reveals, however, a residue of comment of considerable critical interest. Some of these comments deal with the problem of unity and serial publication, but most of them are concerned with aspects of the problem of probability. Are the speech and action of a character convincing or unreal? Is a scene credible or mechanical? Does the setting substantiate the illusion? Does the whole novel give the appearance of real life? In Dickens' remarks, these questions overlap.

If we turn back to the reviews of his novels, it becomes clear why such questions are almost obsessively predominant in what Dickens says of the craft of fiction. The most persistent advice of his reviewers was to avoid exaggeration and imaginative distortion, to portray "real life," to exercise his power "under the broad open sky of nature, instead of in the most brilliant palace of art."[5] This last item of advice was especially in evidence during the final twenty years of Dickens' life. "Art" to these critics was looked down upon as a contrived distortion of reality such as one finds in romances or in poetry

* According to André Maurois, Flaubert was extremely critical of Dickens for never having discussed art: " 'Quel peu d'amour de l'art! dit par exemple Flaubert. Il n'en parle pas une fois.' Et ailleurs: 'Ignorant comme une cruche . . . Un immense bonhomme, mais de second ordre.' " (Maurois, *Un Essai sur Dickens*, Paris, 1927, p. 124.) Because of Maurois' distaste for footnotes, it is difficult to locate the passage in Flaubert, and I, for one, was misled for some years by his authority into repeating what is an unfortunate error. For Flaubert was speaking not of Dickens at all but of Balzac: "Je viens de lire la *Correspondance* de Balzac. . . . Mais quelle préoccupation de l'argent et quel peu d'amour de l'Art! Avez-vous remarqué qu'il n'en parle pas *une* fois? . . . ignorant comme une cruche, . . . un immense bonhomme, mais de second ordre." (Flaubert, *Correspondance*, Paris, 1926-1930, no. 1632, December 31, 1876. Cf. also Maurois' *Dickens*, New York, 1935, p. 120.)

and drama. It was hoped that the novel would be something different from other forms of literature, an untouched transcript of real life as accurate and uncolored as history. Lady Chatterton, a minor mid-Victorian novelist, said proudly of one of her books: "I have followed nature, instead of proceeding on the supposed principles of art."[6]

To realize that such a theory might lead to the de Goncourts, or to Ernest Raymond or James T. Farrell, would have been profoundly shocking to Lady Chatterton, yet the fine borderline between realism and naturalism is suggested by the familiar definition of naturalism as simply realism with scientific pretensions. Much Victorian criticism hovers on that borderline. The first English critic to use the word *realism* was G. H. Lewes in 1855, and four years later Masson referred to Thackeray (in a special sense) as a *naturalist*.[7] Even before the terms became current, in its concern with various shades of probability Victorian criticism was affected by theories which led to naturalism itself.* Sometimes the concern with probability was based on a reasonable and traditional application of Fielding's Aristotelian precepts. Sometimes it originated in the puritan notion (well known to Defoe) that realistic fiction could appear not to be fiction at all,[8] and sometimes that in a scientific age, extraordinary events or characters can no longer be credible. In a passage anticipating Hawthorne's discussion of romance, an *Athenaeum* reviewer observed in 1841:

> Is it not that a *novel* is, or aims at being, a picture of daily life,—a reflex of human nature under the modifications of an actual state of society? . . . A *romance*, on the contrary, pretends to no such fidelity of delineation. It strives to paint man as a being of passion alone; its view of life is taken by the flare of torches . . . dazzling brilliancy and fathomless gloom. . . . If this definition be correct, a romance is at variance with the

---

* For a useful and detailed discussion of the shades of meaning between different *realisms*, see "A Symposium on Realism," ed. Harry Levin, in *Comparative Literature*, III (1951). See also Philip Rahv's essay on naturalism in *Critiques and Essays on Modern Fiction*, ed. J. W. Aldridge (New York, 1952), pp. 415-423.

spirit of the present age. The nineteenth century is distinguished by a craving for the positive and real—it is essentially an age of analysis and criticism.[9]

With G. H. Lewes and other critics, all three of these causes combined to produce a marked hostility to the Dickensian mixture of romance and realism. With mounting dissatisfaction they chorused that Dickens' world was peopled with "grotesque impossibilities."[10] "We cannot recall any single character in his novels, intended to belong to the higher ranks of English life, who is drawn with the slightest approach to truth or probability."[11] In 1848, a *Times* reviewer lamented that an author who had once been "one of the most real of writers" was now losing sight of reality altogether "with the most utter recklessness."[12]

Most of Dickens' prefaces are really replies to some such criticism. And because he was on the defensive in his prefaces, he was led, almost inevitably, into a false position. The prefaces thus give a misleading impression of his concept of fiction. In the Preface to *Bleak House*, for example, he asserted that he was prepared to cite evidence from legal documents to prove that his picture of Chancery was "substantially true." Few things made him more indignant than the succession of conservative critics who found his Circumlocution Offices, Yorkshire schools, and Chancery suits entirely fantastic and without any basis in reality whatever. Like the tennis champion who prefers to be complimented upon his skill at the bridge table (which is ordinary enough) rather than upon his skill on the courts, Dickens thought of himself as an accurate social historian. As Forster wrote:

> What I had most indeed to notice in him, at the very outset of his career, was his indifference to any praise of his performances on the merely literary side, compared with the higher recognition of them as bits of actual life, with the meaning and purpose on their part, and the responsibility on his, of realities rather than creatures of fancy.[13]

When a reviewer in the *Sun* said that Dickens' characters

were "as actual as flesh and blood, as true as humanity,"[14] he earned the novelist's warmest gratitude and friendship.

Thinking of himself as an accurate social historian, and finding his accuracy questioned, Dickens resorted to the same defensive tactics as those of Charles Reade. He would indignantly assert that the conditions pictured do actually *exist*. These defensive tactics are sometimes foolish (as in his reply to G. H. Lewes in a Preface concerning the spontaneous combustion of Krook), and sometimes the tactics are successful (as in his remarks on Jacob's Island in the Preface to *Oliver Twist*). But whether successful or not, such a defense forces him, as was suggested, into the false position of asserting that his imaginary creations are not imaginary and that no element of fantasy exists in his work. The most flagrant example of such an error is his lame reply to Thackeray and other reviewers in his Preface defending the reality of Nancy in *Oliver Twist*. "It is useless to discuss whether the conduct and character of the girl seems natural or unnatural, probable or improbable, right or wrong. IT IS TRUE."

Mere attestation of this kind makes a clumsy defense. As Fielding said, quoting Aristotle, "it is no excuse for the poet who relates what is incredible, that the thing related is really matter of fact." Elsewhere we get a more accurate view of Dickens' attitude towards probability, especially in his letters. He speaks then as a creative artist rather than as a factual chronicler, and he is aware that his flair is the distinctive fantasy which he casts over everything, and that his problem (as Coleridge's had been) is to make this imaginative distortion convincing and, in the best sense, real. For example, in advising another novelist that a coaching scene instead of coming to life was "all working machinery," he spoke of the vital "impression" which the reader must be given:

And exactly because that is not true [i.e. the impression], the conduct of the men . . . is in the last degree improbable. Whereas if the scene were truly and powerfully rendered, the improbability more or less necessary to all tales and allowable in them, would become a part of a thing so true and vivid, that the reader must accept it whether he likes it or not.[15]

This comment brings us closer to Dickens' attitude towards fiction than does the Preface to *Oliver Twist*. Much as he may have wanted to be considered an accurate social historian, his art consisted in the transmutation of a strong impression, sometimes derived from an actual scene, into convincing illusion. Perhaps it was for this reason that when some of his characters were modelled on actual persons, the models usually failed to recognize themselves (Skimpole, Boythorn, and Miss Mowcher are exceptions). Dickens noted with surprise: "I find that a great many people (particularly those who might have sat for the character) consider even Mr. Pecksniff a grotesque impossibility, and Mrs. Nickleby herself, sitting bodily before me in a solid chair, once asked me whether I believed there ever was such a woman."[16]

A reader's sense of probability depends in part upon literary convention and tradition, in part upon his own experience, and in part upon his imagination. To satisfy the demand for probability, the novelist faces more difficulties than the dramatist not only because the theatrical three-sided box is an immediate admission of illusion, but because the novel-reader is more likely to have been affected by realistic or naturalistic convention. In its extreme form, such a convention leads the reader to expect not "a sense of fact" as Pater says, but fact itself. That Dickens recognized his problem is evident in a letter written in 1859 which contains the best defense of his own methods:

It does not seem to me to be enough to say of any description that it is the exact truth. The exact truth must be there; but the merit or art in the narrator, is the manner of stating the truth. As to which thing in literature, it always seems to me that there is a world to be done. And in these times, when the tendency is to be frightfully literal and catalogue-like—to make the thing, in short, a sort of sum in reduction that any miserable creature can do in that way—I have an idea (really founded on the love of what I profess), that the very holding of popular literature through a kind of popular dark age, may depend on such fanciful treatment.[17]

The recognition here of the inadequacy of naturalist cataloguing, a "dreary, arithmetical dustyness that is powerfully depressing" as he said elsewhere,[18] and the recognition of the necessity for color, style, and manner, bring us to the core of Dickens' technique. It is a technique closer to that of poetic drama than of the more conventional novel.

II

Before further consideration of how Victorian critics dealt with this major question in their evaluation of Dickens, it will be best to suspend chronology and to review some examples of the technique itself. An obvious example of its success is the characterization of Mrs. Gamp. Like the Wife of Bath, she is introduced by a brief description of her person, but thereafter, to enable her to take recognizable shape in the reader's mind, Dickens relies almost entirely upon her manner of speech.

"Ah!" repeated Mrs. Gamp; for it was always a safe sentiment in cases of mourning. "Ah dear! When Gamp was summoned to his long home, and I see him a lying in Guy's Hospital with a penny-piece on each eye, and his wooden leg under his left arm, I thought I should have fainted away. But I bore up."

In this initial speech, and the subsequent discussion of Mrs. Harris and the bottle on the "chimley-piece," already caught are the distinctive and completely individual rhythms that characterize Sara Gamp, and the tone of genteel self-satisfaction that differentiates her from her partner Betsey Prig. In subsequent chapters we listen to these same distinctive rhythms during Sara's visits to Mr. Mould, and we witness the mighty clash scene in which Betsey, after a feast of pickled salmon, cucumbers, and several glasses of liquor, makes the epoch-making pronouncement that she does not believe in the existence of Mrs. Harris. As Sara adds afterwards: " 'Wot I have took from Betsey Prig this blessed night, no mortial creetur knows! . . . The words she spoke of Mrs. Harris, lambs could not forgive. No Betsey!' said Mrs. Gamp, in a violent burst of feeling, 'nor worms forget!' "

The illusion here is consistently sustained by distinctive dialogue and not by attestations that Sara is a representative example of conditions in the nursing profession before Florence Nightingale. Like most of Dickens' successful creations, Mrs. Gamp is a "triumph of style" rather than of analysis.[19] The real aim of the novel, says Gide's hero in *The Counterfeiters*, is "to represent reality on the one hand and on the other to stylize it into art." Those who make wholesale charges against improbability and exaggeration in Dickens' novels are usually readers who refuse to admit the desirability of stylization in fiction. Of them Dickens spoke in his Preface to *Chuzzlewit*:

> What is exaggeration to one class of minds . . . is plain truth to another. . . . I sometimes ask myself whether there may occasionally be a difference of this kind between some writers and some readers; whether it is *always* the writer who colours highly, or whether it is now and then the reader whose eye for colour is a little dull?

The most inimitable feature of Dickens, according to George Orwell, is a fertility of invention, "which is invention not so much of characters . . . and situations, as of turns of phrase and concrete details. The outstanding mark of Dickens' writings is the unnecessary detail."[20] Orwell cites as examples Joe Gargery's speech about the robbers stuffing Mr. Pumblechook's mouth "full of flowering annuals to perwent his crying out," and Mr. Murdstone assigning mathematical problems to David Copperfield: "If I go into a cheesemonger's shop, and buy five thousand double-Gloucester cheeses at fourpence-halfpenny each, present payment. . . ."

As Orwell adds, "Dickens' imagination overwhelms him. The picturesque details are too good to be left out."*

In 1864, Dickens was reading some novels by other authors and was irritated by the dialogue. "I have been trying [to read] other books; but so infernally conversational, that I forget who the people are before they have done talking, and don't in the least remember what they talked about before when they begin talking again."[21] In view of Dickens' own practice, his criticism is really levelled not at the quantity of conversation but at its lack of distinctiveness. For purposes of stylization he was prepared to take the risk that his world of sharply marked manners of speech might seem improbable to some sorts of novel readers. It has often been pointed out that if Shakespeare's plays had been printed without the names of the speakers, so distinct are the styles of each one that there would usually be little difficulty is assigning the lines. Dickens' aim is comparable.

A criticism that has been commonly made is that Dickens' characters are all types rather than individuals. Henry James complained instead that they are nearly all individuals and not types.[22] James seems to be closer to the truth, but the whole question of particulars and universals ought to be related to the context in which the characters are placed rather than be settled offhand by rigid prescriptions. The uniqueness of Dickens' most successful creations is readily apparent in their speech. His really flat characters (his insipid heroes and heroines in many instances) have no distinctive style. They are mere types. They are more ordinary, more natural, and hence should supposedly be more probable. Instead they are mechanical and lifeless. Placed in a world of highly stylized, strongly-colored individuals, they are pale and insignificant, and, paradoxically, improbable.

The paradox is reinforced if we consider the dialogue employed by some of the novelists assailed by Dickens. Typical of many is Galsworthy's which is "natural," that is, it has the

* See also R. C. Churchill's discussion of Chuzzlewit: "Throughout, it is the detail which is so masterly. . . always the language of Dickens that is so important; his genius is essentially dramatic." Scrutiny, x (1942), 359.

]

flatness of most ordinary speech. But in sacrificing stylized speech, Galsworthy attains a drabness which finally becomes incredible. After a diet of Dickens, how weary, flat, stale, and unprofitable seem the later volumes of *The Forsyte Saga*. Oscar Wilde once made a breezy remark about a man who wrote novels which were so like life that no one could possibly believe in their possibility.

A second aspect of Dickens' methods is his use of comic exuberance. He was aware that it, too, can lead to improbabilities: "Invention, thank God, seems the easiest thing in the world; and I seem to have such a preposterous sense of the ridiculous . . . as to be constantly requiring to restrain myself from launching into extravagances in the height of my enjoyment."[23] In *A Tale of Two Cities*, he made the experiment of subduing these comic extravagances by reducing dialogue and comic relief to the minimum. The results were disappointing, and he was happy to return to his more characteristic manner in *Great Expectations*, a novel which pivoted, as he said, upon a "grotesque tragi-comic conception."[24]

The tragi-comic mixture is more firmly ingrained in his novels than is sometimes recognized. The obvious place to look for it is in the structure of his books in which we find scenes of dramatic intensity followed by scenes of comedy, a method half-whimsically defended in an introductory chapter in *Oliver Twist*. This method was no doubt attributable to serial publication, but in Dickens it is a more deeply-rooted device which affects both structure and characterization. One suspects that he would have employed it even if his novels had been published as wholes. His letters indicate that he considered the juxaposition of serious and comic necessary not only to the relief of the comic character but of the serious character as well. Lear without his fool is not Lear. Thus he was disappointed in Wilkie Collins' novel *No Name*, in which the heroine is supposed to embody "steadiness and inflexibility of purpose. In Dickens' opinion, Collins failed to make the heroine believable because he told the story "severely and persistently" instead of employing comic contrast. "Contrast in that way is most essential. She [the heroine] cannot possibly be brought out as he wants to bring her out, without it."[25]

The most interesting application of the mixture of genres can be found in the gallery of what may be called, in the general sense, his villains. The mixture here is employed not so much between the characters as within the characters. When Keats was developing his theory of negative capability, he spoke of the poetical character as having "no character." "It enjoys light and shade"; said Keats, "it lives in gusto, be it foul or fair. . . . It has as much delight in conceiving an Iago as an Imogen."[26] Dickens' method accords with Keats' theory. Bumble, Fagin, Squeers, Sampson and Sally Brass, Pecksniff, Uriah Heep, Creakle, Chadband, Podsnap, and other major and minor villains are conceived with gusto and delight. The gusto is apparent in the humor they provoke. They all represent vice or unpleasantness of different kinds, but they all share the characteristic of arousing not only dread but amusement. Stylization is achieved by the mixture of genres in the single character; the flat villain is thus made into something rounder and more complex. The grotesque humor of the scenes between Quilp and his wife may mean that Quilp is a less credible villain, but they make him into a more credible character. Concerning Major Bagstock in *Dombey*, Dickens told his illustrator that the Major was to be shown as "the incarnation of selfishness and small revenge" and hence gloating "in his apoplectico-mephistophelian observation of the scene."[27] Most of the Dickensian villains are similarly conceived; they combine a comic with a serious role. As a rule, it is only when he achieves this combination that his villains are animated and credible. The incredible villains, such as the purely melodramatic Carker and some of the other villains of his Dark Period novels, are played straight.

In the Preface to *Nicholas Nickleby*, Dickens raises the question constantly raised by his critics: how can an altogether evil character be probable?

It is remarkable that what we call the world, which is so very credulous in what professes to be true, is most incredulous in what professes to be imaginary; and that, while, every day in real life, it will allow in one man no blemishes, and in another no virtues, it will seldom admit a very strongly-marked character, either good or bad, in a fictitious narrative, to be within the limits of probability.

Dickens' method is to make such "strongly-marked" black characters probable by greying them not with virtues but with humor. It is a form of complexity, different from George Eliot's for example, but still a form of complexity. For his white characters, whose goodness is "strongly-marked," he often uses no comparable method of greying. That is one of the reasons why the purely virtuous figures such as Little Nell, Agnes, and Little Dorrit, seem improbable. Their flatness is unrelieved. If we compare Nell in her determination never to desert her grandfather with another Dickens character who exclaims "I will never desert Mr. Micawber," the difference will be apparent. Humor is not a sign of illiteracy. It is an integral feature of Dickens' technique. When Dostoevsky was writing *The Idiot*, he noted that Don Quixote and Mr. Pickwick were rare examples of "positively good" characters who are probable. They are made probable because they are ridiculous, and the reader feels a sense of compassion "for the much ridiculed good man who does not know his own worth. . . . This rousing of compassion is the secret of humour."[28]

If we turn to the question of probability of plot and action, we find that Dickens' letters and prefaces provide less clues to his intentions, but there is an excellent substitute in some scattered remarks by Edwin Muir in his *Structure of the Novel*. The latter contains a stimulating analysis of the two kinds of traditional plots used by Dickens. The first is episodic; the characters move from place to place, but they do not develop. They are in this sense static.* The second

---

* Of Mrs. Gamp, R. H. Hutton remarked: "Indeed, just as the great mystery of physiology is said to be how a single living cell multiplied itself into a tissue composed of an indefinite number of similar cells, so the great intellectual mystery of Dickens's fertile genius was his power of reduplicating a single humorous conception of character into an elaborate

kind is designed to show the development of character (such as Pip in *Great Expectations*), and clearly this second kind of plot raises different questions of probability. Instead of asking, as we do of the static character's actions, "Is he simply continuing to behave typically?" we ask instead, "Was his change of character motivated, and is his present behaviour explicable in view of what we have known of him?" Mr. Muir terms this second kind of structure *dramatic*, although there are inconvenient connotations when the term is applied to the novel.

The episodic plot is a device to set the characters "in new situations, to change their relations to one another, and in all of these to make them behave typically." As Muir adds, the task of the novelist who creates static characters is more like the choreographer's than the dramatist's.[29] In this sense, *Pickwick Papers* has the most satisfactory structure of all of Dickens' novels because it is most similar to the ballet. In his later novels, an attempt was made to devise more dramatic plots, to make the best of two traditions. *Dombey and Son*, for example, consists in part of a ballet sequence in which assorted groups of static characters are projected in successive scenes, throughout which they behave typically, and in part of a foreground story of Florence and Walter, who are separated by some extraordinary and improbable accidents and coincidences. In the foreground, also, is Mr. Dombey himself, a serious study in the development of a proud man who, after a series of catastrophic events, is finally restored to humility. Dickens protested in a Preface that readers who failed to be convinced by Mr. Dombey's actions were lacking in knowledge of human nature. "Mr. Dombey undergoes no violent change either in this book, or in real life." But these foreground scenes, in which change occurs, are usually not so convincing as the more static background. One must except some of his last novels from this generalization. Old Dorrit, Pip, Bradley Headstone, show that Dickens was acquiring in his late years a new skill in the presentation of

---

structure of strictly analogous conceptions." *Brief Literary Criticisms* (1906), p. 50.

characters who change during the course of the novel. Usually, however, the static characters tend to crowd the developing characters off the stage. Novelists such as Austen and James, who have successfully used dramatic plot, have demonstrated that the scope of the novel form offers special resources for the exploration of motives of action so that character development seems probable. Dickens dismissed these special resources with the word "dissective."* He preferred to rely not on the resources of fictional drama but on stage drama, often of stage melodrama. "Every writer of fiction," he said, "although he may not adopt the dramatic form, writes, in effect, for the stage."[30] In practice, this meant not merely a reduction of authorial comment and dissection, but a reliance upon stage motivation. Old Martin Chuzzlewit's strange behavior to his grandson, or Mr. Dombey assigning Edith to Carker for instructions in wifely obedience, or John Rokesmith's concealment of his identity—all such incidents might be passably probable in a fast-moving play, but in the slower pace of a novel they arouse incredulity.

As an example of the probability of action of the more static characters, Micawber's behavior in the exposure scene and later in Australia have seemed out of character to many readers. The stylized character does not lend himself to changes. As Muir says, in the novel of static character, "time is assumed, and the action is a static pattern, continuously redistributed and reshuffled in Space." Uncle Toby, Parson Adams, Mr. Collins, and Micawber "are beyond time and change" just as such a character as Pip is "completely enclosed" in time and change. Falstaff, as Muir continues, "remains quite unthreatened by the violent events in the two parts of Henry IV; the world in which Prince Henry and Hotspur fight and the king dies is not his world, but only a dream which passes over it." Falstaff and Micawber dwell in

---

* Concerning *The Woman in White* he wrote to Collins (January 7, 1860): "You know that I always contest your disposition to give an audience credit for nothing, which necessarily involves the forcing of points on their attention." "The three people who write the narratives . . . have a DISSECTIVE property in common, which is essentially not theirs but yours; . . . my own effort would be to strike more of what is got *that way* out of them by collision with one another, and by the working of the story."

"a stationary spatial world in which time has reached an equilibrium."[31] Muir's explanation indicates why many readers have been disappointed by what finally happens to both Falstaff and Micawber; the illusion of permanence is threatened by the intrusion of time and change.

Let us leave the problem of endings, however, for too many discussions of probability are taken up with it exclusively, especially among certain readers (and movie-audiences) who have opinions about nothing else. The main impression Dickens' novels create depends less upon what *finally* happens to the characters than upon the characters themselves and the atmosphere in which they are surrounded. Dickens' lavish use of settings is one more indication of his predominant concern for spatial realities rather than for time realities. Perhaps it is inappropriate to apply the word *probability* in a discussion of Dickens' settings, but if we compare Todgers's boarding house with the Paris pension of Sophia Baines in *The Old Wives' Tale* or even with the Maison Vauquer in *Père Goriot*, the word is applicable. Todgers's is not like any other boarding house; it is not a type but an individual. It is stylized in the same way that the characters are stylized and is therefore equally offensive to the strict realist. And because Todgers's is seen from the same imaginatively distorted angle as the characters, the description is entirely functional and satisfies Henry James' criterion of the organic relationship between the parts of a good novel. The setting of Todgers's and the character of Pecksniff mutually reinforce the credibility of each other. Dickens' awareness of his own method is apparent in some advice he gave to another novelist. It concerned a scene in which the characterization failed because of a lack of "the little subtle touches of description which, by making the country house and the general scene real, would give an air of reality to the people."

The more you set yourself to the illustration of your heroine's passionate nature, the more indispensable this *attendant atmosphere of truth* becomes. It would . . . oblige the reader to believe in her. Whereas, for ever exploding like a great firework *without any background*,

she glares and wheels and hisses, and goes out, and has
lighted nothing.[32]

Descriptions of such background in Dickens are nearly
always atmospheric rather than literal. He rejected one novel
that had been submitted to him because the descriptions "make
no more of the situation than the index might, or a descriptive playbill might."[33] His remark sounds like Willa Cather's
essay, "The Novel Démeublé" which attacks the "popular
superstition that 'realism' asserts itself in the cataloguing of
a great number of material objects" or in explaining "mechanical processes." Our error, she says, consists in taking it
for granted that "whoever can observe . . . can write a novel."[34]
Dickens' novels are certainly as crowded with furnishings as
they are crowded with characters, but although he starts with
observation, he rarely catalogues. His settings are integrated
with what Cather would call "the emotional penumbra of the
characters themselves."[35]

Dickens was his own best critic when he was replying in
a letter to some charge of improbability in one of his novels:

> I work slowly and with great care, and never give way
> to my invention recklessly, but constantly restrain it;
> . . . [but] I think it is my infirmity to fancy or perceive
> relations in things which are not apparent generally.
> Also, I have such an inexpressible enjoyment of what
> I see in a droll light, that I dare say I pet it as if it were
> a spoilt child.[36]

The Circumlocution Office originated in its creator's observation of the excessive reliance upon red tape of government
officials during the Crimean War. But as his invention seized
it for *Little Dorrit*, the Circumlocution Office was transformed
into something rich and strange, something that the civil
servants such as Fitzjames Stephen could only dismiss as
fantastic, yet something which can have, for other readers,
the same nightmare-like reality as Kafka's vision of an intricate bureaucracy under the Austro-Hungarian Empire.

Dickens' comments on the novel which have been quoted
in this section show that he sometimes misunderstood the

nature of his own writings, but in his preoccupation with the problem of probability he was usually trying to reestablish one old and well worn principle about how his novels should be read. Except when forced into a false position by reviewers, he urged that the reality of a novel, as of a play or narrative poem, depends upon imaginative imitation or stylization. His advice to his editorial assistant was the advice he tried to follow himself: "Keep Household Words Imaginative! is the solemn and continual Conductorial Injunction."

III

Most of the assessments of Dickens in the past hundred years have been based on the extent to which his stylized manner and attitude towards probability have been acceptable to the critic. To the Peter Bells of criticism, his novels have been nonsense:

> A primrose by a river's brim
> A yellow primrose was to him,
> And it was nothing more.

To more imaginative readers, his world of fantasy has been vivid and real. In order to distinguish it from the kind of world found in Thackeray or George Eliot, however, some of his contemporaries referred to its creator as a poet. The term was used by David Masson and given currency by Taine. As used by Taine, it refers especially to Dickens' creation of an imaginative fairyland and also to his capacity for stirring the springs of sensibility which subsist under the thick layers of English puritanism and commercialism.[37] In 1872, Robert Buchanan developed the analogy more sympathetically in order to defend Dickens from "superfine" critics who misunderstood his intentions:

> But the amount of the world's interest in Charles Dickens is not to be measured by any quantity of head-shakings on the part of the unsympathetic. . . . And the world decided long ago that Dickens was beyond all parallel the greatest imaginative creator of his genera-

tion, and that his poetry, the best of it, although written in unrhymed speech, is worth more, and will probably last longer, than all the Verse-poetry of this age, splendid as some of that poetry has been. None but a spoony or a pedant doubts the power.*

Although the spoony or pedant might object that the analogy is imprecise, it was an extremely important development in the criticism of Dickens and anticipates the approach used in some of the best twentieth-century studies of his work.

E. P. Whipple, another critic who found Dickens' world a thoroughly credible one for his own tastes, noted that these tastes were not always shared. "He so surcharges his characters with vitality that they seem like persons who have taken something to drink; and, as they burst into the more decorous society delineated by other English novelists, there is a cry raised for the critical police."[38] Three senior inspectors who answered the call between 1850 and 1872 were Hippolyte Taine, Walter Bagehot, and G. H. Lewes, each of whom wrote a lengthy and impressive essay. None of the three really understood Dickens fully, but each is an important representative of some of the ways in which his work has been read and judged and is still read and judged.

Taine's essay, appearing originally in the *Revue des Deux Mondes* for 1856, was incorporated into his *Histoire de la littérature anglaise* in 1863. As two admirable studies of Dickens' reputation in France have shown, Taine's essay made a great stir in his native country,[39] but his influence was likewise very much in evidence across the channel, and no apology ought to be needed for including his celebrated history in an account of literary reputations in England. Of the three critics, Taine was the one who came closest to understanding Dickens. It is strange that in Forster's biography,

---

* Buchanan, "The 'Good Genie' of Fiction," *St. Paul's Magazine*, x (1872), 133-134. In 1857, *The Times* has a reference to "men of imagination" now turning to the writing of novels instead of poetry. "The poets of this day have hung their harps upon the willows and taken to celebrate their 'soul's agonies' and personal inconveniences." (December 24, 1857, p. 4.) For related comments by Clough, Darwin, and Tennyson concerning poetry and novels, see Geoffrey Tillotson, *Criticism and the Nineteenth Century* (1951), pp. 193-196.

he is always treated as a *bête noire* and made to haunt the footnotes whenever examples of critical blunderings are required. Taine did, of course, miss a good deal. He had not read enough Dickens, and (like Edmund Wilson) by concentrating upon the seriousness of such works as *Hard Times* and *Martin Chuzzlewit*, he really underestimated the role of humor in Dickens' writings and character. He nevertheless shared Forster's conviction that the "mainspring" of Dickens' genius was imagination, and most of his essay is taken up with an analysis of its power.[40] His tone is sometimes that of an anthropologist reporting on the strange tribal customs of a South Sea island. "Bizarre!" he exclaims again and again after citing examples of English morality or English imaginative extravagance (the latter he likens to Hoffmann). Taine differs from most naturalistic critics in his zest. Dickens' feverish visions often appal him by their intensity, and he compares them to those of a monomaniac. "It is visionary imagination which forges the phantoms of the madman and creates the personages of the artist,"[41] he writes—a comment which was developed more fully by Lewes. Despite this, Taine's enthusiasm often carries him away into accepting Dickens' world as a convincing reality and one that is certainly never dull. What is more, Taine's is the kind of zest that carries his reader along as well.

One rather suspects that Walter Bagehot was never carried away by anything. If Taine writes like an excited anthropologist, Bagehot writes like an imperturbable judge. In almost every line of his essay, which was first published in 1858, a judgment is passed. It is a quality which may remind one of the pronouncements made more recently in *Scrutiny*, although Bagehot never indulges in the outbursts of temper which enlivened the pages of that interesting magazine. Often his judgments are admirably phrased. Dickens describes London, he says, "like a special correspondent for posterity."[42]

Bagehot has been called the most representative Victorian. It would be more accurate to say that he was most representative of the revival of neo-classical taste in the Victorian age. In his fine essay on "Pure, Ornate, and Grotesque Art in

English Poetry," it is Browning's grotesque exaggeration that receives his strongest condemnation, and it is not difficult to predict how he would respond to Dickens.

Striving to be fair and reasonable, Bagehot admits that Dickens' novels are read "with admiring appreciation by persons of the highest culture at the centre of civilization" as well as by "the roughest settler on Vancouver's Island." But he obviously wishes that the cultured readers would read Scott (or, even better, Wordsworth) instead. According to Louis Cazamian, the most characteristic feature of twentieth-century literature is *discontinuity*.[43] Bagehot finds the same trait in Dickens. "His genius is essentially irregular and unsymmetrical"; his world is a "disconnected" one.[44] To Bagehot, however, it is not merely a characteristic feature; it is a deplorable weakness, an indication of the diseased taste of his contemporaries. He finds such irregularity most deplorable in Dickens' "exaggerated caricature," especially in the novels published after *Copperfield* which, with a shudder, he refuses to discuss.[45] The most important point of Bagehot's essay is that instead of attributing Dickens' wild improbabilities to a powerful imagination, he traces them beyond that to a lack of a proper education. The twisted anti-Johnsonian prose style of Dickens, his lack of "sagacity" and good taste, his "monstrous exaggerations," his sentimental radicalism, are all, in Bagehot's view, the signs of a "brooding irregular mind" which has regrettably not been subjected to the discipline of classical models and educated society.[46] Just as Pope and Boileau had prescribed ridicule as one of the most efficient ways of civilizing the bumpkins of genius, so Bagehot wished that Dickens' wildness had been checked in youth. "Persons more familiar with the ridicule of their equals in station (and this is to most men the great instructress of the college time) well know that of all qualities this one [originality] most requires to be clipped and pared and measured."[47]

All this is traditionally neo-classical, and likewise (although Bagehot was a lawyer rather than a professor) it is fairly representative of an academic attitude towards Dickens' novels which still persists.

Curiously enough, his good friend and learned fellow-critic, R. H. Hutton, took issue with Bagehot on this last question. Touched with a streak of primitivism, perhaps, Hutton argued that book-learning was of little importance to the creative artist.[48] Being thus emancipated, he found Dickens' comic world a probable one and praised him as the greatest of English humorists.*

The remaining critical policeman to be discussed is G. H. Lewes, whose essay, "Dickens in Relation to Criticism," was published in the *Fortnightly Review* in 1872. The ultimate conclusion of this ingenious study combines Bagehot's point concerning Dickens' lack of education with Taine's hypothesis that poetic imagination is close to madness. Lewes concludes, then, that Dickens was simply an ill-educated madman. Because Lewes is one of the most important figures in the history of novel-criticism in England, his essay cannot properly be disposed of so summarily. Of the three critics under discussion, he is the only one who had given a good deal of hard thinking to the novel as a distinct kind of literature. In an able summary of his scattered reviews and articles, Morris Greenhut shows that Lewes had hammered out for himself "a coherent aesthetic of the novel as a literary form."[49] Like Taine and Bagehot, he turned to classical tragedy for his ultimate touchstone, but he was aware that the loose structure of the novel called for a kind of organic unity different from that to be expected in a play.[50] The novel, on its own level, had its own kind of greatness, which, he said, had been obscured by the indiscriminate acceptance of the "profusion of mediocrity" distributed by the Circulating Library.[51] On this level, his touchstones of greatness were *Tom Jones*, *Pride and Prejudice*, *Vanity Fair*, and, later, *Adam Bede*.

Lewes' principles of criticism are those of a realist. Although, with his remarkable versatility, he had devoted a good deal of attention to natural science, its effect on his literary

---

* Hutton, *Brief Literary Criticisms*, pp. 50-59; 66-67. Hutton argues that although Dickens is not a "realist" when dealing with an ordinary character such as Nicholas Nickleby, he is successful in making extraordinary characters convincing because stylization is essential and appropriate for the humorous vein.

taste did not lead him to advocate the use of scientific method or scientific objectivity in the writing of novels. The naturalist's fondness for spinning out a novel from assorted data accumulated in notebooks was censured by Lewes as mere "detailism."[52] In 1865, he complained of this "coat-and-waistcoat realism." "Artists have become photographers, and have turned the camera upon the vulgarities of life, instead of representing the more impassioned movements of life."[53] True realism, such as he found in Fielding and Austen,* depends upon probability of character and action rather than upon physical details. In a great novel, the reader is made to feel "that not only did such events occur, but that there was an inherent necessity in the characters and situations which brought out the events precisely in this order."[54] The function of the experienced critic is to point out to the public whether or not a novel is, as Percy Lubbock later said, "true, vivid, convincing—like life, in fact."[55]

That this distinguished exponent of discriminating taste did not think Dickens deserving of admission to his pantheon is an impressive example of the way in which Dickens' public had split into factions. In his worthy attempt to raise the status of fiction and of the criticism of fiction, Lewes seems to have decided that Dickens' vogue was a deplorable obstacle. His distaste is plainly evident in his review of *Vanity Fair*, but it was not until after Dickens' death that it was expounded at length.

One of the reasons for Lewes' distaste was that he had known the author of *Pickwick* in person from the outset of his career, and although their meetings appear to have been pleasant enough, Lewes never recovered from the shock of having peeped at the young Dickens' empty bookshelves. "Thought is strangely absent from his works. I do not suppose a single thoughtful remark on life or character could be

---

* The Austen-like tone of the opening scenes of *Middlemarch* may reflect the influence of Lewes' tastes upon George Eliot's (they were fond of reading Austen's novels aloud to each other). His praise of Austen's realism is repeated, virtually word for word, in one of Eliot's reviews. See Anna T. Kitchel, *George Lewes and George Eliot* (New York, 1933), p. 103, and *Essays and Reviews of George Eliot* (Boston, 1887), pp. 13-15.

found throughout the twenty volumes. . . . Compared with that of Fielding or Thackeray, his was merely an *animal* intelligence. . . . He never was and never would have been a student."[56] Oddly enough, in *The Principles of Success in Literature* (1865), Lewes had warned his fellow-critics that their most common error was to over-value "an acquaintance with the classics." Culture is relatively abundant, he said, whereas "invention, humour, and originality are excessively rare."

> It may be a painful reflection to those who, having had a great deal of money spent on their education . . . now see genius and original power of all kinds more esteemed than their learning; but they should reflect that what is learning now is only the diffused form of what was once invention. "Solid acquirement" is the genius of wits become the wisdom of reviewers.[57]

Excellent advice this, which might have been heeded by Bagehot as well as by Irving Babbitt. Lewes himself forgot all about it when writing his criticism of Dickens. His expression throughout his essay is as if a bad smell had penetrated into his library. He has gone out to the kitchen to find out what the help have been eating with such enthusiasm, and he has brought back a plateful to his desk for examination and analysis. His own sniff of disapproval is unrelieved, although he does take pains to explain why the kitchen help are under the illusion that the dish is tasty.

The word *illusion* is, in fact, the key to Lewes' attitude towards Dickens. It is as a realist even more than as an intellectual that he finds Dickens' novels distasteful.

"Dickens in Relation to Criticism" is an extremely sophisticated piece of irony. While Fitzjames Stephen had made a head-on attack with a cudgel, Lewes insinuates himself with great skill—the smylere with knyf under the cloke. At the outset he appears to be quarreling not with Dickens but with other critics, *all* of whom (he says with neat malice) disapprove strongly of Dickens' novels, because they have not understood the true nature of his imagination. After what follows in his essay, it seems incredible that anyone could be deceived by such a front, yet at least one scholar, Morris Greenhut, has taken the bait.[58] A typical illustration of Lewes' dialectic is his saying that the primary cause of Dickens' success is the "overflowing fun." This praise is followed by the remark that even critical readers admit its power. "They may be ashamed of their laughter, but they laugh. A revulsion of feeling at the preposterousness or extravagance of the image may follow the burst of laughter, but the laughter is irresistible, whether rational or not. . . ."[59]

Like Taine, Lewes devotes most of his discussion to Dickens' imagination. "If the other higher faculties were singularly deficient in him, this faculty was imperial."[60] Perhaps by *imperial* Lewes was referring here to George the Third for he treats Dickens' imagination as if it were a form of madness. On one page, he assures us that he had "never observed any trace of the insane temperament" in Dickens, but a few pages later, he describes Dickens' "hallucinations" in the very terms he had previously applied to the insane.[61] It is the shading in such discussions which is important. Flaubert once wrote to Taine protesting about his identifying an artist's vision with hallucination (for Flaubert had experienced both), and the debate has been reopened in Lionel Trilling's excellent answer to one of Freud's early essays concerning the neuroticism of the artist.[62] In "Dickens in Relation to Criticism," the shading is consistently directed in such a way as to make Dickens' world a fantastic absurdity. According to Lewes, an insane patient may have an intense conviction that he is a bear and that he can see his hands as claws. Dickens has similar convictions and by his hypnotic power convinces the gullible public that what is false is true. But we, the educated critics, says Lewes, know better. We can test his characters by "experience" and see through their "falsity." Dickens' figures are not characters. They are "merely masks . . . caricatures and distortions of human nature" which the public has accepted because of "the vividness of their presentation." "Unreal and impossible as these types were, speaking a language never heard in life, moving like pieces of simple mechanism always in one way (instead of moving with the infinite fluctuations of organisms . . .) these unreal figures affected the uncritical reader with the force of reality."[63]

Lewes' analysis of Dickens' static characters is harsh here, but not inaccurate. What is disconcerting is that he never considers for a moment that such stylization may be effective and even probable in its own way, as even Taine, for example found it. Lewes' concept of realism is so rigid that he cannot find a place for an artist whose pictures consist of "artistic daubs" instead of delicately finished scenes from everyday life.[64] "When one thinks of Mr. Micawber . . . one is reminded of the frogs whose brains have been taken out for physiological purposes, and whose actions henceforth want the distinctive peculiarity of organic action, that of fluctuating spontaneity."[65]

The most telling example of Lewes' limitations can be detected in his main criticism:

> Give a child a wooden horse, with hair for mane and tail, and wafer-spots for colouring, he will never be disturbed by the fact that this horse does not move its legs, but runs on wheels—the general suggestion suffices for his belief; and this wooden horse . . . is believed in more than a pictured horse by a Wouvermanns or an Ansdell. It may be said of Dickens's human figures that they too are wooden, and run on wheels; but these are details which scarcely disturb the belief of admirers.[66]

This striking comparison may have been suggested to Lewes by the second chapter of *Our Mutual Friend*. At the Veneerings' dinner party, the characters are first described as they appear in a mirror. The effect is extremely sinister: "Reflects Mrs. Podsnap; fine woman for Professor Owen, quantity of bone, neck and nostrils like a rocking-horse, hard features, majestic head-dress in which Podsnap has hung gold offerings." On later occasions, Mrs. Podsnap is likened to a rocking-horse again and again, and that Lewes would miss the appropriateness of the simile is typical of his inflexibility. She is being presented to us at the driest of parties in a novel which has, as its central symbol, a dust-heap. A rocking-horse is filled with dusty stuffings, and its external lacquered rigidity is ideally appropriate to represent the artificiality of the person described.* Mrs. Podsnap is not "real" in the sense that a minor character in George Eliot's novels is real. Her reality is of the same terrifying kind as we find in the simplified and expressive figures of Elmer Rice's play, *The Adding Machine*.

Lewes' analysis suffers not so much from inaccuracy, then, but from his being hide-bound to a theory which premised only one kind of probability in novels about contemporary life. The poet who strayed into novel-writing was to Lewes an anomaly (that George Eliot wrote verse as well as fiction does not affect the argument). If his premises are accepted, his essay still stands as the most effective attack on Dickens ever written. Even when disagreeing with it, one can admire its skillful argument, and especially its tone. Like the walrus and the carpenter, Lewes weeps over the oysters he is consuming, and he assures his victim and his audience that it is all for the best.

IV

In summary, the period from 1848 to 1872 witnessed not the decline and fall of Dickens' status but rather the undermining of his seemingly impregnable position by important and vocal sections of the reading public. When he died in 1870, he was still unquestionably the monarch of Victorian literature. Even such novels as *Little Dorrit* had consolidated his position with his thousands of devoted readers, for whom he was a king who could do no wrong, and among whom there were some who had gained a genuine insight into his intentions as an artist. His books as well as his public readings had made him a beloved national institution, seemingly above criticism. Also evident, however, is that during the same

---

* In Dickens' sketch, "A Christmas Tree," there is a further account of the reality of a rocking-horse as seen by the eyes of a child, and there is a discussion of why masks are terrifying because of their resemblance to reality. At least in his saner moments, Dickens would appear to have been aware of the differences pointed out by Lewes.

period, the seeds of revolution were being sown by gifted and perceptive readers who had outgrown his books.

It was to be a revolution initiated by a critical aristocracy, through whose efforts Thackeray, and later, Eliot and Meredith, were to be thrust forward as leading contenders for the eminence occupied by Dickens. The manifestoes for such a revolution were published during this period. They include the reviews in which Fitzjames Stephen demonstrated that a romantic's criticism of society was both repulsive and fatuous, and they include the essays in which G. H. Lewes demonstrated that a romantic's handling of probability was naively out of keeping with the requirements of realism and of mature taste.

In terms of these manifestoes, almost all the ingredients of the Dickens novel could be represented as stale. The sentimentality which had warmed the heart of Jeffrey was becoming laughable; the exposure of a materialistic society which had pleased Hood and Ruskin was becoming the tiresome rant of a Cockney ignorant of Political Economy; the command of an audience's sense of fear which had held Crabb Robinson spellbound was mere theatricality; the seemingly wondrous vitality and vividness of characterization was a sleight of hand trick, easily seen through except by children. The revolutionaries were willing to leave the small principality of humor as Dickens' sole domain; for the other responsibilities of his kingdom his hands (they contended) had been quite unworthy. It is also evident that before 1872, theirs was a minority verdict, yet because it originated not merely in jaded palates but in a growing desire among readers for a different kind of novel from what Dickens had provided, it was a verdict that was to become increasingly important and prevalent in the succeeding decades.

PART THREE

[1872-1952]

"The function of criticism . . . is that of dealing with the subconscious part of the author's mind which only the critic can express, and not with the conscious part of the author's mind, which the author himself can express. . . . Criticism means saying about an author the very things that would have made him jump out of his boots."—G. K. Chesterton

CHAPTER 8

BIOGRAPHY

"THE Literary Heavens of Two Hemispheres Hung in Black"—so ran a newspaper headline during the second week of June, 1870,[1] and the biographers at once set hastily to work. Several funeral-baked versions of Dickens' life made their timely appearance in the same year.[2] These were fortunately superseded by John Forster's more accurate account, which began to be published two years later. If Forster's book is also sometimes marred by hasty preparation, it was the pardonable haste of an aging biographer who feared that death might intervene before his task was finished. Forster did die, in fact, within two years of completing his *Life of Charles Dickens*. The interval was long enough for him to realize that his book was having a mixed effect upon the reputation of his friend.

Whether biographical information ought to affect literary reputations at all is a nice point. Some of the so-called New Critics have ably argued that it ought not to do so,[3] and the present study has also suggested, with reference to Little Nell, the limitations of such information. In empirical terms, however, whether it ought to do so or not, there can be no doubt that biography has had a marked effect upon literary judgments. The reader who shares Mark Rampion's opinion that Shelley the man was a white slug will read *Prometheus Unbound* in a different spirit from the reader who considers Shelley a martyred saint.[4] The reader who persists in thinking of Dickens the man as a kind of Santa Claus will probably not understand *Little Dorrit*, although neither instance should lead to the absurd conclusion that Shelley the man or Dickens the man is more important than his writings.

During Dickens' lifetime, the need for a biography was not a pressing one. Although reticent concerning his own background and circumstances (except upon the occasion of separating from his wife), he had established an extraordinarily personal relationship with his public. Direct addresses to the reader are much less frequent in his novels than in those of Thackeray or Eliot, yet Dickens contrived to make his readers feel that they were listening to a speaking voice whose tones were familiar and dear to them. As Tolstoy recorded in his notebook: "The first condition of an author's popularity, the prime means to make people like him, is the love with which he treats his characters. That is why Dickens's characters are the friends of all mankind: they are a bond of union between man in America and man in Petersburg."[5] This warm bond between author and public was reinforced by the personal tone of *Household Words* and *All the Year Round* and more especially by Dickens' public appearances as a reader. The enjoyment which Dickens himself derived from his readings is abundantly recorded in his letters. By this direct contact with his public he seems to have satisfied a craving which love and friendship could not fill. That his audiences were more than satisfied is also evident. A few, such as Henry James, were unimpressed, but the majority of listeners were astounded by his wizard-like demonstrations. The man who could provoke emotion and laughter from his writing-desk had an even more infallible power at his public reading-desk. Above all, the readings stamped on the minds of thousands an impression of a personality which seemed warm-hearted in indignation, sorrow, or joviality, and, like that of the Queen herself, sincere. Dickens anticipated George Bernard Shaw and Somerset Maugham in his ability to give the reader a pleasurable sense of being on speaking terms with the writer. In 1858, when he was trying to decide whether it would be proper for him to earn money as a reader in public, his sole concern, he told Forster, was what would be the effect of such an action "on that particular relation (personally affectionate and like no other man's) which subsists between me and the public."[6]

When the voice at last was still, Forster was faced with the difficult task of trying to keep before the public their idealized conception of Dickens' character and, at the same time, to paint an accurate portrait of one of his closest friends.

That he failed to satisfy either his contemporaries or posterity was almost inevitable.* Swinburne considered it extraordinary that when Forster wrote biographies of men he had never seen, such as Goldsmith, his work was of high quality, but that when he wrote of Landor and Dickens, his work was "execrable."[7] There was nothing extraordinary about the difference; Forster was simply overwhelmed by the difficulties of writing about a contemporary to whom he had been too closely attached. In his role as a critic, his attachments were likewise too close. Lewes once described Forster as "Pungent, the editor of the 'Exterminator,'" and complained that his literary criticism was always marred by asperity.[8] But because Forster had acted as Dickens' constant sounding-board, there is not much pungency in his discussion of novels which had been partly shaped by his own editorial advice. Hence his discussions are packed with valuable information, but as criticism they are not distinguished.

In most twentieth-century studies of Dickens, Forster is used as a mere butt. The absurd pomposity of his character, his elephantine manner of managing his protégés, his insularity and egotism were sometimes oppressively evident to Dickens in his later years. In the biography itself, it is the egotism which is especially evident. One wit described it as "The Autobiography of John Forster with Recollections of Charles Dickens."[9] Another reviewer protested that the theme of the book suggested that "Codlin was the friend, not Short."[10] Subsequently, it has often been pointed out that Forster's obtrusiveness is marked not only by the large role he assigns to himself in the story of Dickens' life, but in his omission of the importance of other friends, in particular his petulant overlooking of Wilkie Collins. Like all subsequent biographers (with the exception of Edgar Johnson), Forster was at his weakest in describing the last dozen years of Dickens' life, the period during which Collins was most closely associated with the Inimitable.

* He even failed to satisfy Dickens' family; there was talk of Charles Dickens the Younger publishing a rejoinder to vindicate his mother's role, which, it was felt, Forster had distorted. The Forster collection includes several accounts from the newspapers describing the family's dissatisfaction.

Despite these important omissions and shortcomings, the surprising quality of Forster's work is its permanence. If his sprawling volumes are studied with care, one often encounters evidence of his awareness of aspects of Dickens' character which have later been hailed as discoveries. The hearty and cheerful extrovert aspects of Dickens are, of course, predominant, and they established the tone of Dickensian biography for sixty years. But Forster knew his subject well enough to perceive many of the conflicts which had obsessed him even though he did not underline them. Oddly enough, it was this redeeming quality of awareness that displeased Forster's early readers. Old Samuel Carter Hall, wedded to the impression of a simple and cheerful Dickens, considered that a new and more genial biographer was needed. Dickens' memory, he said, had "received tarnish rather than glory from the efforts of his friend."[11]

The first volume, unlike the later two, was well received on the whole, especially because of its revelation of the blacking-warehouse incident. It was the dramatic story of the self-made man, a story summarized best in some lines of a play by Bulwer-Lytton. They are lines which Dickens knew by heart:

> Then did I seek to rise
> Out of the prison of my mean estate;
> And, with such jewels as the exploring mind
> Brings from the caves of knowledge, buy my ransom
> From those twin jailers of the daring heart—
> Low birth and iron fortune.[12]

To most readers, such a story was moving; to others, it was primarily a confirmation of their suspicions that Dickens' irregularities as a writer were the fruits of a lack of education and suitable social background. *The Times* noted that Dickens the man was "often vulgar in manners and dress, . . . ill at ease in his intercourse with gentlemen; . . . something of a Bohemian in his best moments."[13] The *British Quarterly Review* drew attention to the shallowness of a man improperly educated.[14] One amusing *jeu d'esprit* on this point was an article which used the Baconian theory to prove that Dickens could not have written his novels and that they were all from the pen of Mr. Gladstone: "We can . . . learn enough from Forster's 'Life of Dickens' to see that neither by position nor by training was he likely to become the author of works in which politics, science, art, and literature are dealt with confidently and boldly."[15]

A second aspect of Forster's biography which lowered Dickens' reputation in other quarters was his emphasis, in the later volumes, upon pounds, shillings, and pence. Inevitably, much of the correspondence between Dickens and his financial advisor was concerned with profit and loss—horrifying to aesthetes. The unfavorable impression was not modified until the later publication of letters to other correspondents culminating, in 1938, in the handsomely printed Nonesuch collection. Most offensively, Forster's final volume gave the impression that Dickens drove himself to death in a greedy effort to make an ample fortune more ample.[16] That Forster failed to perceive Dickens' more complex motives in this final phase is understandable. Dickens took great pains to screen them not only from his old friend but from himself. The total effect of these impressions and disclosures was summed up by an essayist of 1880 who commented upon the undeniable irony of Forster's efforts. "The popular estimate of Dickens was distinctly lowered by a work, every line of which was inspired by an almost infatuated admiration for him."*

Later biographers were able to supplement Forster's account with a considerable quantity of fresh information drawn from reminiscences, most of it reinforcing Carlyle's reference to "the good, the gentle . . . noble Dickens,—every inch of him an Honest Man."[17] The fresh information thus seemed to leave the picture unchanged. As Ralph Straus complained,

* *Appleton's Journal*, January 1880, p. 72. An exception to this reaction was George Gissing, who admired Dickens' capacity to combine artistic zeal with financial success. In moods of depression, Gissing used to reread Forster's account of Dickens at work. He considered it "one of the most bracing and inspiring in the history of literature." According to Gissing, there was a great difference between Dickens' industrious "fervour" and the tradesman-like habits of "the broad-based Trollope." See *The Private Papers of Henry Ryecroft* (New York, 1918), pp. 182-183.

such a biography as F. G. Kitton's *Charles Dickens* (1902), despite Kitton's "encyclopedic" knowledge, added virtually nothing of significance to Forster's version. Not until more than sixty years after Forster was any really epoch-making addition made, but the addition was enough to modify the whole portrait. It gave a glimpse into aspects of Dickens about which his literary executor could offer hardly a hint. For if Forster was unwittingly responsible for lowering Dickens' reputation by disclosures about his lowly background and his lust for profits, he was nevertheless careful to steer clear of anything smacking of scandal. Some were horrified by his account of Dickens' attitude towards his mother, but there was little comment from readers about the separation from his wife—a ticklish incident which the biographer steered round with skill, leaving his hero relatively undamaged. G. K. Chesterton, it should be noted, was much less charitable; even on the basis of inadequate evidence he was sharply critical of Dickens' behavior as a husband.[18]

That great writers must have led blameless existences was an ingrained mid-Victorian assumption. When Geraldine Jewsbury had enjoyed reading a novel by Collins, she wrote to Jane Carlyle: "I am sure Wilkie Collins must be a good man."[19] Had she been aware of Collins' actual domestic arrangements, she would have had to revise her estimate of his book. For Dickens, a spotless reputation was more obviously indispensable. Blanchard Jerrold said of him that "every sentiment [was] pure, every emotional opinion instinctively right—like a woman's."[20] Forster was not in a position to challenge such sugary sentiments which may still persist. Why is Dickens popular? asked Marie Corelli in 1920: "Why? Because he is sane, pure and wholesome! Because he never soiled his pen with degrading 'sex-problems,' and because . . . in his healthy brain there were no deceptive subterfuges."[21] The man's life seemed, then, to confirm the impression derived from his novels. Bagehot even suggested that the unsullied propriety of Dickens' writings was owing to his being so innocent that he had never experienced the temptation to write in any other way.[22] Bagehot's compliment was published in 1858. According to later biographers, this was the same year in which Dickens had set about establishing Ellen Ternan as his mistress.

In his sermon on Dickens in 1870, Benjamin Jowett suggested, somewhat mysteriously, that the lives of men of genius are so special and unusual that they should not be pried into too deeply by other mortals.[23] From the time of Dickens' domestic upheaval, rumors had circulated hinting at the existence of a Shelley-like affair with Georgina Hogarth, or of an affair with an actress.[24] The *Saturday Review* made a sly allusion to these in attacking the vulgarity of Dickens' Will,[25] and George Sala later whetted the appetites of the curious by asserting that he possessed an important secret about Dickens which he could not divulge.[26] In 1880, J. C. Watt speculated that Dickens must have had "some rare hidden experiences" which had been passed over by Forster,[27] and in 1896, the rumor was fanned once more. Mrs. Lynn Linton, who had been acquainted with Thackeray as well as with Dickens, remarked in an article: "Both men could, and did, love deeply, passionately, madly, and the secret history of their lives has yet to be written. It never will be written now, and it is best that it should not be."[28]

After the turn of the century, a few glimpses into the "secret history" were provided. In 1906, the correspondence with Christiana Weller was published, and a small stir was created. Innocent enough, the letters nevertheless showed up Dickens' capacity for strange infatuations, an impression heightened by the charming correspondence with Maria Beadnell, which was published two years later.[29] Not in the least innocent, however, were the sensational disclosures made in 1934 by the Reverend Thomas Wright concerning Ellen Ternan. As a biography, Wright's book is dull, but the bombshell included in it was of major significance. In the opinion of Hugh Kingsmill, it was "the most important contribution to the biography of Dickens in this century."*

* Kingsmill, *The Sentimental Journey* (1934), postscript. Wright's findings first appeared in the *Daily Express*, April 3, 1934, and were incorporated into his biography in 1935. Cf. the indignant replies by J. W. T. Ley in the *Dickensian*, xxxii (1936), 15-21; xxxiii (1937), 47-

The Dickensians who refused to accept Wright's disclosures had little difficulty in pointing out that his evidence was slim and questionable. Also somewhat questionable was Gladys Storey's *Dickens and Daughter* (1939) in which the public legend of Dickens as a sweet and gentle parent seemed to be destroyed by his daughter's reported comments: "He did not care a damn what happened to any of us. Nothing could surpass the misery and unhappiness of our home."[30] Yet however insubstantial the evidence was, the story of Ellen Ternan seemed to fit into place as the missing piece of a jig-saw puzzle. The biographers accepted it without hesitation. It was first extensively exploited by Edmund Wilson in his essays of 1941, and later in the biographies by Una Pope-Hennessy, Hesketh Pearson, Jack Lindsay, and Julian Symons. In 1952, the verdict of these biographers was finally confirmed by a fresh exploration (with the aid of infrared photography) of Dickens' manuscripts in America. Ada Nisbet's *Dickens and Ellen Ternan* makes a thorough and reasonable presentation of the facts, and Edgar Johnson's *Charles Dickens: His Tragedy and Triumph* incorporates many of these facts into an exhaustive two-volume analysis of Dickens' life and character. As a topic for angry debate, the Ellen Ternan case would appear now to be a closed one.

The effect of such disclosures has been twofold. One learned professor in Toronto published an article called "Literary Idols with Feet of Clay," in which he castigated the "solemn ruffianism" of Dickens' treatment of his wife.[31] Such a reaction explains why many Dickensians have honestly believed that to appreciate Dickens' writings, it is essential to keep his name spotless. Other readers have felt that an idol is dull and that only by recognizing a man's weaknesses may his character be understood or even appreciated. The reputation of Wordsworth offers an interesting example of such twentieth-century tastes. As Douglas Bush wittily said, Victorian readers valued Wordsworth because he gave the world a natural religion whereas we have acquired a new respect for

---

51, and by Edward Wagenknecht in *College English*, XI (1950), 373-382, and in *An Introduction to Dickens* (Chicago, 1952), pp. 424-426.

him because he gave the world a natural daughter.[32] It is certainly true that the disclosures concerning Annette Vallon prompted an extensive and valuable reconsideration of the poet's character and writings. The importance of the Ellen Ternan story is parallel. It is important not so much in itself as a morsel of gossip but because it leads to fresh evaluation of the complexities behind Dickens' work. Virginia Woolf affirmed haughtily in 1925 that she would not trouble to cross the street in order to meet Charles Dickens. Of all great writers, she said, he was "the least personally charming" because of his masculine self-assurance and his freedom "from the foibles and eccentricities and charms of genius."[33] Had Mrs. Woolf lived to read Edmund Wilson's analysis of Dickens' character, it is possible that she might have found the novelist a more interesting and sympathetic figure.

We hear much in the twentieth century concerning the lonely isolation of the artist, yet it would be difficult to find a more disturbing account of an artist and his public than the following passage from the final chapter of *Edwin Drood*: "Constantly exercising an Art which brought him into mechanical harmony with others, and which could not have been pursued unless he and they had been in the nicest mechanical relations and unison, it is curious to consider that the spirit of the man was in moral accordance or interchange with nothing around him." The function of the traditional biographers is to remind us that the passage is a picture of John Jasper, respected organist in a respectable cathedral city, who is also a haunted criminal and an enemy of social order. The function of later biographers has been to remind us that the passage is also a picture of Charles Dickens.

Some of these later biographers have obscured the hearty exuberance and zest for experience which had been stressed in the previous accounts of Dickens' life. The traditional Dickens still lingers in Pope-Hennessy's common-sensical version and in Hesketh Pearson's lively sketch, but in Jack Lindsay's ambitious and disappointing book, the traditional Dickens disappears under a welter of Freudian solemnities. In 1951, Julian Symons summed up this later view by diagnosing

Dickens' personality as that of a *manic-depressive* and by making fun of earlier biographers who pictured Dickens, he says, as "an amiable mixture of Santa Claus and his own Mark Tapley."[34]

In perspective, the Ellen Ternan affair was essentially a catalyst. The clear and simple portrait of the happy, successful, sane, and well-adjusted author, which the Dickensians found inspiring and which others found insipid, was suddenly clouded over. A much more complex and interesting figure remained to be discerned. In all of these later biographies, our attention is shifted to the unhappiness behind the lacquered mask of his triumphs: his obsessions, fears, restlessness, and rebellious failure to adjust himself to the social scene of England.* Much the most comprehensive of these later portraits is Edgar Johnson's. In his vigorous, full-length study, this American biographer displays as much hero-worship for his subject as Forster or F. G. Kitton had displayed; his Dickens is pictured as a Titan toiling to transform the inadequate social conscience of the Victorian middle classes. The difference is that this later Titan is a more recognizable and sympathetic figure, one whose career was as much a tragedy as a triumph.

What has been gained can be tested by contrasting the traditional and the more recent pictures of Dickens attending the banquet held in his honor before his second voyage to America. In the newer context, we see not only the extraordinary spectacle of a living man of letters fêted with splendors beyond the reach of kings; we sense also that this literary monarch was a disappointed human being. We know that there was the taste of dust in his mouth. The pedestal has been taken away, but our understanding of his struggles has

* An early essay which anticipates parts of Edmund Wilson's interpretation appeared in 1877 in the *Encyclopaedia Britannica* (ninth edition). The author, William Minto, stressed Dickens' isolation from Victorian society, an isolation prompted by "a lurking fear" that the circumstances of his youth "exposed him to contempt." Hence there was "something of the defensive, even of the aggressive" in his attitude towards society, especially "cultured society." "He faced towards society with . . . the consciousness of a vast popular multitude behind him, to which he could appeal if they refused him what was his due."

been enriched, and Dickens is left, a more than life-size figure, even in his unhappiness. Feet of clay have been exposed
more fully than the traditional admirer would like, but, as
one Dickensian has consolingly added, the clay was at least
human clay.[35]

CHAPTER 9

THE COMMON READER

"This cheap edition of my books is dedicated to the English people, in whose approval, if the books be true in spirit, they will live, and out of whose memory, if they be false, they will very soon die."—(Dedication proposed for the People's Edition, 1847)

HAVING weathered the early failure of *Martin Chuzzlewit* and the batterings administered by critics of the 1850's and 1860's, the reputation of Dickens was subjected to its most severe testing after his death. One assertion most persistently repeated from that day to the present has been that his books are no longer read. It is admitted that they once served a useful function of revealing "the masses to the classes," but such days are past, and these formerly useful volumes now repose "undisturbed on the shelves of libraries in country houses."[1] The opinion summarized here is from an essay of 1895, but it might have appeared in 1875 or 1925. To demolish a writer's reputation, a full-scale critical attack, such as Lewes' analysis of Dickens, may be effective. But much more damaging, and much less troublesome to prepare, is an essay asserting that the writer's books are no longer fashionable. Of Victorian writers, Tennyson has suffered most from this treatment; the 1920's made it bad form to mention his name except in jest. In the instance of Dickens, as the circulation records of any library can show, it has usually been difficult to say that his work is not read at all. It has been affirmed, instead, that he is not read by those who know better. According to the *London Quarterly Review*:

> Though Dickens' works are still [1871] by far the most popular of his age, we have never met a single man of high cultivation who regarded Dickens in the light of an artist at all, or looked upon his books as greatly worthy the attention of persons capable of appreciating better things.[2]

For at least sixty years after Dickens' death, this kind of attack was a commonplace one. It is interesting to place beside it George Gissing's report that by 1898 a similar neglect prevailed at the opposite end of the social scale. "How the London poor should love Dickens!" Gissing wrote. "But—with his books always obtainable—they can scarce be said to read him at all."[3] That during Dickens' lifetime there were important limits to his popularity among the poor has already been discussed; Gissing's impression would indicate that it later became even more necessary to remember these limits when referring to Dickens as The Novelist of the People.

Of the several articles which have replied to the charge that Dickens is obsolete among all levels of readers, W. H. Mallock's is the most cogent. In 1893, Mallock raised the question which plagues all investigations of literary reputation. In reply to those who assert that Dickens is not read, he asks: *How do you know?* We reach such conclusions, Mallock says, by trusting to impressions derived from our own "social observation" which is limited by our age, class, and pursuits, and it is from some such limited circles that the erroneous impression derives that Dickens is everywhere despised.[4] From his own observation of country houses in the nineties, Mallock cites contrary evidence demonstrating the extent to which Dickens' novels had become household words. Even young guardsmen read them, he notes, and he then cites statistics from Dickens' publishers showing that instead of declining, the popularity of Dickens had increased since his death. The gradual exhaustion of copyrights by the end of the century prevented Chapman and Hall from acquiring precise figures for total sales in England, but their own figures are sufficient to demonstrate that sales by 1891 were four times greater than in 1869, that the annual sales averaged 330,000 copies, and that further increases followed after 1900.[5] The sale of Carlyle's writings, which were published by the same firm, began to slump before 1900, and never recovered. "If it wasn't for Dickens" said an employee of Chapman and Hall, "we might as well put up the shutters tomorrow."[6] During the first two decades of the twentieth century, thirteen editions of his works were published,[7] and individual novels continued to appear in astonishing numbers. By 1944, no less than sixty different editions of *A Tale of Two Cities* were published by presses in Great Britain.[8] A further indication of continued sale is provided by Everyman's Library. In 1948, Richard Aldington pointed out that of the thousand and more titles of this "best collection of general literature extant in English," the book with the highest annual sale is *David Copperfield.*[9]

If even during the eighties and nineties (supposedly the nadir of Dickens' literary status), the sales increased rather than declined, the only real question was, as Mallock said, by whom were the books being read? One could answer that they were being read by Gissing and Conrad, Kipling and Hopkins, Swinburne and Henley, the aging William Morris and the young Bernard Shaw, and (with some grumblings) even by George Saintsbury. The importance of such powerful and articulate readers in sustaining a dead writer's fame is enormous, yet in Dickens' case, the less articulate have also played an unusually prominent part. During the eighties and nineties, thousands of common readers continued to buy and read Dickens, and thousands have been buying and reading him ever since.

According to Arnold Bennett, it is the small critical minority, the "passionate few," who initiate and sustain literary reputations. "The majority can make a reputation, but it is too careless to maintain it. . . . Do you suppose that if the fame of Shakespeare depended on the man in the street it would survive a fortnight? . . . This is not cynicism; but truth."* If Dickens' name is substituted for Shakespeare's, Bennett's theory seems inadequate. The dogged loyalty of the provincial Dickensian has been phenomenal; changes in literary fashions seem to leave him quite unruffled. His understanding of Dickens may be limited, but his persistent enthusiasm has been a powerful support. In 1922, Middleton

* Bennett, *Literary Taste* (1909), pp. 22-24. The theory of the passionate few appears many times in Bennett's work. In *Clayhanger*, the hero's study of *Gulliver's Travels* provokes a similar comment from the author. See also his *Fame and Fiction* (1901), pp. 11-16; 197. Cf. J. W. T. Ley, "Dickens's Popularity," *Dickensian*, I (1905), 154-155.

Murry published an article in *The Times* entitled "The Dickens Revival." He rightly argued that an adequate appreciation of Dickens is a much more genuine test of taste than the conventional highbrow's professed love for *Emma*, and he rejoiced that Dickens' work had not gone "the way of wax fruit."[10] His article was succeeded by letters to the editor pointing out that the "revival" was the work not of the likes of Mr. Murry but of the Dickens Fellowship. Eleven years later, in a fashion distinctly his own, Robert Graves confirmed the impression that Dickensians are important. According to Mr. Graves, Dickens had become boring to even the "middle public" because he was "emotionally connected with aspidistras," and so "he is abandoned to the great backward public of the depressed provinces and semi-residential suburbs."[11]

It would seem, then, that Arnold Bennett's premise is only partially applicable. The buoyancy of a literary reputation is ultimately tested in the critical vortex at the centers of civilization, but a reputation may also be kept afloat for long periods in the quieter provincial backwaters. The qualities which have sustained Dickens' fame among less critical readers have included those already discussed as making the strongest appeal to the general Victorian public. It is said that a public may begin, and sometimes end, by admiring a great artist for the wrong things.[12] The quality most admired after Dickens' death remained his reputed cheerfulness. In 1879, it was pointed out by the historian, Justin McCarthy, that although Dickens had "gifts of far higher artistic value," his fame depended upon his having "set forth life in cheerful lights and colours."[13] Much of the so-called Dickensian literature today reinforces McCarthy's impression. In addition, for some readers, has been the charm of familiarity. Trollope reports that dealers in tea who stimulated the purchase of their product by giving books as prizes to "their poorer customers" had found Dickens' works to be the most reliable inducements. One dealer had ordered 18,000 copies of Dickens' novels and would accept no substitutes. "He had found," says Trollope gravely, "that the tea-consuming world preferred Dickens."[14] If, in some circles, Dickens has seemed what is called old hat, in others he is rather an old shoe, comfortably broken in by use. In Henry Green's novel, *Living* (1929), there is a foundry worker called Mr. Craigan whose custom is to read the works of Dickens "over and over again." He will read nothing else. To him, *Little Dorrit* is a habit, rather like a favorite brand of marmalade or pipe tobacco; he has no interest whatever in trying another.

Mr. Craigan is a charming example of the non-unionized Dickensian. Much more vocal, if less numerous, have been the organized Dickensians, whose Fellowship was founded in 1902. Mention should also be made of another organized group, the Boz Club, which was founded two years earlier. The Boz Club, a somewhat exclusive assemblage of diners, featured among its 150 members several representatives of the aristocracy of rank if not the aristocracy of intellect. Its chairman, Sir Henry Dickens, defined its aims by declaring proudly: "We had no concern with academic discussions as to whether Dickens's methods were . . . of the highest order; all we cared for was to try to show that he had secured for himself the love and affections of his readers." After defining these aims, Sir Henry proceeds to describe one of the feasts at which love and affection were to be aired. The occasion included a very long speech by Lord James in praise of Dickens as a social reformer. His speech prompted a heated reply from the Lord Chancellor who protested that Dickens was simply a politician, whereupon Sir Henry, in turn, had to leap into the fray with "a very strong protest."[15] The group "narrowly escaped destruction," Sir Henry admitted, but his failure to realize the incongruity of the scene, which his father would have relished, is of a solemnity almost monumental. Even more significant quarreling had broken out in 1902 when the more appropriately democratic Dickens Fellowship was likened to the House of Commons and the Boz Club to the House of Lords.[16]

The Boz Club expired in 1914 but the Dickens Fellowship continued to flourish and to spread its branches over the whole English-speaking world. Although the interests and backgrounds of its thousands of members are, in reality, widely varied, the tone of the Dickens Fellowship has been commonly identified by its critics with a single kind of reader who is represented as a harmless old duffer at best and an ignorant zealot at worst. If Sir Max Beerbohm had followed up his celebrated picture of Browning drinking tea in the company of members of the Browning Society by drawing a comparable scene of the organized Dickensians, he might have gone back to Phiz's illustrations from *Pickwick Papers* for models. The Transactions of the Pickwick Club seem indeed to repeat themselves in the transactions of provincial branches of the Dickens Fellowship. Instead of "Speculations on the Source of Hampstead Ponds, with some Observations on the Theory of Tittlebats," there are apt to be speculations about which room of the White Hart Inn was occupied by Samuel Weller.*

Topographical detective work is a pastime especially attractive to amateurs. A somewhat different kind of amateur has been lured by *The Mystery of Edwin Drood*, and the number of books and articles provoked by that tantalizing fragment is breathtaking. One collection of *Droodiana*, assembled over a period of fifty years, is said to have filled every shelf on all four sides of a great exhibition hall used by the Grolier Club in New York.[17] With some valuable but rare exceptions, most of these publications have been the work of amateurs whose enthusiasm is equalled only by their critical and scholarly innocence.

To satirize the activities of the organized readers of Dickens is too easy and also presupposes that there must be only one way of reading his novels. Aside from their good works of charity, the Dickensians in their zeal have been largely responsible for preserving Dickens' house on Doughty Street

* For a list of topographical writings, see William Miller, *The Dickens Student and Collector*, pp. 257-274. Topographical speculations exemplify the Dickensians' tendency to insist upon the naturalistic correspondence between Dickens' characters and people of the everyday world. They are apt to be suspicious of any praise of Dickens' imagination. H. D. Traill says, in a pleasant essay, that for the true Dickensian the likeness between Dickens' world and "some objective reality in nature is his *signum stantis aut cadentis ecclesiae.*" *The New Fiction and other Essays* (1897), p. 142.

not only as a shrine but as a valuable museum and library, and, by the efforts of some of them, Rochester may eventually be transformed into another literary Mecca like Stratford-on-Avon.* Their prolific antiquarianism sometimes brings to light information of importance and value.† The stones of London, already rich with associations of Dickens, are made richer. Many Dickensians suffer, however, from a certain exclusiveness of their own. As custodians of a shrine, they will have it that the Inimitable can do no wrong, as man or writer, and they are inclined to look with suspicion upon even well-intentioned criticism. Their antiquarianism, instead of being subservient to literary criticism, tends to crowd any fresh interpretations off the bookshelf. Moreover, by extension of this antiquarianism, there develops the tendency to read Dickens' novels not as novels but as social history. The dangers to the social historian from reading the novels in this fashion have been ably demonstrated in *The Dickens World* by Humphry House. The dangers to the reader of novels are even more significant.

What distinguishes the Dickensians since Dickens' death from the most devoted readers among his contemporaries is that the later ones have discovered a new pleasure in his writings: the charm of the past. "Yoho, down the pebbly dip, and through the merry water-splash, and up at a canter to the level road again. Yoho! Yoho!" Even in 1844 there was a degree of quaintness about Tom Pinch's ride. After a hundred years and more, it can evoke a dim nostalgia for a past age which seems warmer, heartier, happier than anything since. Not only are such scenes colorfully picturesque, they seem also to have an eighteenth-century quality of stability and order

* The delightfully colorful and lavish Dickens pageant staged at Rochester during the Festival of Britain in 1951 was a great success in all respects except (it is reported) financially. It may be some time before Rochester pilgrimages will be as profitable as those described in *This Shakespeare Industry* by Ivor Brown and George Fearon (1939).

† Antiquarian studies such as J. H. McNulty's *Concerning Dickens and other Literary Characters* or E. Beresford Chancellor's *The London of Charles Dickens* are fresh and unpretentious by comparison with the work of critical dabblers such as Albert S. G. Canning, whose three books on Dickens are distinguished by an unrelieved triteness. See e.g. the latter's *Dickens Studied in Six Novels* (1912).

(however unlike the muddle of Victorian life). Dickens himself was susceptible to the charms of the recent past as a haven from problems of his own day, and it is perhaps pointless to bewail the modern Dickensian's comparable absorption in it. Yet the Christmas card elements have certainly received more prominence and attention than their presence in Dickens' novels warrants. In a discussion of G. K. Chesterton in the final chapter, this question can be reconsidered; here it should only be noted that this eloquent spokesman for the Christmas Dickens was at one time president of the Dickens Fellowship.

Another interesting explanation of the sustainment of Dickens' popular reputation after his death was offered by Arthur Waugh, of Chapman and Hall. From the point of view of the "general reader," said Waugh, his greatest strength, like Scott's and Cervantes', consisted in his not having relied too much upon story, for stories cannot often be reread. "Their books are not episodes of life but life seen whole and presented whole through art."[18] Waugh is speaking here of lasting popularity; for a temporary popularity, good story-telling seems to be enough in itself.

If Dickens' hold upon critical readers after 1860 was loosened by the attractions of Flaubert, Henry James, and George Meredith, his command of the general public was threatened by competition from a different quarter. One of the earliest and best of these rivals was his own disciple, Wilkie Collins, an extraordinarily skillful contriver of tales, the sales of which were enormous during the sixties, seventies, and eighties.[19] Although many of Collins' novels appealed (like his Master's) to a variety of levels of taste, the general effect of his writing was to limit the scope of the Dickensian novel, and to make one of its elements—the sensationalism of suspense—prevail over all others.[20] In Collins' imitators, such as Mrs. Henry Wood, the author of *East Lynne*, and Mary Elizabeth Braddon, author of *Lady Audley's Secret*, the tendency is further developed towards the ubiquitous detective story of the twentieth century. With Ouida it is pushed to an extreme in which exotic and sensational situations are not even sustained by a well-contrived story. The popular roll call thereafter is a very long one, and, if pursued to its logical conclusion through Edgar Wallace, Marie Corelli, and Mickey Spillane, would lead to the writers of Hollywood.

It is said that early moving picture producers learned certain screening techniques from a study of Dickens' novels, especially the method of increasing tension by means of alternate shots from a parallel series of events. It could also be said that much more indirectly, they had learned from him some of the requirements of mass entertainment. As the *Saturday Review* complained, he was the embodiment not only of a revolution in politics but of a revolution in taste. "People mutht be amuthed, Thquire, thomehow," said Mr. Sleary of the horse-riding; "they can't be alwayth a working, nor yet they can't be alwayth a learning. Make the betht of uth; not the wurtht." A similar compassion for the common man's need for entertainment appears in Dickens' letters and in his early tract, *Sunday Under Three Heads*. One wonders how far his compassion could be stretched. As we have seen, it did not include the trashy entertainments of G. W. M. Reynolds, whose novels Dickens described as "a national reproach." Would his compassion have been wide enough to embrace the works of Marie Corelli and other purveyors of entertainments which, for brief periods, have attracted audiences much vaster than his? "What is progress?" asked Malcolm Elwin in 1934. "At the beginning of the Victorian era, Dickens sold in tens of thousands; after a century of progress, Conrad counted his sales for years in hundreds, and Edgar Wallace in hundreds of thousands."[21]

That Dickens himself contributed to the development is obvious. As editor of *Household Words* and *All the Year Round*, he fostered the growth of the popular fiction magazines, and his own success as a novelist, even more than Scott's, showed the possible resources of a new public which could be exploited by the unscrupulous. Like most initiators of revolutions, however, he would have been bewildered by the later developments through which the novelist of quality has become isolated, and the common reader often left to content himself with a diet of trash. Dickens shared his century's faith in the progress of taste and knowledge through education, and he considered his own novels as in part a contribution towards such an end. Their continued survival among a large public, even when they are sometimes inadequately understood, is an indication that his faith was not altogether misplaced. A discouraging corrective to any such optimism is the more typical public fare. As Santayana admitted, Dickens himself had more genius than taste.[22] Most of his best-selling successors have displayed somewhat less of his taste and of his genius almost none.

CHAPTER 10

THE DISCOVERY OF THE SOUL

" 'Incidents in the development of a soul! little else is
worth study.'—Browning."—From the notebooks of
Thomas Hardy, 1889.

I

IN "The Soul of Man under Socialism" (1891), Oscar
Wilde paid tribute to the "incomparable" genius of George
Meredith as a novelist. There were better artists in France,
he admitted, but artists whose view of life was more restricted. And in Russia there were writers with "a more vivid
sense of what pain in fiction may be." But to Meredith "belongs philosophy in fiction." "His people not merely live, but
they live in thought. . . . There is soul in them and around
them. . . . And he who made them . . . has never asked the
public what they wanted."[1] Without mentioning Dickens, this
passage tells a great deal about his status among many
cultivated readers. It has already been demonstrated that such
readers were abandoning Dickens in the fifties, a process that
was accelerated by the publication of novels by Thackeray and
the Brontës, and later, more markedly, by those of George
Eliot and George Meredith, for the gradual undermining of
Dickens' reputation owed a great deal to his critics' being able
to compare his books unfavorably with the writings of other
major novelists whose aims differed from his. That is, the
process of dethroning (which was to be most in evidence about
1900) really depended upon a combination of interdependent
factors. There was a shift of taste; there was a development of
new theories of the novel, and there was a recognition by English readers of fresh talents among the novelists of England,
France, America, and Russia, a recognition stimulated partly
because these talents were in accord with the shift of taste.
This combination of factors will be the subject of the present
chapter and of the one which follows.

In 1854, Thackeray was wondering how soon it would be before "some young fellow" would arrive to knock Dickens and himself "both off the stage."[2] He did not have to wait long, but the young fellow turned out to be a woman of almost forty years of age. Just as *Vanity Fair* had made many readers dissatisfied with the vulgarity of Dickens' novels, so *Adam Bede* made readers dissatisfied with Thackeray as well as with Dickens. Beside the prodigious erudition of George Eliot, Thackeray's learning seemed almost schoolboy-like, and beside the warm-hearted earnestness of her tone, his half-cynical airs (Thackeray's most glaring fault, in Victorian eyes) seemed meretricious.

Even though the expression has been sanctioned by Thackeray as well as by Ernest Hemingway, to speak of one novelist knocking another off the stage is an obvious historical simplification. Many readers were content to enjoy all three novelists equally. In general, however, *Adam Bede* was as timely a publication as *Pickwick* had been earlier, and as damaging to other novelists. It seemed to satisfy the demands being made of the novel by cultivated critics, demands which Dickens and Thackeray had failed to satisfy. A few years later, William Cory, an admirer of the French Academy, was looking back upon the decline of taste since the time of Wordsworth. "I think it is Dickens that has brought us down," he wrote, and added that it was "wonderful" how George Eliot had risen "so very far above him and his dominant set."[3] Here is the note of the representative Victorian admirer of George Eliot—a sense of having successfully taken flight into higher realms. When a reviewer praised *Adam Bede* as "one of the best novels we have read for a long time," G. H. Lewes was indignant. "The nincompoop couldn't see the difference between *Adam* and the mass of novels he had been reading."[4]

Aside from the effect of her novels upon other readers, George Eliot is of interest as a critical reader of fiction. Like many of her contemporaries, her literary diet in childhood included a feast of Scott's novels, which was later followed by a period of revulsion from fiction during which she looked upon novel-reading as a sinful waste of time. "Have I, then, any time to spend on things that never existed?"[5] The Evangelical phase was soon outgrown but left its mark on her mature attitude towards fiction. Some writers such as Rousseau and George Sand she was prepared to accept because they swept her away with their cascade of emotions,[6] but, as a general rule, she argued that the novelist's special forte ought to be an unsensational record of everyday life. Observation ought to be colored by sentiment but by nothing else.[7] The happiness of her union with Lewes must have been augmented by their mutual love of Jane Austen's novels. As a reviewer in the fifties, she used Austen as a standard by which to measure "silly novels by lady novelists," and her sarcasm fell most heavily upon theatrical exaggeration. "Only cultivated minds fairly appreciate the exquisite art of Miss Austen. Those who demand the stimulus of 'effects,' those who can only see by strong lights and shadows, will find her tame and uninteresting."[8] Even Mrs. Gaskell, she said, "seems to me to be constantly misled by a love of sharp contrasts—of 'dramatic' effects. She is not contented with the subdued coloring, the half-tints, of real life."[9]

Although in Eliot's own novels there are some lapses into sensationalism in the endings of *Adam Bede* and *The Mill on the Floss*, and in the Raffles incident in *Middlemarch*, she usually achieved the plain, unvarnished tale which she had recommended as a critic. Her realism was, however, of a much more revolutionary turn than has so far been indicated. "You see, it was really George Eliot who started it all," so the young D. H. Lawrence said to a friend. "And how wild they all were with her for doing it. It was she who started putting all the action inside. Before, you know, with Fielding and the others, it had been outside. Now I wonder which is right?"[10] Lawrence was perceptive to include Fielding with "all the others." Eliot's admiration for Fielding has misled some of her critics.[11] The general direction of her novels is Richardsonian. As H. D. Traill said in 1897, Fielding's triumph had made readers forget how Richardson ("that great but exasperating artist") had displayed human nature by "working away

. . . at 'how he felt,' 'how she felt,' 'what he thought' . . . until he has traced . . . a human soul."[12] George Eliot and Henry James thus restored a balance.

It is not surprising that Eliot seldom refers to Dickens' novels in her letters, novels, or criticism, and her most important comment upon them (published a year before *Scenes from Clerical Life*) is a manifesto for her own fictional revolution:

> We have one great novelist who is gifted with the utmost power of rendering the external traits of our town population; and if he could give us their psychological character—their conception of life, and their emotions—with the same truth as their idiom and manners, his books would be the greatest contribution Art has ever made to the awakening of social sympathies. But . . . he scarcely ever passes from the humorous and external to the emotional and tragic, without becoming . . . transcendent in his unreality.[13]

Eliot's criticism here is parallel to George Brimley's review of *Bleak House* in which he had pointed out Dickens' concentration upon the "purely outward" aspects of character and his failure (with Tulkinghorn for example) to deal with motives.[14] Such were the readers who were more than ready to welcome Eliot's novels. Parenthetically, it should be noted that one of the warmest welcomes came from an unexpected source, from Dickens himself. Eliot had looked for encouragement from Thackeray, thinking him "as I suppose the majority of people with any intellect do, on the whole the most powerful of living novelists." It was Dickens, however, who characteristically overwhelmed her with his enthusiasm for her first two novels.[15]

With the possible exception of Thomas Hardy, George Eliot was the last English novelist to succeed fully in the same way as Dickens, with his early novels, had succeeded. She gained the highest acclaim from critical readers, and she satisfied the tastes of a large public. R. E. Francillon reports that in 1859, the *annus mirabilis* of English publishing, *Adam*

Bede "threw the whole nation into excitement."[16] As *The Times* indicated, George Eliot could challenge Dickens successfully on his own ground. Mrs. Poyser, "the gem of the novel," is "likely to outvie all the characters of recent fiction" with the single exception, according to *The Times*, of Mr. Samuel Weller.[17] In addition, with such characters as Arthur Donnithorne, there was a painstaking exploration of motives which was quite beyond Dickens' methods. In the eighties, one reviewer looked back with satisfaction upon Eliot's accomplishment in changing the direction of the novel away from Dickens and Collins: "Within the past twenty-five or thirty years English fiction has taken on itself an introspective hue, and the taste of readers of fiction is all for analysis of character and motive, while the taste of the period immediately preceding was entirely for the display of character and motive in action."[18]

The reception by the reviewers of some of her later novels was not always so triumphant. Fatuous attacks on the immorality of *The Mill on the Floss* (to which she was painfully vulnerable) are said to have affected her artistic development by accentuating her concern with the exposition of a moral system.[19] The sale of her novels nevertheless continued, and the eight thousand pounds she received from the *Cornhill* for *Romola* caused Meredith (who lacked a popular audience) to gasp with astonishment.*

It is interesting that one of Meredith's most ardent admirers, the poet James Thomson, complimented the novel-reading public of the seventies upon their choice of George Eliot as a popular favorite.[20] Popularity did not, as in Dickens' case, cost her the following of the cultivated. John Addington Symonds, a very discriminating reader, said that if Balzac had been less fantastic and less sceptical, he "would certainly be one of the two greatest novelists of the world, Miss Evans the other."[21] For the most extravagant praise, however, one should turn to the American poet, Sidney Lanier,

---

* *Letters of George Meredith* (New York, 1912), I, 74. See also *The Autobiography of Mrs. Oliphant* (New York, 1899), p. 326. Mrs. Oliphant considered George Eliot to have been the most highly paid author of the age.

whose lectures on the history of the English novel were delivered in 1881.[22] An expert upon prosody, Lanier was virtually an ignoramus concerning the art of fiction. His book being one of the most inept studies of the novel, the kind of book which gives the false impression that no one in the nineteenth century knew how to read, it is embarrassing to find that George Eliot was its heroine. For Lanier, as for others during the seventies and eighties, when her fame was at its apex, George Eliot was not a novelist but a high priestess whose pronouncements solved the religious dilemmas of a troubled age. In "Daniel Deronda: A Conversation," Henry James gives a delightful portrait of another such devotee and pits her against a lively reader who finds *Daniel Deronda* dull.

In time the sibyl-phase exhausted itself. By 1897, Clement Shorter had the impression that unlike Dickens and Thackeray, George Eliot had failed to maintain her hold upon readers. "Of the idolatry which almost made her a prophetess of a new cult we hear nothing now."[23] Some of the Victorian poets such as Hopkins, Fitzgerald, Swinburne, and Rossetti had detected a prosy dullness in her novels which they compared unfavorably with the liveliness of Dickens.[24] Their verdict came to be more and more accepted after the turn of the century. Although her own reputation became temporarily dimmed by this development, Eliot's achievement in revolutionizing the English novel left its mark. It was her method of analyzing Bulstrode's hypocrisy rather than Dickens' method of presenting Pecksniff which became the norm not only for major novelists but for critical readers.[25] When Matthew Arnold was recommending Tolstoy's *Anna Karenina* to English readers in 1887, he used virtually the same terms which Eliot had used in her manifesto against Dickens: "The Russian novelist is thus master of a spell to which the secrets of human nature—both what is external and what is internal, gesture and manner no less than thought and feeling—willingly make themselves known."[26]

I I

In their own special way, George Meredith's novels reflect

the same development. To expose the inner lives of his characters, to present a minute analysis of human motives, to impart an air of philosophical discussion into the novel were certainly among Meredith's objectives. He is, however, so many-sided a figure that he keeps breaking out of the brown paper wrapping in which literary historians have attempted to package him.

In 1887, the poet Gerard Manly Hopkins observed to Robert Bridges that "the abundance of genius in English romance in this age appears to me comparable with its abundance in drama in the Elizabethan."[27] This fictional renaissance, which still continues despite annual predictions to the contrary, has had a marked effect on writers of what booksellers call *non-fiction*. As a contemporary poet complained: "Your novel is a great thief." The progressive pressure of a predominant literary form has driven poets such as Hardy and essayists such as Aldous Huxley into attempting a form not altogether congenial. Meredith is an early example of the somewhat reluctant novelist. One might say that he was a promising poet who could have been a major essayist but chose, instead, to make his name as a novelist. Under the circumstances, it was inevitable that he would set about making changes in the traditional form which had come down through Smollett to Dickens. It saddened him that Thackeray, who was "Titan enough" to have animated his puppets "with positive brainstuff," had failed to make the changes required. Had he done so, "he would . . . have raised the art in dignity on a level with history."[28] In Dickens he had no comparable confidence. "Dickens gone!" he wrote in a letter of 1870. "The 'Spectator' says he beat Shakespeare at his best, and instances Mrs. Gamp as superior to Juliet's nurse. This in a critical newspaper!"[29] His dislike of Dickens was not qualified with any of George Eliot's indulgent benevolence:

> Not much of Dickens will live, because it has so little correspondence to life. He was the incarnation of cockneydom, a caricaturist who aped the moralist; he should have kept to short stories. If his novels are read at all in

the future, people will wonder what we saw in them. . . .
The world will never let Mr. Pickwick, who to me is full
of the lumber of imbecility, share honours with Don
Quixote.[30]

In 1899, Meredith was obliged to reconsider his verdict when
his friend Alice Meynell published an excellent essay "in de-
fence of a slumbering popular favourite." By means of well-
chosen quotations (Meredith called them "plums") Miss Meynell set about proving that Dickens had been "very much a
craftsman," a great literary artist, a stylist of the first magni-
tude.[31] "Portia is not to be withstood," wrote Meredith gal-
lantly and added that he had been won over by the "very handsome pleading" to restore "his Homer to the Cockney."[32]

In this last phrase, rather than in his comments on realism,
we seem to have the principal reason for Meredith's dislike.
His own novels are not realistic in the sense that Trollope's
and Eliot's are realistic.[33] As his fugue-like dialogues illustrate, he is an even more stylized novelist than Dickens, and,
in his early work, he sometimes imitated Dickens' manner.[34]
What he disliked was the lack of intellectual challenge. As
Dr. Alvan says in *The Tragic Comedians* (1880), vulgar
readers demand "to have pleasures in their own likeness" instead of learning about life from "noble fiction," in which
the positive brainstuff, rather than mere narrative, engages
the reader's attention.[35] An early reviewer commented: "No
man we know of has more resolutely gone into literature with
a total disregard of popularity. . . . His novels are not amusing;
they require thought."[36] Meredith replied bluntly that reviewers and critics had become so slavishly obsessed with whether
or not a writer was popular that they were mere "umpires"
recording failure or success. "Now the pig supplies the most
popular of dishes, but it is not accounted the most honoured
of animals, unless it be by the cottager. Our public might
surely be led to try other, perhaps finer, meat."[37]

After baffling and astonishing the reviewers with his independent style, philosophical virtuosity, and dazzling experiments, Meredith's novels finally won a considerable recogni-

tion. In summary, the detailed studies which have been made of his reception indicate that Meredith exaggerated the unkindness of his early critics. Although they did not become popular, his early novels gained him a small but enthusiastic following among the elite. According to René Galland: "the seventies mark the turning of the tide"; the reviews of *Beauchamp's Career* (1876) were extremely friendly. In the eighties he became fashionable, and by 1890, his defenders had "won the day."[38] Meredith had a special appeal for a new generation which had outgrown Dickens and become tired of the praises lavished on George Eliot. His young defenders included Wilde, James Thomson, Barrie, and Stevenson.[39] As one of them wrote concerning Oxford in the 1880's: "For us youngsters George Meredith was what Dickens had been to our seniors, and our joy in him was, I fear, just a little enhanced by his being—then, at least—caviare to the general."[40] Although to an even later generation, the point may seem somewhat quaint, Meredith's value for the young was enhanced because he had daringly challenged Victorian prudery. "In 'Richard Feverel,' what a loosening of the bonds!" exclaimed Arnold Bennett.[41] While Meredith's vogue lasted, Dickens seemed especially antiquated.

In his energetic effort to add seriousness to the novel not, like Henry James, by making it a serious art but by making it a device for testing serious ideas, Meredith paved the way for such twentieth-century novels as *Howard's End* and *A Passage to India*, to say nothing of such extreme examples as *The Magic Mountain*. By making the readers of his novels accustomed to a fare of serious ideas, he even paved the way for writers as different from himself as Hardy and Dostoevsky.

III

In the case of Hardy, Meredith's role was more obviously helpful. Of one of his own novels, Meredith once admitted: "This cursed desire I have haunting me to show the reason for things is a perpetual obstruction to movement. I *do* want the dash of Smollett and know it."[42] Perhaps with his own experience in mind, he advised Hardy to learn the art of narrative from Wilkie Collins. That Hardy profited from his advice is most evident in early novels such as *Desperate Remedies*, but there is a fondness for sensational narrative and melodramatic situation running through all his works, and he is much less concerned than Meredith or Eliot with a slow paced analysis of motives. Like Paul Dombey, Hardy had a somewhat old-fashioned air.[43] George Eliot was to him one of the great "thinkers" of the century, superior to Newman and Carlyle, but "not a born storyteller."[44] Throughout his scattered comments about the novel's having advanced to a thoughtful "analytic stage," Hardy still clung to a more primitive, Dickens-like belief in extraordinary incident. It is typical of his taste that he found realistic landscape-painting boring. "The much decried, mad, late-Turner rendering is now necessary to create my interest" he confessed in 1887.[45] For this reason the devoted reader of Hardy is much less apt to be allergic to Dickens' novels than is the devoted reader of Meredith.

In his admirable essay on "The Profitable Reading of Fiction" (1888), Hardy himself investigates the novel from the point of view of different levels of readers. He notes that the "perspicacious reader" may have insights into a novel's meaning of which the novelist himself is unaware. Unlike most artists, Hardy welcomed such insights and recommended that the perspicacious reader ought to look for a novelist's "special gift" which is "frequently not that feature in an author's work which common repute has given him credit for." The "popular attribute" and "more obvious" talent may overshadow the author's true "specialty" which the critic ought to seek. "Behind the broad humour of one popular pen he discerns startling touches of weirdness."[46]

Hardy's comment seems almost a prophecy of the critical reinterpretations of Dickens in the 1940's and 1950's. It is also applicable to later evaluations of his own novels. In his provocative study of Hardy published in 1949, Albert Guerard argued that such readers as Lord David Cecil have been at fault in their dislike of Hardy's melodrama and in their attempt to circumvent it. Speaking for a later generation of readers, Guerard finds Hardy's "deliberate anti-realism" a virtue rather than a defect:

> We have rediscovered, to our sorrow, the demonic in human nature as well as in political process; our everyday experience has been both intolerable and improbable, but even more improbable than intolerable. . . . Between the two wars the most vital literary movements . . . arrived at the same conclusions . . . that experience is more often macabre than not.[47]

I cite this interesting passage partly because it effectively summarizes the direction being taken in recent interpretations of Dickens as well as of Hardy. Although Hardy, for the most part, worked independently of Dickens towards what Guerard calls the "grotesque, macabre and symbolic," he arrived at a similar juxtaposition of "the fantastic and everyday."[48]

Finally, according to this interpretation, Hardy was first of all a story-teller rather than a commentator upon Victorian problems. To thoughtful readers of an earlier period, as any list of books and articles about Hardy testifies, the contrary was true. Although he had arrived at different conclusions concerning the intentions of the President of the Immortals, Hardy was valued as George Eliot and Meredith were valued. He was a commentator upon the profound disturbance created by Darwin and his predecessors, a disturbance with which Dickens was apparently too ignorant to be concerned. Again the comparison was implicit. The philosophy of Dickens (what there was of it) was a philosophy for children. The philosophy of Hardy was a challenge to the adult.

I V

When we turn to the reception of the Russian novelists in England, the word *adult* becomes even more prevalent. In an article published during the first World War entitled "Redemption and Dostoevsky," Rebecca West described *The Pilgrim's Progress* as an allegory for the world's childhood and *The Brothers Karamazov* as "an allegory for the world's maturity."[49] Much of the appeal of Russian fiction has been the sense it gives readers of a literature liberated not only from the butler's pantry but from the nursery. Two years after Dickens' death, Charles Yonge spoke of the novel as one of the "triumphs of British genius," and of British novelists as "certainly above all competition."[50] Such insular confidence was to be sorely tried by successive invasions from abroad of French, Russian, and American novels. The effect of Russian novels in particular was to develop an inferiority complex among English readers which has had a marked effect on Dickens' status. In 1917, Somerset Maugham recorded in his notebook that his delight in Turgenev, Tolstoy, and Dostoevsky had made him unfair to such Victorian novelists as Dickens whose work seemed, by comparison, conventional and artificial.[51] E. M. Forster's *Aspects of the Novel* (1927) opens with the airing of an "unpatriotic truth." "No English novelist is as great as Tolstoy—that is to say has given so complete a picture of man's life, both on its domestic and heroic side. No English novelist has explored man's soul as deeply as Dostoevsky."[52] A similar point was made in 1947 by Clifford Bax who remarked, somewhat naively, that the Russian novelists who "mysteriously" admired Dickens have made it difficult for English readers to enjoy his novels any more.[53]

The cult of Russian fiction in England, which began to be evident in the 1880's, can be followed in several studies, especially in Helen Muchnic's able and detailed history of Dostoevsky's reputation between 1881 and 1936. Turgenev was the first of the three to attract attention. Some of his sketches even appeared in *Household Words* during the Crimean War, and in succeeding decades he became the favorite and model for several notable English novelists, especially of Henry James, Galsworthy, and Ford Madox Ford.[54] One of James' three essays on Turgenev (1884) includes a comparison between Dickens' agile improvisations and Turgenev's more artful style and design, but such comparisons belong more appropriately to the chapter which follows. That no novelist had been "more unreservedly intelligent," as James said, was the prevailing estimate of Turgenev among a restricted circle of admirers.[55] Turgenev's intelligence did not preclude his admiring Dickens more than any other nine-teenth-century English author—a taste which must have been disconcerting to some of his disciples such as Ford Madox Ford in whose eyes Turgenev was greater than Shakespeare and Dickens a hack for children.[56]

Tolstoy's breathtaking achievement began to be recognized in the eighties, and after the turn of the century, critical super-latives had made him into a colossus in whose shadow the reputation of all English novelists seemed dim.* Tolstoy himself did his best to make sure that there would be room left for Dickens in the sunlight. He consistently maintained that Dickens was one of the greatest novelists of the century, and that his writings, inspired by a benevolent love of good men and a contempt for worthless institutions such as Parlia-ment, had been of great benefit to mankind. "All his char-acters are my personal friends—I am constantly comparing them with living persons, and living persons with them, and what a spirit there was in all he wrote."[57] When news of Tolstoy's high recommendation trickled back to England in 1903, Swinburne, who had been fighting a noisy rear-guard action in defense of Dickens, was overjoyed:

> The appreciation of . . . so glorious a genius . . . does what no other living man's could do—it adds a crowning ray of glory to the fame of Dickens. Above all, what a superb and crushing reply to the vulgar insults of such malignant boobies . . . as G. H. Lewes & Co. (too numer-ous a Co.!) is the witness of such a man as this.[58]

A French critic of the same period was impressed by the failure of intelligent readers in England to consider Dickens as anything more than a humorist. Like Tolstoy, he said, Dickens is a great religious teacher. *Bleak House* teaches us a detestation of mere bourgeois virtue, and anticipates Tol-

---

* Arnold's essay (1887) is a useful summary of the estimate of Tolstoy appearing in late Victorian reviews. He was admired for his insight into the souls of his characters, for his realism which was considered to be relatively unsullied by the troughs of Zolaism, and especially for his contribution as a religious thinker. See Clarence Decker, "Victorian Com-ment on Russian Realism," *PMLA*, LII (1937), 542-549.

stoy's *Resurrection* in interpreting the divine message: "Tu ne jugeras pas!"[59]

> Aux yeux du public russe . . . Dickens est surtout le créateur de la petite Nell, le poète des 'humiliés' et des 'offensés': c'est par là surtout qu'il a été le maître de Dostoievsky comme du comte Tolstoï.[60]

It is true that Tolstoy's appreciation of Dickens in later years was enhanced by his own progressive obsession with religious problems. *What is Art?* rests on the quixotic premise that the story of Nell and her grandfather is greater art than *King Lear*.[61]

At one point in this strange treatise, Tolstoy does make an interesting comparison when he links together Dickens and Dostoevsky as artists of the highest type.[62] In England, whenever such comparisons have been made, and a faint resemblance recognized, Dickens has usually been treated as a progenitor outmoded by a dazzling successor, a poor relation to be kept out of sight in the attic. In 1930, for example, Aldous Huxley contrasted the death of Ilusha in *The Brothers Karamazov* with the death of Little Nell. "Why is this history so agonizingly moving, when the tale of Little Nell leaves us not merely cold, but derisive?"[63] Huxley's question is not easy to answer (as has been indicated in the previous discussion of Little Nell), but he has made it unnecessarily difficult by using Dostoevsky's most mature novel for his comparison. If he had referred, instead, to *The Insulted and the Injured* (1862), there would be less special pleading. The life and death of the young girl, Nellie Valkovsky, as critics have recognized, is modelled directly upon *The Old Curiosity Shop*, and Dostoevsky's sentimentality is often as excruciatingly gauche as that of his model.*

Like German readers of Shakespeare, Dostoevsky believed that Russian readers had a perfect understanding of the foreign writer whom he referred to as "the great Christian— Dickens."[64] It is said that during his imprisonment, the only books he would read were *David Copperfield* and *Pickwick*

---

* Dostoevsky's Nellie combines the role of Little Nell with that of the Marchioness, which makes her a more interesting figure.

Papers,[65] and the influence of Dickens is very marked in the short novels which he wrote in Siberia: *Uncle's Dream* and *The Friend of the Family* (1859). According to E. H. Carr, the lack of merit in these Siberian novels is attributable to the alien influence of Dickens which results in a substitution of caricature for analysis and in an inept attempt to write in a vein of sustained humor.[66] Some of the early reviewers of Dostoevsky's novels in England during the 1880's also noted the "glaring similarities" to Dickens, which they found rather bewildering.[67] The *Spectator* described the hero of *The Friend of the Family* as a "Muscovite Mr. Pecksniff," but a Pecksniff at whom it was difficult to laugh. *The Gambler* had a similar effect because of the unpredictability of its Pickwickian humor,[68] and even *Crime and Punishment*, according to Gissing, "abounds in Dickens-like touches in its lighter passages," especially in its "extravagances of character."[69] In 1949, a learned article entitled "Steerforth and Stavrogin" demonstrated that the debt to *David Copperfield* in *The Possessed* was an extensive one and by no means confined to the "lighter passages."[70]

If Dostoevsky can be considered to have been in some respects Dickens' disciple, the reception of his novels in England is an ideal illustration of a Toynbee-like pattern of history. The export returns in modified form to the country of its origin and obliterates the original product, idea, or technique. As the cult of Dostoevsky gathered momentum in England, it was not the similarity to Dickens which was pointed out but his superiority. Gissing in 1898 admitted that Raskolnikoff's confession to Sonia "is beyond Dickens, as we know him," and that in general Dostoevsky surpassed Dickens in power, imagination, and tragic sense.[71] In 1951, virtually the same conclusion was reached by Julian Symons, in whose eyes Dickens' contemporaries seem to be men from Mars: "The comparison . . . shows us the vast landscapes of the soul which Dickens never knew, the terrible corridors of the spirit down which this respectable member of the Victorian bourgeoisie never walked."[72]

According to Dr. Muchnic, the high point of Dostoevsky's

English reputation began in 1912 (with the first Garnett translation) and lasted until 1921. Although it was difficult to surpass the superlatives already bestowed upon Turgenev and Tolstoy, Dostoevsky's admirers did their frantic best. Like George Eliot, he became a prophet and one whose insight into the soul was considered to be beyond the reach of all other writers. Virginia Woolf affirmed that his novels "are composed purely and wholly of the stuff of the soul,"[73] and her own efforts in fiction were directed to the same end. According to Walter Neuschäffer, Dostoevsky's influence appears not only in the novels of Virginia Woolf, but in those of Maugham, Huxley, Dorothy Richardson, and even of Conrad and Lawrence, who did not altogether share the awe in which Dostoevsky was held.[74] During the 1920's and 1930's, the appreciation of Dostoevsky became a little less farfetched; one critic even had the temerity to point out that "as material for literature the soul is formless, it lacks variety, it has no sense of humour."[75] Even though the cult of Dostoevsky among the elite may have diminished in intensity, his is still something of a sacred name in twentieth-century literature. Insofar as that literature has been characterized by an anti-rational and anti-utilitarian quality, so have his novels been congenial to readers. James Joyce, for example, may seem to have little in common with the great Russian melodrama-tist, but Mrs. Woolf was able to yoke them, as Dr. Johnson would say, with some violence together. *Ulysses* and Russian novels are both, she says, "spiritual."[76]

The principal question remains. Why was it that Dickens could not be harnessed to the same yoke? From Mrs. Woolf's essay on "David Copperfield" it would appear that to her there was no connection. Although she elevates him to highbrow status, she treats him as if he belonged to a cruder, clumsier, and inferior school of materialists.[77] As Edmund Wilson complained: "The Bloomsbury that talked about Dostoevsky ignored Dostoevsky's master, Dickens."[78] One is inclined to explain this phenomenon of taste as mere snobbishness. A kind of *xenophilia* has been a prominent quality of much English criticism since Matthew Arnold helped to break down mid-

Victorian insularity. The very critic who admires Dostoevsky's overflowing sentiments for the poor and oppressed—his violent melodrama and extravagant passion—will find these same traits in Dickens to be distasteful. When Mrs. Woolf said that in all Russian novels the main theme is a recommendation of sympathy for our fellow man, a sympathy of the heart and not of the mind, she seemed unconscious that she was likewise stating the theme of *David Copperfield*.

V

It is pointless, of course, to push such parallels too far. If the English reception of Dostoevsky is reviewed more closely, it is apparent that his novels provided a satisfaction which Dickens had seemingly overlooked. The Dostoevsky character asks questions endlessly, and the reader is made to share the intense preoccupation of a saint or sinner who asks *Why? Why?* As in *Hamlet*, the answer may not necessarily matter; the poetry is in the question itself. The terrifying questions which confront Mrs. Moore after her visit to the Marabar Caves in *A Passage to India* go echoing through all of Dostoevsky's major works. The stimulus such questioning provides seems to be absent from those of Dickens. Jonas Chuzzlewit lacks not only the self-consciousness of Raskolnikov or Stavrogin; he lacks the world-consciousness. When such a character as Jo in *Bleak House* does ask *Why?*, the answer has seemed to many readers to be too pat, too bourgeois, too childishly superficial. As Edward Dowden wrote:

> We rejoice that Dickens should have quickened the sensibility of the English middle class for the . . . sorrows of the poor; we rejoice that he should have gladdened the world with inexhaustible comedy and farce. But it were better if he had discovered that for . . . the life of man there is something needful over and above good spirits. . . . His ideal of human happiness was that of his readers; their middle-class notions of human well-being . . . he gave them back, animated by his own vigorous animal spirits. . . . Banish from earth some few

monsters of selfishness, malignity, and hypocrisy, set to rights a few obvious imperfections in the machinery of society, inspire all men with a cheery benevolence, and everything will go right well with this excellent world of ours.[79]

This late Victorian verdict, appearing in 1887, is admirably typical of the kind of indictment which still persists among readers who find Dickens somewhat naive at best. F. R. Leavis tells us that "The adult mind doesn't as a rule find in Dickens a challenge to an unusual and sustained seriousness."[80] Julian Symons writes of the "childish fantasy" of Dickens' love stories, and their lack of appeal to the "adult."[81]

The discovery of the soul by later novelists and the tendency to use fiction as a proving-ground for the latest intellectual modes have presented Dickens' later-day admirers with a most challenging task. The task is to show (if it can be shown) that *Martin Chuzzlewit* and *Great Expectations* are like *Gulliver's Travels* and *Alice in Wonderland*, that is, books which are capable of catering to the adult reader as well as to the child. That Dickens can serve, like Shakespeare, as a childhood classic is all very well, but that he should be considered a childhood classic exclusively would be an unhappy fate.* His books belong "to the memories and myths of life, and not to its esthetic experience," was the somewhat curious verdict of Virginia Woolf.[82] And Elizabeth Bowen admitted candidly in 1946 that she could no longer read Dickens, not because of distaste, but "because I read him exhaustively as a child," and having "absorbed him into myself . . . there is no more oxygen left, for me, anywhere in the atmosphere of his writing."[83] Such candor is admirable, but the question lingers whether or not childhood reading *can* ex-

---

* Frederic Harrison is an interesting example of a critic who laments because children now (1910) may miss the rapture of reading Dickens that he had enjoyed in childhood. Yet he has really little respect for Dickens as fare for adults and confesses that he rarely reads his novels. See his *Among My Books* (1912), p. 110; *Autobiographic Memoirs* (1912), I, 23. Harrison's essay on Dickens in his *Studies in Early Victorian Literature* (1895), pp. 136-154, is a conventional estimate in which a distaste for Dickens' exaggeration is occasionally obscured by bursts of platitudinous eulogies.

haust the potential pleasures of Dickens any more than it exhausts the pleasures of Shakespeare or Swift. When Edmund Wilson was comparing his undergraduate impressions of Henry James' novels with his impressions upon rereading them, twenty years later, he noted that in the sense of a reader himself changing constantly, "one can never read the same book twice."[84]

As a critic of Dickens, Mr. Wilson has endeavored to reintroduce some of his novels to the attention of adult readers, and much of the best criticism, which remains to be discussed in a final chapter, has been moving in the same direction. Our survey has indicated, however, that since 1872, Dickens has been regarded in many quarters as a writer whom critical readers outgrow, and who cannot bear comparison with later novelists whose interests were less restricted by the traditionally external preoccupations of English fiction and by Victorian superficiality. In 1880, Dostoevsky was recommending a list of books for a child to read. The list included, together with Scott, Pushkin, Gogol, and Cervantes, "all Dickens's works without exception." Concerning his own novels, he warned: "I don't think that all of them are suitable for your daughter."[85] For an adult in the twentieth century, such a qualification is in itself a recommendation.

In Virginia Woolf's essay on George Eliot, there is a comment made upon *Middlemarch* which sums up the development traced in this chapter. When Mrs. Woolf's own theories of the novel are recalled, her preoccupation with stream of consciousness and especially her enthusiasm for the maturity and greatness of Russian fiction, the comment suggests why Dickens' novels have so often been under a critical cloud. *Middlemarch* she describes as "the magnificent book which with all its imperfections is one of the few English novels written for grown-up people."[86]

CHAPTER 11

THE HIGH AESTHETIC LINE

"The difference between French and English novels is
that of their and our fowls at table. Theirs are better
trussed."—(Journal of William Cory, 1874)

I

IN the autobiography of Henry Green (1940), there is an
account of the cult of Proust's novels among Oxford undergraduates in the 1920's. After remarking upon the seemingly
incredible fact that there had once been an earlier generation
of undergraduates who had waited for new books by Kipling
with "an almost unendurable suspense," Mr. Green suggests
to his own contemporaries that if they want to realize "how
painful it will be to grow old," let them think forward to
the time when a future generation "will treat Proust as we
treated Kipling."[1]

The story of Dickens' declining reputation among critical
readers after his death, which we have already been following, illustrates the identical pattern suggested by Mr. Green.
To be subjected to the undergraduate treatment is the inevitable fate of the overly-admired author. Many never survive this second stage as such nineteenth-century figures as
Barry Cornwall, Samuel Rogers, or even Bulwer-Lytton
will suggest. And Mr. Green's word "painful" is an accurate
one to describe the sensations of the older generation of
readers during the second stage. For them there is no way of
knowing that it may not be the final stage. In 1895, the
elderly William Hale White was distressed to realize that he
had lived through a golden age as glorious as the Elizabethan,
which had come to an irrevocable end:

> Ruskin now is the last, and after him the deluge. To
> understand to what we are coming, you ought to borrow
> from a circulating library one of the widely-read novels.

I don't mean the confessed trash, but one praised by "culture."[2]

Perhaps White had in mind such novels as Oscar Wilde's *Picture of Dorian Gray*,[*] George Moore's *Esther Waters*, Arthur Morrison's *A Child of the Jago*, or some recent translations of Zola or Maupassant. In his *Mid-Victorian Memories*, R. E. Francillon was likewise pained because readers of the nineties valued cleverness more than greatness.[3] And during the same period Andrew Lang was bewildered by the spectacle of Dickens' works being tested by the "dismal seriousness"[4] of the young aesthetes and being found "too gutterly gutter." "Can this fastidiousness be anything but a casual passing phase of taste?" Lang asked. "Are all people over thirty who cling to their Dickens and their Scott old fogies?"[5] It should be added that when Lang set about writing a series of critical introductions for the Gadshill edition of Dickens (1899), he found himself in an unenviable position. Badgered on one side by fanatical Dickensians such as Swinburne and Henley who considered him unfit to speak of Dickens, and painfully aware of the indifference of the majority of fastidious readers on the other, Lang offered a mild compromise. He presented a Dickens cut down to size for a new generation. To save the humorous parts, he was prepared to jettison the social critic, story-teller, melodramatist, and in effect "the genius which, even in its errors, so delighted our fathers."[†]

As earlier chapters have indicated, the fathers of Lang's generation had been by no means blind to Dickens' "errors," but because they were not such ardent soul-seekers in their reading, and because they were not so obsessed with self-conscious artistry, they could be somewhat indulgent. Moreover,

---

[*] An expert literary detective might be able to trace the indirect influence of Dickens upon Wilde's novel by analyzing the Dickensian elements in *À rebours*, for Huysmans, Wilde's model, had a strange passion for Dickens' books.

[†] Lang, "Charles Dickens," *Fortnightly Review*, LXX (1898), 945. The introduction to *Great Expectations* shows Lang at his best, probably because that novel embarrassed him less than any of the others. In general, Lang was more at ease with Scott than with Dickens. Concerning Swinburne's attack upon him, see Lang's introduction to *Pickwick Papers* in the Waverley edition and W. E. Henley's article on Dickens in the *Pall Mall Magazine*, XVIII (1899), 578.

the later generation had new standards of comparison. If comparisons with Meredith, Eliot, Hardy, and the Russians exposed Dickens' philosophical and psychological ineptitude, comparisons with Flaubert, Maupassant, Henry James, and Conrad exposed his artistic ineptitude. In 1906, in an article called "Dickens as Artist, or Genius and the Cry of 'Art for Art's Sake,'" R. Brimley Johnson summed up the results:

> It can scarcely be questioned . . . that Charles Dickens has suffered more than any other eminent English writer from the arrogance of aesthetic criticism. His work has not merely been complacently dismissed as "bad art"; it has been cited again and again as a conspicuous example of degraded popular taste.[6]

One of the signs of the impact of aestheticism upon the reading of fiction was a growing interest in a definition of aims. In 1884, Walter Besant's lecture on *The Art of Fiction* was published, stirring up a flurry of replies from James, Stevenson, and Howells. A few years later appeared *The Novel: What it Is* by Marion Crawford, another novelist. Crawford's Pateresque study defines the novel as "an intellectual artistic luxury,"[7] a definition which corresponds to Oscar Wilde's in *The Decay of Lying*. All this preoccupation with statements of intention and with the novel as a work of art had roots, as we have seen, in the mid-Victorian critical interest in problems of plot and probability of character, but the distinctive mark of the later aesthetic flowering was self-consciousness. According to Henry James, the English novel had hitherto been characterized by "no air of having a theory, . . . a consciousness of itself behind it—of being the expression of an artistic faith."[8]

Unanimity among the theorists we can hardly look for, and it is perhaps foolish to link together Howells, who despised imagination, with Wilde, who made fun of mere realism. Yet there is a point at which the theories of aestheticism and those of realism and naturalism intersect. An obvious example is in a mutual recommendation of objectivity, whether the recommendation is urged for scientific or artistic reasons.

More significant is a mutual agreement that earlier techniques have been outmoded. Both aestheticism and naturalism are committed to what Herbert Butterfield called "the Whig interpretation of history." The very title of one historical survey, *The Advance of the English Novel*,[9] is indicative. Howells' *Criticism and Fiction* (1891) is dominated by a conviction that "the stone age of fiction and criticism" is now over. Of Dickens, a stone age artist, he says: "in the light of the truer work which has since been done his literary principles seem almost as grotesque as his theories of political economy." "The pathos appears false and strained; the humor largely horse-play; the characters theatrical; the joviality pumped; the psychology commonplace; the sociology alone funny."[10] In waggish vein, there appeared a few years later a review in the *Nation* in which it was assumed that *Pickwick Papers* was a new novel by an unknown author. The reviewer gravely commended the novelist upon his knowledge of stage coaches but urged that it would be essential for him to study the great novelists (that is, the "modern" novelists as Howells would say) with care.[11]

A corrective to Howells' Whiggish dogmatism was provided by Robert Louis Stevenson who plunged into the debate by calling Howells "the bondslave, the zealot of his school; he dreams of an advance in art like what there is in science; he thinks of past things as radically dead; he thinks a form can be outlived: . . . a strange forgetfulness of the history of the race!"[12] This blast of common sense sounds strange coming from the delicate craftsman credited by James with having revolutionized English fiction by making it a conscious art, and one whose style could be a model of aesthetic prose. Stevenson, however, was an eclectic reader whose choice of novelists included Meredith and Dostoevsky on one hand, and Dumas and even G. P. R. James on the other.[13] Such eclectic tastes enabled him to discuss earlier Victorian novelists without rancor. Of Dickens he does not often speak, but at least he does not find a "literary method" offensive which consists of seeking something "more definite than nature." It is typical of Stevenson's eclecticism that he disliked such novels as *Bleak House* but admired *Our Mutual Friend*. The "fierce intensity of design" in the portrait of Bradley Headstone he considered to be "one of Dickens's superlative achievements."[14] If Stevenson was a literary revolutionary, he was the kind whose respect for the past prevents any violent break with traditional predecessors.

II

To some extent, this generalization also applies to Stevenson's friend, Henry James, although James' tastes were much more fastidious and discriminating, and they require more extensive consideration. Indeed when writing of Henry James today, a critic may feel like a piano pupil as he sits down to play his Bach number at the recital. James is now being treated, deservedly, as one of the saints of literature. And even when his novels sometimes appear cloying to us, if we turn back to his critical essays, prefaces, and notebooks, with their pure enthusiasms, their wisdom and taste, we are inclined to face east. To the discussion of fiction James brought a quality which he sought in other writers: the rare quality of charm. Sharing Dickens' conviction that the novel is an art form of which its creators have no cause to be ashamed, he went further by developing what Dickens had shied away from—an exposition of theories of the novel and of its technical problems. And when he talked of the distinctive qualities of its artists, by some miracle he was able to talk without clap-trap. His remarks upon Dickens constitute what he himself would have called an especially interesting "case."

When *David Copperfield* began appearing as a serial in 1849, one of the many tributes to its potency was paid by a small boy in New York City. One evening, while a relative was reading aloud a chapter about the cruelty of the Murdstones, the seven-year-old Henry James, hiding under a table to listen, broke into "sobs of sympathy" and was promptly sent to bed.[15] It is sometimes disconcerting to encounter reminders that James began as a representative Victorian reader (the Atlantic not being of much consequence in his remarkable household). "We were practically contemporary . . . [with]

the fluttering monthly numbers," he notes, and "the general contagious consciousness, and our own household response not least, breathed heavily through Hard Times, Bleak House and Little Dorrit. . . . I was to feel that I had been born . . . to a rich awareness." James' boyhood experience even included the crude theatrical versions of *Nickleby* and *Oliver Twist* which in old age he was able to recall vividly. The "force of the Dickens imprint . . . in the soft clay of our generation" was such that it was to resist serenely "the wash of the waves of time."[16]

The wistfulness of such evocations may remind us of Dickens' account of his own boyhood reading of Smollett and Fielding, but there is a difference. James' wistfulness is that of a man who has outgrown the home of his boyhood. Its mark on him and on his work was to be permanent, and in old age he considered it fruitless to scoff, "to overhaul" impressions by letting in "the intellectual air." Yet it is evident that James was also typical of his generation in having exerted himself to break away.

The next glimpse we get is from James' account of meeting "the master" in person in 1867, a meeting which, as he reports in his Notebooks, deeply affected his attitude towards the man and his works. The public readings James had found "monstrous" and "charmless," but the brief glimpse of the aging "extremely handsome" man inspired him with a curious and overwhelming tenderness.[17] James was twenty-four on this occasion, "a yearning dabbler in the mystery" who trembled in every limb as he came face to face with one who embodied the "sublimity of mastership" more, he says, than any other writer, for his generation.

In the midst of this reverential account, James does not add that two years before the meeting he had reviewed *Our Mutual Friend* in a spirit not in the least reverential. Hypocrisy is, of course, not the issue. The young critic had found new ties in Thackeray, Eliot, and French fiction, and in the act of striking out for his own independence he had to utter harsh sayings. The affection, however, remained.*

* Describing his life in Boston in the 1860's, James notes: "Dickens at

What James says of *Our Mutual Friend* is similar to George Eliot's comment upon Dickens. It is both a declaration of independence and a manifesto of his own aims as a future novelist. He affirms that Dickens "reconciles us to what is commonplace, and he reconciles us to what is odd," but because "he has added nothing to our understanding of human character" and because he fails to "see beneath the surface of things," he is "the greatest of superficial novelists." Disagreeing with Stevenson, James contends that the study of Bradley Headstone, with immense possibilities, fails in Dickens' hands because he neglects to produce true "sparks" in the conflict between Headstone and Wrayburn. "Humanity is . . . what men have in common with each other, and not what they have in distinction." Dickens' characters therefore lack humanity.[18]

James' own concerns as a novelist are evident here: the attempt to make full exploitation of dramatic situations, the concern with *nuance* and sober exploration of motive, and the representation of the typical rather than of the extraordinary. Nineteen years later, in discussing Turgenev, he returned to the same area of disagreement. He was surprised that Turgenev rated so highly Dickens' "power of presenting to the eye a vivid, salient feature":

> If Dickens fail to live long, it will be because his figures are particular without being general; . . . because we do not feel their continuity with the rest of humanity— see the matching of the pattern with the piece out of which all the creations of the novelist and dramatist are cut.[19]

James was aware that Turgenev resembled Dickens in "this habit of specializing people by vivid oddities," but there was a difference not only on the score of the particular-universal; there was a difference of method. Dickens, he said, was "an

that time went a great way with us, the best of him falling after this fashion well within the compass of our life; and Thackeray, for my own circle, went, I think, a greater way still." James, "Mr. and Mrs. Fields," *The Cornhill Magazine*, n.s., XXXIX (1915), 34. See also *Notes of a Son and Brother* (New York, 1914), pp. 20-22.

improvisatore; the practice, for him, was a lawless revel of the imagination."[20] Turgenev, by contrast, was an artist who embodied, for James, one of the most reassuring of qualities, and one most needed in English fiction: the quality of taking pains.

As Rebecca West has noted, the prevalent impression that James was an unqualified admirer of Flaubert must derive from those who have never read what James actually said of Flaubert. In a different way from Dickens, Flaubert seemed to James lacking in humanity (except in *Madame Bovary*).[21] Of French naturalists generally, James made similar complaints. In such a mood he preferred the healthy tone of Trollope.[22] Yet his later essays show that the general impression is well founded that he learned much from Flaubert about the technical problem of point of view and a general concern for careful workmanship. It was the wildness of the earlier English novelists (as well as of Balzac) which James sought to correct by his criticism and example. While discussing the careless abuses of Trollope, he speaks of his objection to "a certain English ideal" that "it is rather dangerous to be explicitly or consciously an artist."[23] Although James' aestheticism, like Pater's, is strongly restricted by moral preoccupations, he is part of the movement. Much of his criticism of Balzac expresses the ambivalence of his attitude towards Dickens, and in reading Balzac's letters he was conscious of the "striking" analogy between them.

> In intensity of imaginative power, the power of evoking visible objects and figures, seeing them themselves with the force of hallucination and making others see them all but just as vividly, they [Dickens and Balzac] were almost equal. Here there is little to choose between them; they have had no rivals but each other and Shakespeare. But they most of all resemble each other in the fact that they treated their extraordinary imaginative force as a matter of business; that they worked it as a gold-mine, violently and brutally; overworked and ravaged it.[24]

And they produced, as he was later to complain of his *bête noire*, *War and Peace*, and of *The Newcomes*, "large loose baggy monsters" instead of "an absolutely premeditated art." "I delight in a deep-breathing economy and an organic form," he wrote.[25]

It has been pointed out by R. P. Blackmur, a sympathetic critic, that a preoccupation with "executive form," that is, the craft or technique, led James' criticism astray by making him fail to see that Tolstoy's novel has an "organic form" of its own, as has *Don Quixote*.[26] Our survey has indicated how James' blind spots were typical among his more enlightened contemporaries. And it is in his passionate concern for executive form, his aesthetic conviction that mere vitality is not enough, that James is most alien to Dickens' native wood-notes wild.

The application of these theories in James' novels produced a mixed reaction. Except for the brief flurry occasioned by *Daisy Miller*, his work, as might be expected, was not popular, and the lack of understanding among many of his reviewers was as crude as had been the *Saturday Review*'s attitude towards Dickens. He was, nevertheless, talked about. Even in such remote communities as Toronto, the literary magazines of the eighties were discussing the relative merits of James versus the old school of Dickens.* When Maurice Hewlett read *Roderick Hudson*, he recommended it to a friend as "mental cayenne pepper" for the "jaded novel monger" be-

* See Claude T. Bissell in the *Canadian Historical Review*, September 1950, p. 246. The controversy was continued elsewhere in Richard Burton's *Forces in Fiction* [1902] which records that James' "deification of technic" and high art of the "scenario" had a "chilling" effect upon the patrons. James' failure, says Burton, is attributable to his overlooking the primary importance of characterization. "Who . . . are the living personages in the stories of Henry James?" "This fact . . . explains the relatively limited appeal of leaders cried up by critics whose admiration for construction, description, and style make them forget the preëminent thing." Dickens, by comparison, is a "giant." (pp. 7-17.) A study of five hundred English reviews of James made by Donald W. Murray shows that during the nineties Burton's conclusions would have been typical of the "middle and lower rank critics." In H. G. Wells' *Boon* (1916), the objections to Jamesian preciousness are maliciously summarized. On the other hand, during this same period, James' novels were winning more sympathetic attention from serious reviews such as the *Academy* and *The Times*. See *The Periodical Post Boy* (Chapel Hill, North Carolina, no. 8, December 1950).

cause James "dissects motives like a surgeon does corpses."[27]
Hewlett, a young novelist, was typical of the special audience
which was to be drawn to James and to share some of his
zest for new techniques, a group which included Conrad,
Ford, Percy Lubbock, and Edith Wharton. But as Elizabeth
Bowen notes, there were other enthusiastic readers as well.
In a broadcast devoted to Trollope in 1945, Miss Bowen
evokes an imaginary reader of the turn of the century, Uncle
Jaspar, who explains why Trollope and his contemporaries
had gone out of fashion. We looked on life as "a psychological
battle," Uncle Jaspar says, in reminiscent vein. "And into
that battle we took our three novelists—Hardy, Meredith,
James. Yes, those were the great names." These novelists
wrote for minds that "wanted to be adult."[28]

In the midst of the see-sawing stages of James' subsequent
reputation in the twentieth century, much excellent criticism
has been devoted to an analysis of the subtleties of his technique[29] and to the differentiation of his fine skill from the
clumsy blundering of his predecessors. More recently, there
has been an increased recognition of his concern with the
problem of evil, and by shifting attention from his role as a
revolutionary theorist of the art of fiction, there is more opportunity to see that his break with the traditional novel was
not a violent divorce. Jacques Barzun's provocative essay on
James as a melodramatist tries to establish that although
James criticized the melodrama of Dickens and Balzac, he
was not turning his back on their "exaggeration" and "romanticism"; he desired only "to purge and renovate" but not
to deny their basic concern for moral problems and for the
stimulation of the reader. By differentiating between Meredith
and James, Barzun indicates how the latter had really gone
back over the heads of such realists as Flaubert to the earlier
romantic generation.[30] That Balzac was more important to
the mature James than Dickens is obvious enough, but that
there was a carry-over into maturity from all that extensive
exposure to Dickens in James' youth seems highly probable.

Much of James' criticism consists simply of the rendering
of an impression, and I have reserved for this place his most

striking account of the impression made upon him by Dickens'
novels. In *The Middle Years*, describing his "*initiation*" into
the English scene in 1869, he mentions a visit to Craven
Street in search of "atmosphere." The visit seemed to him
epoch-making because the street "absolutely reeked, to my
fond fancy, with associations of the particular ancient piety
embodied in one's private altar to Dickens." All this sounds
like the tourist's familiar wistfulness, but it was more. The
"hallucination" of the "whole Dickens procession . . . inter-
fused the aesthetic dream in presence of its subject with the
mortal drop of despair."

> The whole Dickens world looked out of its queer, quite
> sinister windows—for it was the socially sinister Dick-
> ens . . . rather than the socially encouraging or con-
> foundingly comic who still at that moment was most apt
> to meet me with his reasons. Such a reason was just that
> look of the inscrutable riverward street, packed to black-
> ness with accumulations of suffered experience.[31]

This evocation of the "socially sinister Dickens" is interesting
in its own right, especially when the date is considered, but
it also leads one to speculate in what ways this overwhelming
impression left its mark on James' novels. *The Princess Casamassima* seems to "reek," as he would say, with the same atmosphere, and in the Preface he explains that his novel was
inspired by impressions derived from London streets "especially during the younger, the initiatory time." That the single,
strong impression of 1869 contained the germ of a book
written sixteen years later would be a far-fetched contention
if the novelist were other than Henry James, whose gestations
were sometimes of great length.

James' critics have noted that *The Princess Casamassima*,
like *The Bostonians*, represents "his curious excursion into
the Dickens kind of social novel."[32] Lionel Trilling has
grouped it with *Our Mutual Friend* and with *Howard's End*
as one of the greatest novels of this class, and he has also
pointed out the similarity between the crippled, bed-ridden
Rosy Muniment and the figure of Jenny Wren, the doll's

dressmaker in *Our Mutual Friend*.[33] If Jenny Wren did contribute to *The Princess Casamassima*, it is amusing to recall that James had singled her out, in his review of 1865, as an example of "a little monster" who "belongs to the troop of hunchbacks" among Dickens' sentimental failures. It is also possible that Daudet, as well as Dickens, may have contributed to the formation of Rosy Muniment. In his essay on Daudet (1883), James had praised the portrait of M. Delobelle's lame daughter in *Fromont Jeune* "who makes butterflies and humming-birds for ladies' head-dresses."[34]

In this same essay, James raises the question which plagued Daudet for years, the question of his imitation of Dickens. After making a tactful distinction between "gross imitation" and "conscious sympathy," he notes simply that there are pages in Daudet's books "which seem to say to us that at one moment of his life Dickens had been a revelation to him."[35] Of *The Princess Casamassima* the same might certainly be said.

The infinitely complex problem of Dickens' influence on other novelists has been deliberately made peripheral in this study partly because it would swamp everything else, and partly because with a novel (unlike a poem) the study of influence seems to be an elaborate exercise in walking upon eggs. *The Princess Casamassima* is itself a useful example. If Rosy Muniment owes something to Dickens through Daudet, it is also possible that the whole book owes much to Dickens through Gissing, a writer for whom James had considerable admiration.[36] So far as I know, no one has drawn attention to the parallels between Gissing's first novel, *Workers in the Dawn* (1880) and James' *Princess*. Gissing's story is of a sensitive, orphaned youth, Arthur Golding, who is brought up by a bookseller and printer. Like Hyacinth's, his experiences develop against a background of London slums, working-class politics, and women philanthropists who are trying to better conditions. Gissing's novel, itself an imitation of Dickens, is yet much more like *The Princess Casamassima* than is any work by Dickens, including *Our Mutual Friend*. I do not know whether James had read Gissing's novel, but the problem suggested by the triangle of resemblances does exemplify the complexities one encounters when tracing fictional influences.

In general, the kind of "Dickensisms," as James calls them, which are most readily identified in post-Dickens novels are characters whose eccentricities are strongly marked. E. M. Forster's phrase "flat characters" has become a useful label in novel-criticism, although readers sometimes seem to assume that great novels contain no flat characters. All novels, including those by Forster, do of course contain them, and in many novels before *Pickwick Papers* there were strongly marked eccentrics. Dickens has nevertheless usually been given the credit for inspiring those which have followed. They are encountered in novelists as diverse as Conrad and Bennett, Joyce Cary and H. G. Wells. Thus in *Loving*, by Henry Green, a novelist who disapproves of Dickens (and of Tolstoy) because of their excessive descriptions has yet created a talkative, gin-drinking cook, Mrs. Welch, who was described by reviewers as "Dickensian." And everyone knows what is meant. Similar examples can be found in James' novels. Strether in *The Ambassadors* is remote from anything created by Dickens, but the same cannot be said of Waymarsh. Whenever Waymarsh appears, it is like a Dickensian ballet-sequence. We are amused by repeated phrases such as "Quit this," or references to "the sacred rage" or to "Sitting Bull." Waymarsh is triumphantly flat. In *The Bostonians*, Miss Birdseye might be cited not only as a flat eccentric, but as one seemingly modelled directly upon Mrs. Jellyby in *Bleak House*.

Other parallels have been noted by F. R. Leavis who describes *Roderick Hudson* as *Martin Chuzzlewit* "redone by an enormously more intelligent and better educated mind."[37] That James did learn a lesson from the master is the interesting thing. With Walter Besant, or William De Morgan, or H. G. Wells, one encounters the Dickensisms without surprise.[38] James, who is assumed to have remained altogether outside the orbit, is a more significant example. All this is not to forget that the two were poles apart, that James revolutionized the Dickens novel, and that his work had the effect of discrediting his predecessor's reputation. It is nevertheless a valuable corrective to shake the kaleidoscope occasionally and to observe a different pattern, one made up of resemblances. In his independence from naturalism and his creed that art is convincing illusion, in his fondness for sinister atmospheres and for what Barzun calls melodrama, there are signs that James was powerfully affected by his youthful absorption in Dickens' novels, and that unlike Virginia Woolf, for example, he never altogether outgrew it. There are pages which seem to say that Dickens had been a revelation to him. As Barzun writes: "The wickedness of being cold, of deliberately sacrificing others to one's lusts, of taking advantage of another through legal or social or emotional privilege, obsesses James."[39] These were also Dickens' obsessions, humorously presented in the early novels through Quilp or Sally Brass and the Marchioness, but becoming progressively more Jamesian in Mr. Dombey and his treatment of Florence, Murdstone of David Copperfield, Miss Wade of Tattycoram, Miss Havisham of Pip. By avoiding the stagey note of Dickens, and the allegory of Hawthorne, James was able to present these romantic themes with the skill of a mature art. As a result, James' position in relation to Dickens has something in common with Dryden's in relation to Shakespeare. Each was affected by the literary movements of his day, the one by neoclassicism, the other by aestheticism, to a point at which his predecessor seemed barbarous. Yet both Dryden and James were also aware of something lost:

> Our age was cultivated thus at length,
> But what we gain'd in skill we lost in strength.

III

After discussing the tortuous case of Henry James at some length, we can dispense with Joseph Conrad very briefly, for almost everything that has been said of James' relationship to Dickens and to his readers applies equally well to Conrad. *Nicholas Nickleby* was his first introduction to English literature. "It is extraordinary how well Mrs. Nickleby could chatter disconnectedly in Polish and the sinister Ralph rage in that language."[40] When Conrad began to write, the English novelists who "counted most for stimulus" he said were Dickens and Thackeray, with "Dickens easily first." Like James, he referred to Dickens in later life as "the master," and mentioned in particular his admiration for *Bleak House*, a novel which he had read "innumerable times" and continued to read. "Its very weaknesses are more precious to me than the strength of other men's work."[41] Again, like James, he later came under the influence of Flaubert, and his aesthetic bent obscured from his readers his roots in the romanticism of Hugo and Dickens. *The Secret Agent*, like *The Princess Casamassima*, represents Conrad's bid for popular favor by drawing upon Dickens as a model. To say nothing of the London scene, there is Stevie, the sensitive half-wit who perishes in an anarchist plot. Stevie, with his love of animals, and participation in events of which his ignorance renders him innocent, is strikingly reminiscent of Barnaby Rudge during the Gordon Riots.[42]

Perhaps because humor is usually absent, and even more because of the veil of mystery which shrouds all issues in Conrad's most typical writing, the play of evil forces in his work is more sinister than in Dickens or in James. But he, too, was content to get along with a few simple ideas. In Dickens, the Smallweeds and Jonas Chuzzlewits are pitted against the kind of heart; in Conrad the corrupt gangsters who can make the world a jungle are pitted against the brave and dutiful who serve. The basic conflict, the implied standards, are much alike, although in Conrad the cocky confidence of the early Dickens is rarely present. The bewilderment is closer to the muddled tone of *Bleak House* and the other dark period novels.

What impressed Edwardian readers more were the obvious differences, and Conrad's reception was similar to that of James: much early misunderstanding, the growth of a fit audience though few, and a gradual recognition accentuated, in his case, by a public admiration for his exotic settings.

Unlike the naturalists, Conrad did not offend his readers; he baffled them.[43] Part of the baffling could be attributed to what readers called his Slavic sense of mystery, and part to his experimental techniques. Despite his protests against Dostoevsky, he became identified with the Russian invasion, and as Dostoevsky's reputation among the critical elite reached its apogee, Conrad's satellite rose with it. *Heart of Darkness*, with its hair-raising hints of evil glimpsed through layers of mystery, appealed to the same taste that responded to *The Brothers Karamazov*.

In addition, Conrad was part of the invasion from France, as well as from Russia, not in its naturalistic manifestations but in its aesthetic concern for the novel as conscious art.[44] A sea-captain's adventure stories were made endlessly complex by painstaking experiments with point of view. In *Nostromo*, the Dickensian flow of narrative has been dammed up into the most intricately contrived of watercourses.

So much attention has been devoted by twentieth-century novel-criticism to a consideration of point of view that one can share the impatience of a distinguished critic who dismissed it as a superstition.[45] So far as Dickens' status is concerned, however, it has had important consequences. Point of view is in part an angle of vision (which interested James and Conrad), and in part the author's degree of detachment from his narrative (which interested Flaubert). In the former sense, *Bleak House* is a groping experiment anticipating Conrad, but not by any means successfully. In the latter sense, in the search for detachment, Dickens was even less satisfactory in the eyes of aesthetic criticism: "It's one of my principles that one must never write down *one's self*. The artist must be present in his work like God in Creation, invisible and almighty, everywhere felt but nowhere seen." Flaubert's credo, as quoted here by Henry James, reappears almost word for word in James Joyce's *Portrait of the Artist*.[46] On the desirability of detachment, the aesthetic, realistic, and naturalistic critics could see eye to eye. Tolstoy and Dostoevsky erred here, it seems, as Dickens had erred. In fact Tolstoy considered that Dickens' relationship to his characters was an ideal one, and said of him: "It is well when an author stands only just outside his subject, so that one continually doubts whether the treatment is subjective or objective."[47] Tolstoy's reasonable principle applies, in practice, to James and Conrad, and could even be stretched to include Flaubert, but a less reasonable fetish of unqualified objectivity became predominant after 1885 when Flaubert's influence began to make itself felt in English critical theory.

I V

Studies which have been made of the reception of French fiction in England bring out the curious fact that the reputations of Balzac, Flaubert, and Zola followed almost identical patterns.[48] Each in turn was neglected for many years; translation was delayed, and such references as were made were usually devoted to proving the inferiority of the immoral French product by comparison with the sturdy good health of Dickens and Scott. In the second phase, there would be a full scale debate among the reviewers, fought on the same issues, in which the epithet "garbage" was replied to by the epithet "Philistine." Finally, the old guard reviewers would grumblingly give ground, and Balzac, Flaubert, and even Zola, to a more limited extent, were installed on English soil as classics.

About 1885, the debate reached its crucial stage. Balzac was already accepted, but the first translation of Zola had been delayed until only the previous year, and *Madame Bovary*, the first translation from Flaubert, appeared a year later. Despite the setback caused by the prosecution of Zola's publisher, translations appeared in rapid succession, and in the nineties, Flaubert's turn to be accepted had been established.

Because it widened the split between various levels of readers, the debate was to have unhappy consequences for Dickens' reputation. Broadly speaking, there were three questions at issue: what subjects are proper to the province of the novel? What should be the novelist's moral attitude towards his subjects? How much play should be allowed to the novelist's imagination?

Bedroom and washroom, accurately portrayed, especially slum bedroom and slum washroom, over these the debate was to wax hotly. During the debate, the adherents of the early Victorian conventions of family reading adopted Dickens as their chief exemplar. In *Bleak House*, Dickens had given a vivid picture of slums. There was, for example, the ghastly household of a drunken brickmaker who was in the habit of beating his wife. It was vulgar, perhaps, but not "sordid" because it could be read aloud to an assembled family. Not so Zola's account of the miner's household in *Germinal*. And the picture of Edith Dombey with Carker in the hotel room at Dijon was in a very different strain from the picture of Emma Bovary with M. Léon in the hotel room at Rouen. As the latter mode became accepted in the 1890's, and as the range of subjects and vocabulary was extended further in the 1920's, Dickens became identified with the narrow-minded Philistines who had used his books to prove that such liberty was unnecessary.[49] A reviewer of some of Daudet's experiments in the naturalistic vein in 1891 used the delicacy of Dickens as his measuring stick to show the inferiority of the French writer.[50] However well-intentioned, and however gratifying to Dickensians, such praise constituted a kiss of death, and still does for those critics who fear that literature's hard won victory over the circulating libraries is yet in jeopardy.

If the French novel stood for a considerable extension of the subject matter of fiction, it also stood for a new kind of restrictiveness. Sex might come in but the author was to step out. Authorial intervention and moral commentary destroy the reality of a fictional work of art, as Flaubert argued, or they destroy the scientific validity of the case, as Zola argued. An article praising Flaubert's objectivity, which appeared in the *Westminster Review* in 1895, contains this contrast:

> To Flaubert the silly idea of Dickens that a novel might be useful for exposing the mismanagement of schools and workhouses would have been the best proof that the man who wrote *Oliver Twist* and *Nicholas Nickleby* was a

sorry botch, for whom literature was not an art but an ignoble trade.[51]

Flaubert's more tolerant acceptance of Dickens as one of the greatest of his contemporaries was not shared by his English disciples.[52] Again we encounter the most persistent of ironies concerning Dickens' reputation. While his fame in France, Russia, and Germany[53] was skyrocketing to an eminence only slightly behind that of Shakespeare, in England he was being displaced by the very continental writers who had admired him.

The third aspect of the debate over French fiction was ultimately concerned with the problem of probability. The argument (already discussed in a previous chapter) was extended and intensified by Zola's theoretical attempt to make the novel into a Darwinian document in which many of its familiar Dickensian components such as imagination, humor, and story (let alone authorial comment) were said to distort the desired transcript of actuality. At this point, the realist and naturalist may part company, but what is significant here is that the quasi-scientific study of externals was even more antipathetic to Dickens' violently colored world than was the high aesthetic line of Flaubert and James.

V

George Moore, during one of the many phases of his fantastic career, was the chief bearer of glad tidings from France. He told of a new kind of art which would be "based on science, in opposition to the art of the old world that was based on imagination, an art that would explain all things and embrace modern life in its entirety."[54] As a character in *A Modern Lover* explains, the novel is to be "an exact and complete reproduction of social surroundings of the age we live in."[55] For such purposes, Moore believed that humor was to be avoided. Although he knew Dickens "by heart," he considered that the earlier novelist's jesting destroyed the soberly impersonal study of life required by both naturalistic and aesthetic canons: "He [Dickens] had more talent than Flaubert, Zola, Goncourt, Daudet; but he would have learnt from them the value of seriousness. . . . He would have learnt that humour is more commercial than literary."* The difference between the presentations of Esther Waters and the Marchioness illustrate Moore's modification.

In *A Christmas Garland*, Max Beerbohm offers an essay supposedly written by George Moore after his discovering *Pickwick Papers* for the first time. This best of parodies captures Moore's casual tone as reader and critic, a tone that here becomes endearingly fatuous, especially in his chat about Arabella as Winkle's mistress. "The disengaging of the erotic motive is everything," says the imaginary Moore.[56] It is a pity that Robert Graves did not read Beerbohm's essay with care before composing his earnest bedroom scene between David Copperfield and Emily in *The Real David Copperfield*.

To say anything about Moore and Dickens after Beerbohm is a hopeless task, but the Moore of real life, despite his fluctuations of taste, does seem to have been affected in his development as a novelist by his steady relishing of Dickens. Like Arnold Bennett, after beginning with imitations of French naturalism, he moved off into other directions. In his *Confessions of a Young Man* (1886) he stated that "the healthy school is played out in England" and added that "the successors of Dickens, Thackeray, and George Eliot have . . . nothing new to say."[57] In the defense of the "unhealthy" school, he was one of the most prominent advocates, but even in his first novel, a *Spectator* reviewer observed that Moore differed from the hogs of Zola's sty because of a strain of tenderness.[58] Later, in 1894, *Esther Waters*, in spite of its air of detachment and its similarity to *Germinie Lacerteux*, was hailed as a return to the "English" school.[59] *Esther Waters* is one of the purest examples of the scope and limitations of realism. It is not really in the Dickensian vein, yet by com-

---

* Moore, *Avowals* (New York, 1923), p. 79; *Confessions of a Young Man* (New York, 1923), pp. 307, 455; Geraint Goodwin, *Conversations with George Moore* (1929), p. 58. It might have been disconcerting to Moore to discover that Bagehot also disapproved of humor in Dickens: "You take up the esteemed writers, Thucydides and the *Saturday Review*; after all, they do not make you laugh. It is not the function of really artistic productions to contribute to the mirth of human beings." *Works of Walter Bagehot* (1915), III, 105.

parison with Moore's earlier novels, it seems to be. What is significant is that this iconoclastic disciple of art for art's sake and of naturalism should have felt the pull of a tradition he considered outmoded, and that his novel should have affected readers as Dickens had affected them, even to the extent of one reader founding a home for unmarried mothers![60]

The novels of Arnold Bennett are a more clear-cut illustration of the same development. Such early works as *A Man from the North* (1898) are imitations of Flaubert, Zola, the Goncourts, Maupassant, and George Moore's early writings. By 1908, as his critics have indicated, Bennett's novels show a marked change, and traces of Dickens, whom he had formerly ridiculed, begin to appear in his work. As can be discerned in his journals and essays, this development as a novelist corresponds to his development as a reader. Unlike James or H. G. Wells, Bennett had not read Dickens extensively in his youth (he was thirty when he first read *David Copperfield*), and what he had read seemed to him distinctly inferior to his French favorites. As he said in 1901: "It is strange that Turgenev, whose work marks him as a hater of exaggeration in any form, was an enthusiastic admirer of Dickens. He put Dickens above Balzac, and was never tired of his praises."[61] Bennett's bewilderment continued for a few years afterwards. In 1904, when a friend recommended the style of the opening of *Hard Times* as one of the finest passages in English, Bennett recorded in his journal: "Of course I disagreed."[62] One of his strangest notions, at this time, was that Dickens had no "feeling for words." This impression was part of his total indictment of the Victorian novelists: they were not craftsmen, they had been unconcerned with technique.[63] Moreover, Bennett had the complaint to make, typical of his generation, that Dickens had treated sex dishonestly; he had failed to face the facts of life.[64]

Within a few years, Bennett's estimate of Dickens seems to have undergone a change. In 1909, the year following *Buried Alive* and *The Old Wives' Tale*, he published a manual called *Literary Taste: How to Form It*. Of the sixteen nineteenth-century novelists on his list, he recommends, as a rule, only one novel of each. Dickens is treated as a class apart; his *Works* in eighteen volumes are recommended.[65] Nor was this recommendation a mere concession to public taste. The journals and essays show that he was becoming dissatisfied with the arrogance of naturalistic theory and the aesthetic emphasis upon self-conscious technique. "With the single exception of Turgenev," he said, the great novelists of the world had "either ignored technique or . . . failed to understand it."[66]

It has been said that the real danger in research is that unless we are very careful we always find what we are seeking. As a result of Bennett's breaking away from his French idols, we expect to find a Dickensian strain in the novels written after 1907, and we do find it. Mr. Critchlow has been cited as a Dickensian character,[67] and it is probable that Bennett's fondness for such flat eccentrics was stimulated by Dickens. A late entry in his journals speaks of the similarity between Dickens' "conventionalized" and "simplified" characters and his own, and he mentions his agreement with T. S. Eliot that such characters have the virtue of remaining fixed in the reader's mind.[68] In this, however, as I suggested above, Bennett's partiality is not unusual. What is more distinctive in these later books is the occasional intrusion of exuberance and affection. When Edwin Clayhanger is showing Hilda Lessways the tawdry little theatre of the Five Towns called *The Blood Tub*, she is depressed by it, but he reminds her that "it's our form of poetry."* Ironic juxtapositions are Bennett's special province, but he seems to have been exposed to a fresh stimulus which released the zest he was capable of feeling for such settings and such lives, especially in his extraordinary farewell address to the reader on the subject of Mr. Povey's death. A trickle of Dickensian warmth throughout the drab story of Constance in *The Old Wives' Tale* saves his masterpiece from the calculated dreariness of Maupassant's *Une vie*. The warmth is most Dickensian, however, not in the occasional strain of tenderness but in the exuberant de-

---

* *Clayhanger*, Bk. II, ch. XX. The fourth chapter, picturing the grim childhood of Darius Clayhanger, is Dickens-like in its grimly jocular irony. The eighteen-hour working day was performed, Bennett says, by a "man of seven."

scriptions of the commonplace. The following passage in *Buried Alive* is from a chapter called "The Simple Joy of Life" in which some street advertisements are described:

> In every available space gigantic posters were exhibited. They all had to do with food or pleasure. There were York hams eight feet high, that a regiment could not have eaten in a month; shaggy and ferocious oxen peeping out of monstrous teacups in their anxiety to be consumed; spouting bottles of ale whose froth alone would have floated the mail steamers pictured on an adjoining sheet. . . . Then after a few score yards of invitation to debauch there came . . . a cure for indigestion, so large that it would have given ease to a mastodon who had by inadvertence swallowed an elephant.[69]

This is certainly Pickwickian, the very vein of which the early Bennett had disapproved. It is a vein that was more fully exploited by H. G. Wells than by Bennett. From early in his career, Wells was hailed as a disciple of Dickens, the upholder of the Dickens tradition against the fastidiousness of Henry James, which, in many respects, he may have been. At the outset, however, it ought to be pointed out that Wells, like Bennett, did not comprehend the whole of Dickens by any means. The obvious Dickensisms he absorbed and used to good effect; the rest he ignored. There is a sense in which James and Conrad can be regarded as being much closer to the essential nature of Dickens' work than are Bennett and Wells. Such a paradox depends upon how a critic defines the "essential nature" of Dickens—a problem to be discussed in the final chapter. Meanwhile, the more obvious connections remain to be considered.

In his *Experiment in Autobiography* (1934), Wells looked back upon the last decade of the nineteenth century as a time extraordinarily favorable for new novelists. The predominance of Dickens and Thackeray and their successors was passing:

> For a generation the prestige of the great Victorians remained like the shadow of vast trees in a forest, but now

that it was lifting, every weed and sapling had its chance, provided only that it was a different species from its predecessors. When woods are burnt, it is a different tree which reconstitutes the forest. The habit of reading was spreading to new classes. . . . Even the humours of Dickens no longer fitted into their everyday experiences.[70]

To capture this new market, which he succeeded in doing for many years, Wells had his own kind of newness. Unlike most of his contemporaries, he did not begin by imitating the French naturalists. In fiction, his early diet had been English, especially the novels of Dickens.[71] What he brought that was new was not the literary techniques of naturalism but the ideas behind the techniques. The ideas of Darwin and Huxley and Spencer are more important in his typical discussion-novels (such as *The World of William Clissold*) than in his scientific fantasies. In the former, with their once sparkling modernity, Wells achieved a kind of novel which might have satisfied even Mr. Gradgrind. Wells was himself aware of his affinities with Mr. Gradgrind. As the hero of *A Modern Utopia* purringly admits: "I'm a Gradgrind—it's quite right—anything you can say about Herbert Spencer, vivisectors, materialistic Science or Atheists, applies without correction to me."[72] The speech could have been spoken by Wells himself, and the basic gap between his standards and those of Dickens is yawning enough. Yet it is also characteristic of Wells that his hero is accompanied by an eccentric individual who is not at all happy in the streamlined world of the Samurai. From his own experiences in life (which have been compared to those of Dickens),[73] and from his absorption in Dickens' novels, Wells acquired a concern for the differences between individuals. This concern humanized his Spencerian hardness, and it also affected his technique as a novelist during an important phase of his career.

In such novels as *Kipps*, *Tono-Bungay*, and *The History of Mr. Polly*, critics of Wells have found a marked Dickens phase. "It was under the spell of Charles Dickens that this great anti-Victorian was most creative."[74] Although V. S. Pritchett has warned us that the similarities are superficial,[75] most readers have readily sensed that Edward Ponderevo, for example, is an offspring of Micawber. As his nephew observes of him: "One felt that he was silly and wild, but in some way silly and wild after the fashion of the universe."[76] There is a hearty, bouncing tone in these novels, the tone which G. K. Chesterton enjoyed in Dickens. As a recent critic suggests, Wells "winks at the reader" and assumes a "genial charitableness" in the Dickensian manner. There are also certain similarities in their imagery.[77]

Wells' own comment upon the resemblances is a sensible one. In the early stages of a novelist's career, he said, it is useful to be called "a second Dickens," as he had found, but after a time, it can be harmful. "Pett Ridge for instance pinned himself down as a second Dickens to the end of his days. I was saved from a parallel fate by the perplexing variety of my early attributions."[78]

Even in *Tono-Bungay*, the variety is evident. George Ponderevo has to assure us at one point by asserting: "But this is a novel, not a treatise." In Dickens' novels, even in *Hard Times* or *Little Dorrit*, the reader does not often need such assurances. The abuses of Chancery become transformed into literature. With the effort required for such transformation, Wells became progressively impatient. He was only too willing to admit that he found the "novel proper" somewhat dull. "The plain fact is that I have never been willing . . . to accept the Novel as an art form."[79] That such an opinion seemed disconcertingly heretical to Henry James is to be expected. It is important to recall that Dickens would also have found it heretical, and the same could be said of how he would have reacted to Wells' confessed "indifference to intensity of effect"—an indifference which bewildered Conrad.[80]

After *Ann Veronica* was published, Henry James complimented Wells upon his "objective vividness" with a typical sentence: "You must at moments make dear old Dickens turn —for envy of the eye and the ear and the nose and the mouth of you—in his grave."[81] Perhaps so. Wells certainly shows the persistence of certain Dickensian elements into the twentieth-century novel. Yet just as the example of Keats was narrowed or distorted by some of his later imitators such as Rossetti or Wilde, so was Dickens' example narrowed by Wells. As a critic of fiction, Wells was a cocky defender of Dickens. In an essay of 1912, he took the line that aesthetic critics had failed to do justice to his greatness.[82] By that date, as a writer, he had himself outgrown his model. Despite his interest in history, Wells, like Carlyle, became too absorbed in time future to concern himself whole-heartedly with time past or even with time present. His dissatisfaction was therefore almost inevitable.

V I

Equally inevitable was that the novel after Dickens' death would develop in a variety of new directions. Although in this chapter some examples of his persistent influence have been indicated, there has been no intention of suggesting that it was in any way predominant. His importance to later novelists, especially from the time of his death until the first World War, was that he served as a corrective. If to critics who shone in the high aesthetic line Dickens seemed a clumsy cave-artist, and to the naturalists merely fantastic, and to those who sought topicality in fiction merely antique, he was never altogether ignored. One reason that he could not be ignored was that virtually all the important novelists (and George Gissing must be added to the list) were affected by his work. To find examples of "pure" naturalism, for example, is always difficult anywhere. In England, where Moore, Gissing, and Bennett were drawn off into eclecticism, it is almost impossible.

For the period following the first World War, it becomes progressively hazardous to speak of Dickens' influence. Novelists as various as Graham Greene, George Orwell, Somerset Maugham, and Joyce Cary have written discerning appreciations of his genius,[83] yet it would take a critical Geiger counter of infinite delicacy to detect the Dickens element and to isolate it from other compounds under the surface of their writings. For this period, it is more useful to consider some indications of how his work weathered the criticisms which had been raised during the nineties against his artless art of narrative.

If Henry James' concern as a novelist with executive form has captured the attention of novelists and critics alike, his concern as a critic with the allowance of a legitimate variety of techniques has also left its mark.[84] The difference, generally, is between an age that spoke of Dickens' technique as hopelessly inadequate, and a later age to whom it is merely different. In 1922, J. W. Beach analyzed the technical inadequacies of *David Copperfield* by showing that its method failed because it was that of a "moving picture" instead of a drama.[85] In view of the successful adaptations of Dickens' novels to the moving picture medium, this is interesting criticism. It assumes, however, that "drama" (in James' sense) is essential to fiction. Other critics have been less dogmatic. E. M. Forster, for example, concludes that the theory of point of view has been overemphasized. To prove his point, he cites *Bleak House* and contends that although Dickens may have shifted the viewpoint carelessly, he has shown a power "to bounce the reader into accepting what he says" which is of far greater importance.[86] His conclusion is echoed by Somerset Maugham in *The Summing Up*: "The artist is absorbed by his technique only when his theme is of no pressing interest to him."[87]

Perhaps Mr. Forster's word "bounce" is too elusive. Another novelist, C. E. Montague, raises the question more effectively. After discussing "Dickens's magnificently artless art," Montague simply asks whether the new and exacting technique, which was evolved by James and "a few middle-nineteenth-century Frenchmen," really serves its intended function of increasing illusion:

> Or is there some bigger truth that they have not got hold of?—does it arise from something still unexplored, in the very nature of narrative fiction, that its richest and strongest practitioners should look like very standard-bearers of the cause of technical looseness? In some moods one may find oneself thinking that the curious state of absorption and semi-belief (never literal belief),

which we call illusion in a reader's mind, may be actually favoured by a certain easy-going way of the writer's,
an unguarded-looking habit, an unprofessional-seeming
lack of technical apparatus.[88]

In *The Craft of Fiction* (1921), Percy Lubbock does not
face Montague's searching question head on, but he does
show that a variety of methods work. As we have seen, Lubbock was somewhat disturbed that Dickens followed an "uncritical instinct," but he demonstrated how in *Bleak House*
and *Copperfield* that instinct led Dickens to a technique which
was "sound and good" and by no means a simple one.[89] Another novelist, Phyllis Bentley, in her short study of the art
of narrative (1947), also refers to Dickens' mastery of scene
and summary.[90] The subject is one of many which remains for
someone to investigate fully,[91] just as Edwin Muir, in his
Structure of the Novel, showed the possibilities of a sympathetic investigation of Dickens' plots. It has been raised here
primarily to show that since the first World War, there has
been a gradual shift away from the rigidity of an earlier
aestheticism—a shift confirmed by the recent revival of interest in D. H. Lawrence. As James' methods have been
absorbed by later novelists, there has been less squeamishness
in the evaluation of other methods on the part of critical
readers (as Forster says, the less critical readers usually do
not find the question of much interest). There are signs that
the technical experiments of Woolf and Joyce are being
similarly digested, all of which leads to a less condescending
way of regarding Dickens' craftsmanship. The shift was anticipated by Katherine Mansfield, a fastidious artist who, as
an adult, read Dickens without condescension. Three or four
years before her death, she was absorbed in several of Dickens' novels which, as she said, she was not reading "*idly*."
"Have you read *Our Mutual Friend*?" she asked Middleton
Murry. "Some of it is really *damned good*." And after a diet
of *David Copperfield*, she exclaimed: "Yes—doesn't Charley
D. make our little men smaller than ever—and such pencil
sharpeners—"[92]

CHAPTER 12

THE UNCOMMON READER

I

HOW good it is to meet someone who enjoys Dickens, and how rarely this happens!" So begins an essay by the English novelist, Rex Warner, which appeared in 1947.[1] In 1952, the American critic, Lionel Trilling, begins an essay with the following assertion: "No one, I think, is any longer under any illusion about Dickens. It is now manifest that he is one of the two greatest novelists of England (Jane Austen being the other)."[2] From these contradictory statements, one might infer either that a miracle has taken place in five years, or that there exists a radical disagreement about literary preferences on opposite sides of the Atlantic. A more reasonable explanation is simply that Mr. Warner and Mr. Trilling must enjoy a different circle of acquaintances and that they must have been reading different books and magazines. As W. H. Mallock reminded us, whenever the assertion is made that Dickens is no longer read, we must ask the essential question: *How do you know?*

In discussing the so-called common reader, I referred to the annual sale of such novels as *David Copperfield*, and librarians in England still report that Dickens is approached only by Scott in having the largest circulation of any "classic" writer.* Among those members of the general public who are prepared to read books from earlier times, Dickens has continued to hold a remarkable lead. A further sign of vitality has been the successful adaptation of such novels as *Great Expectations* and *Oliver Twist* into the medium of the film. The fact that the film seems a much more effective medium for

---

* See *TLS*, June 20, 1952, p. 404. —In his history of Scott's reputation, J. T. Hillhouse observed with some dismay that by 1936, even among critical readers, Dickens had gained the highest reputation of any English novelist, whereas, Scott had gone into serious decline. See *The Waverley Novels and their Critics* (Minneapolis, 1936), p. 340.

his work than the stage has been raises a number of interesting enquiries which cannot, however, be pursued here.

Our survey has indicated that it is not among the common readers but among the more critical and vocal sections of the reading public that we can detect the significant variations in Dickens' status since 1872. Here again the signs are difficult to read, but it can be said with confidence that Mr. Warner is mistaken in assuming that Dickens' reputation in the 1940's was much lower than it was at the turn of the century. It was in the latter period that Dickens' status among critical readers reached its lowest point, although desperate attempts were made, during the 1920's, to push it even lower. When Chesterton set about his defense of Dickens in 1906, he had to admit that the principal literary movements of his time— naturalism, aestheticism, and what I have called the discovery of the soul—had by-passed his favorite novelist.

Estimates of critical status must be made on the basis of quantity as well as the quality of comment that a writer's work continues to evoke. Since the 1939-1945 war, the quantity of writing stimulated by Dickens is enormous. In England, biographies and critical studies have appeared including those by Una Pope-Hennessy, Hesketh Pearson, Jack Lindsay, and Julian Symons, and numerous appreciative essays including the one by Rex Warner himself. Under the editorship of Humphry House, a vast new edition of the letters is being prepared to supersede the already vast collection available in the Nonesuch version. In America, during the same period, a considerable quantity of scholarly investigation and criticism has been climaxed by Edgar Johnson's two-volume biography—the sale of which would have made even Dickens envious. Within a month of its publication, three other books about Dickens also appeared. Most encouraging of all, however, to the admirer of Dickens, are signs that the appreciation of his novels is moving in a new direction— or perhaps there is simply a return to a direction once followed and subsequently abandoned. Chesterton's further explanation of the neglect of Dickens by his critical contemporaries was that Dickens had not only exaggerated; he had exaggerated the wrong things.[3] There is considerable indication that for our generation, as for some of Dickens' early readers, his kind of exaggeration is once more appropriate.

"He is tremendous, his taste is abominable." In these words, Percy Lubbock summed up the problem of Balzac. His comment applies equally well to the problem of Dickens. To sum up what it is that readers have found to be abominable, I must resort to the clumsy device of an itemized list:

1. that Dickens' criticism of society is childish, misinformed, and based upon a fatuous optimism;
2. that his novels violate the canons of The Novel by their emphasis upon sensationalism, by their improbabilities and general failure in realism;
3. that his novels fail to explore the inner lives of the characters;
4. that his novels violate the canons of The Novel because they must have been written without due attention to art; their author is a mere entertainer, not an artist;
5. that his novels fail to deal with sexual relations;
6. that because he was self-educated, his writings can have nothing to say of interest to educated readers;
7. that when he resorts to sentimentality, his style is unbearable.

Most of the critics who remain to be discussed have been engaged in the reiteration or refutation of these seven counts. At the outset it must be noted that very few defenders of Dickens have attempted to cope with the last item on the list; they prefer to regard Nell as a blemish to put up with—like Touchstone's puns. Even such a champion as Swinburne was prepared to jettison Nell from the troika and leave her to the wolf-pack led by G. H. Lewes—a critic loathed by Swinburne with the most intense Swinburnian loathing. The above list is based, in fact, upon Lewes' essay of 1872 (with the exception of the reference to sex), for Lewes anticipated the shifts of taste which were to welcome Tolstoy, Flaubert, Meredith, and James. Lewes even anticipated a review by Anthony West, appearing early in 1953, in which all seven items on the list are restated once more almost as if they were novelties.[5] In the midst of the current reevaluation of Dickens, Mr. West's article is a chastening reminder that critical hostility in some quarters may have been scotch'd but not kill'd.

Many of the postulates in Lewes' list have also reappeared in some of the academic criticism of Dickens, as, for example, in Ernest Baker's *History of the English Novel*. For such criticism at its best, we can turn to the writer responsible for the article on Dickens in the *Cambridge History of English Literature*: Professor George Saintsbury. As a boy, Saintsbury had enjoyed Dickens so heartily that when he first read Thackeray, at the age of fifteen, he found *Vanity Fair* disagreeable. After remaining in this state of sin (as it later seemed to him) for two years, he became converted to the position that a novelist's task is to represent a stable, everyday reality, and that Thackeray had come closer to this ideal than any other English writer, including even Fielding and Austen. A zestful and omnivorous reading of continental fiction only served to reinforce this conviction. For the rest of his life Saintsbury nevertheless continued to expose his finely developed critical palate to the coarse Dickensian vintages, and to report his verdicts to the public. The early, sparkling bottlings of the *Pickwick* variety, he could often savor with pleasure; the later, heavy-bodied ones he found sour. As a political conservative, he considered Dickens' social criticism to be, at best, boring, and *Our Mutual Friend* he ranked just below *Hard Times* as the worst of the novels. But what bothered him most of all was his realization that none of these books conformed to his theory of what he called "the novel proper." In moods of exasperation, he was ready to dismiss them all as *vin ordinaire*. Thus in an essay of 1895, his impatience with Dickensian exaggeration led to his treating the novels as minor works of humor. Dickens' "unfortunate want of early education" had produced a rant which is "disgusting." Repetitions such as Panks and the "tug" are examples of "damnable iteration."[6]

Twenty years later, Saintsbury had somewhat revised these

impressions. For one thing, he admitted that he found himself going back to Dickens' novels with pleasure. "You can read him again and again with unceasing delight."[7] His own prose, like Ruskin's, teems with images drawn from Dickens.[8] For another, as he wisely observed, the fact of a writer's popularity persisting long after his death "cannot, without danger, be slightly recognised by the critic, and, especially, by the historical critic."[9] On the basis of these revised impressions, Saintsbury was even prepared to admit that Dickens had somehow "mastered . . . the Aristotelian doctrine of the impossibility rendered probable."[10] But it is evident, even in this *Cambridge History* essay, that he was bewildered. Saintsbury is an excellent example of a critic with a theory of The Novel and with a concept of reality to which the novelist must conform. If certain novels fail to conform, then they must be abandoned, or reclassified, or clipped into the prescribed shape. A fourth possibility, that the theory might be modified, and a new theory constructed inductively, does not seem to have occurred to this uncommonly lively and perceptive historical critic.

Equally lively but less perceptive were the attacks which appeared during the 1920's and 1930's, such as Bechhofer Roberts' *This Side Idolatry.* In these the front has been narrowed. Instead of attacking Dickens' lack of realism in general, attention was concentrated upon the lack of realism in sex and in social criticism. In his valuable study, *Freudianism and the Literary Mind*, F. J. Hoffman has demonstrated why the generation which survived the 1914-1918 war was dissatisfied with Dickens' evasiveness in his treatment of sex.[11] If Robert Graves may serve as a representative of this generation, the word *dissatisfied* is not strong enough. The word *contempt* would be closer. In 1933, Mr. Graves published his curious revision of Dickens entitled *The Real David Copperfield* in which he attempted to weed out the most dreadful passages (especially those concerned with Agnes) and to add enough bedroom scenes so that the book might be palatable for post-war tastes. His *jeu d'esprit* is about as effective as Pope's attempts to translate Donne's satires into elegant neo-classical verses and will remain an equally amusing specimen for future literary historians. One of its most striking features is Mr. Graves' assumption that Dickens is no longer read. "The advanced public has so long outgrown him that Mr. Osbert Sitwell . . . is now able to add to a reputation for waggery by a serio-comic championship of Dickens as writer and man."*

The Real David Copperfield was succeeded by *The Sentimental Journey*, a surprisingly mild explanation of Dickens' failure from the pen of that indefatigable exposer of Victorian absurdities, the late Hugh Kingsmill. Two years later, the ultimate obituary notice was published when Sean O'Faolain delivered his considered judgment:

> Dickens hitched his star to the wagon of conventional thought and conventional morality, one of the shakiest wagons ever known. He became the novelist of bourgeois thought, and in the drawing room . . . he lay side by side with the family Bible. . . . He is, in short, the great comforter of the nineteenth century, and unhappily for him the nineteenth century is gone.†

One wonders how the reviewers of the 1850's, who considered Dickens anything but comforting, would react if they could return to witness such a verdict—rude in any age, but in 1936 virtually libellous. Mr. O'Faolain was not alone in his opinion. According to Philip Henderson, Dickens had obscured the "root causes" of nineteenth-century poverty by his concern with "raucous humour" and with sentiment

---

* *The Real David Copperfield* (1933), p. 5. Because Mr. Graves considers Dickens' most tiresome fault to be "his continual readiness to sacrifice straightforwardness in writing to a tradesman-like exploitation of the now extinct Dear Reader," it is surprising to encounter a similar habit in Mr. Graves' own works. In *Sergeant Lamb of the Ninth*, for example, Mr. Graves is not above interrupting his lively narrative with long and rather clumsy lectures on history. It may also be remarked that the expression *Dear Reader* never appears (to the best of my knowledge) in Dickens' writings.

† *The English Novelists*, ed. Derek Verschoyle (1936), pp. 146-148. Mr. O'Faolain also notes that Dickens is no longer a "Novelist's novelist." He is a "master without pupils." At least one popular novelist was of a contrary opinion. In the same year as his essay was published, there appeared an article by Pearl Buck entitled "My Debt to Dickens," in the *English Review*, LXII, 408-412.

"which recommended him to the vast middle-class reading public of his day." Hence, "he is, for a generation nurtured on Bernard Shaw, D. H. Lawrence and Aldous Huxley, of all the Victorians the most difficult to read."[12]

That Shaw should appear in this context is a further example of the process already considered with reference to Turgenev, Dostoevsky, Tolstoy, and Flaubert. Once again we find a writer who deeply admired Dickens used by his disciples to show the inferiority of Dickens.

I I

If the attacks on Dickens since 1872 seem to be variations on a theme by Lewes, the assorted critical essays in his defense also seem to follow recurrent patterns. Of these there are chiefly four. The first is represented by Shaw and others, the second by G. K. Chesterton, the third by George Gissing, and the fourth by Edmund Wilson.

George Bernard Shaw once told Alexander Woollcott (another zealous reader of Dickens) that a concordance of his own writings would reveal the Dickens allusions as running from four to one against any other writer.[13] To those who think of Dickens as the respectable comforter of the Victorian middle-classes, such praise from the eminent socialist and iconoclast seems puzzling. When Shaw describes Dickens as "one of the greatest writers in the world," they would like to write off the praise as another example of waggery. If it was waggery, the joke was repeated too often in his essays to sustain itself. Shaw was both emphatic and serious when he remarked that all of Dickens' detractors "were, and are, second-raters at best."[14]

Strong and distinctive personalities make the most engaging but not the soundest of critics. Shaw's Dickens is certainly not the complete Dickens—if the complete Dickens does exist anywhere in criticism. Like Matthew Arnold, Shaw was looking for an ally. Upon finding one in Dickens, his hug is hugely affectionate but so powerful that the object of his affections is squeezed out of shape. It is significant that Shaw's first love was for *Little Dorrit* not for *Pickwick Papers*, and

Dickens' habit of describing "the gorgings and guzzlings which make Christmas our annual national disgrace" was offensive to his basic asceticism.[15] Hence an important phase of Dickens he was content to leave to G. K. Chesterton. Much less offensive to him was that his idol had never acquired a taste for Bach; the lacking was part of the necessary price to be paid for the indispensable "Sam Weller training" which Dickens had mastered. The lack of Bach in Dickens' equipment is related, however, to a more significant lack of "the great synthetic ideals"[16]—that is, of a realization of the need for an intellectually planned reorganization of world economy so that life may be efficiently and rationally controlled. Shaw's love of Dickens was so deep that he seldom examined the implications of the difference between a writer whose ideal was a happy society and another whose ideal was a sensible one.[17]

If there was a difference in ultimate objectives, there remained, nevertheless, a large meeting-ground both for subject and method. What Shaw valued, first of all, was the criticism of society. In a letter of 1919 to Frank Harris (who loathed Dickens), he said bluntly:

> Your ignorance of Dickens is a frightful gap in your literary education. He was by far the greatest man since Shakespear that England has produced in that line. Read *Little Dorrit*, *Our Mutual Friend*, and *Great Expectations*. Until you do, you will not have the very faintest notion of what the name Dickens means. . . . He did not come of age until Ruskin and Carlyle probed his social conscience to the depth, and he made a beginning of his great period with *Hard Times*. But when it came, it *was* great.[18]

This "great period" Shaw later likened to Beethoven's "third manner," in which were produced works that had never been fully appreciated by the artist's contemporaries, but which were extremely pertinent for later generations.[19] In his Introduction to the Waverley edition of *Hard Times*, Shaw speaks of Dickens' "conversion," during the Dark Period novels, to a sense of "social sin," and of his realization that middle-class civilization is a "disease" to be cured, "that it is not our disorder but our order that is horrible; that it is not our criminals but our magnates that are robbing and murdering us."

To have reasserted the importance of Dickens' indignant exposure of abuses—the aspects of his work which had delighted Thomas Hood and John Ruskin earlier—was an extremely important task performed by Shaw, and much recent criticism has simply followed his lead. Also important but much less obvious has been his absorption of Dickens' basic methods into his plays. His criticism of society may owe more to Morris, Butler,* and even Carlyle than it owes to Dickens; it is his tone that is Dickensian. Of one of Shaw's earlier works, Stevenson remarked with amusement that the young author was pretending to be a realist while actually soaring away on the wings of a romantic griffon. The griffon, he added, is "shouting with laughter" as he cleaves the air.[20] In 1934, Shaw himself pointed out that for this characteristic tone he was indebted to Dickens. Only the "stupendous illiteracy of modern criticism" (he said) could account for his debt to Dickens being overlooked:

> especially my continual exploitation of Dickens's demonstration that it is possible to combine a mirrorlike exactness of character drawing with the wildest extravagances of humorous expression and grotesque situation. I have actually transferred characters of Dickens to my plays . . . with complete success. . . . Dickens could not only draw a character more accurately than any of the novelists of the nineteenth century, but could do it without ceasing . . . to be not merely impossible but outrageous in his unrestrained fantasy and fertility of imagination. . . . That is what I call mastery: knowing exactly how to be unerringly true and serious whilst entertain-

* Butler protested against Dickens' being buried in the Abbey next to the remains of the greatest artist of all time: Handel. "It pained me to think that people who could do this could become Deans of Westminster." Nevertheless, according to Ernest Baker, certain resemblances between Butler's writings and Dickens' can be detected. See his *History of the English Novel* (1936), VII, 247n., and *The Note-Books of Samuel Butler* (1913), p. 134.

ing your reader with every freak . . . that imagination
and humour can conceive at their freest and wildest.[21]

With this passage in mind, it could be argued that Dickens'
mark is more evident in twentieth-century drama than in many
of the novels which supposedly reflect his influence.

In his reassertion of the importance of Dickens' social
criticism, Shaw has been followed by several other writers,
most notably by Edgar Johnson, whose biography stresses
Dickens' importance as an exposer of the abuses of Victorian
society. Another group has recommended him as the great
exponent of the common man and has produced studies with
such characteristic titles as *Dickens and Democracy*, *The
Apostle of the People*, and *Challenge to Oppression*.[22] This
view of Dickens was not shared by Shaw, and anyone who has
read a sketch called "The Ruffian" in *The Uncommercial
Traveller* will also be aware of its serious limitations. One
other group related to Shaw has attempted to represent Dickens
as a forerunner of Marxism, a great revolutionary writer
whose later books are aimed at the overthrow of the whole
capitalist economy. T. A. Jackson's ingenious interpretation,
which appeared in 1937, is the principal work devoted to
this thesis, but it reappears, in a more subdued and fuzzier
form, in a biography by Jack Lindsay in 1950. That Mr.
Jackson was able to dress Dickens in Marxian robes has one
important advantage. It offsets the crudely simplified versions
which represent him as the great comforter of the bourgeoisie.
That it has the disadvantage of setting up an equally crude
and simplified version is also evident. The Marxian robes are
borrowed robes; in very few places do they fit. As the Spanish
civil war demonstrated, there may be times when the liberal
anarchist has to join forces with the Communist, but the
temporary alliance does not make the momentous differences
disappear. It is significant that another Marxian critic, Ralph
Fox, was dissatisfied with Dickens. In *The Novel and the
People* (1937), the thesis is developed that art will flourish
only when there is a "harmony between writer and public."
We might expect from this premise that Dickens would surely

meet Fox's requirements, for Fox admits that the harmony certainly existed. "He and his London were one." But by some curious reasoning, Fox decides that Dickens failed *because* he was in harmony with his readers. It is an interesting comment on Fox's position that he really prefers the aristocratic reading public of the eighteenth century to the more democratic reading public of the Victorian age. Speaking of the decline of the novel in the age of Dickens, he remarks: "The appearance of the reader on the scene as a force almost as important as the writer, finished off the process."[23]

As a critic of society, as in many other respects, Dickens was not one but many. It was suggested earlier that he was in part a solid middle-class father of ten, with the middle-class horror of mobs, and in part he was also an indignant anarchist, with the anarchist's horror of institutional oppression. To the seeker for clear-cut political and social panaceas, the mixture is a disconcerting one. To the reader of novels, it is rich with endless possibilities. The universal dilemma of the individual pursued by the inhuman mob *or* caught in the web of the inhuman institution provides Dickens with his major themes. Those admirers of Charlie Chaplin who have likened his funny-sad pictures to the world of Dickens come closer than most to explaining the latter's position. The most perceptive essay on the subject which has so far appeared was written, appropriately, by George Orwell. Orwell is one of the few critics who has recognized some of the complexities and contradictions of the social criticism in Dickens' novels and yet retained a respect and love for them.

III

The second cluster of critics replying to Lewes' list consists of G. K. Chesterton, Swinburne, J. B. Priestley, and others whose interest in Dickens is certainly not concentrated upon determining whether he sang us a song of social significance.* In general, they try to convey, for wavering readers,

* "We do not read him now for his social reform, and neither did our grandfathers. He was only successful as a social reformer because he commanded a large audience, but he did not command that audience as a social reformer." J. B. Priestley, *The English Novel* (1935) [1927], p. 66.

the zestful enjoyment still to be found in Dickens' fiction. *Look! look!*, they say to us. *Do but see what you have been missing!* What they are usually recommending, in their impressionistic books and essays, are characters. "Here in England, . . ." writes J. B. Priestley, "one standard of judgment in fiction has remained. We English have always had a zest for character, for sharply defined and vivid personalities."[24] Mr. Priestley's observation is undoubtedly correct as a statement of fact, but more recent critics have been led quite properly to protest against a common error which may stem from this preoccupation with vivid characters. It is the error of discussing the characters without reference to the context in which they appear. A. C. Bradley has been said to have forgotten that Iago is a character in a play by Shakespeare; G. K. Chesterton certainly forgets sometimes that Toots is a character in a novel by Dickens. For this reason, among others, Chesterton's reputation is, at the moment, under a cloud. What follows does not seek to reinstate him and his group, although by relating them to the overall survey of Dickens' status, some explanatory apology may emerge.

In a previous discussion of the aesthetic criticism of the 1890's, reference was made to the dismally serious young readers whose fondness for Meredith and Tolstoy led to their banishing Dickens as "too gutterly gutter." It is not surprising that such comments provoked a reply from William Ernest Henley, a belligerent Dickensian whose tastes ran counter to the main stream of the nineties.[25] That the anti-Dickensians also provoked a lengthy reply from Algernon Swinburne (published in 1902) was much more unexpected,[26] but only to those unfamiliar with his reading-habits. Beginning with the monthly numbers of *Dombey* in 1848, Swinburne had devoured Dickens' novels with an anxiety so intense that his French biographer, M. Lafourcade, describes it as almost morbid.* M. Lafourcade even suggests that this

---

* In 1853, Swinburne startled an acquaintance by asking him unexpectedly: "Have you seen the murder in London?" He was speaking of the murder of Tulkinghorn as if it were an actual "case." See Georges Lafourcade, *La jeunesse de Swinburne* (Paris, 1928), I, pp. 89-90. —Clara Watts-Dunton, who witnessed Swinburne's feverish absorption in Dickens'

early reading may have been responsible for the faults of Swinburne's prose style, which is probably the unkindest remark ever made about Dickens.

I assume that Lafourcade was referring to the essays, for in Swinburne's remarkable novels, *Love's Cross-Currents* and *Lesbia Brandon*, there is no apparent sign of Dickens' influence on the style or in any other respect. The only resemblance between the two novelists is one that seems so fantastic and far-fetched that to mention it may be productive of apoplexy in many quarters. It is their common interest in sadism and masochism. With Swinburne, the interest is obvious and open; no other English novelist has described with such power the relish of the whipper and the biter, the ecstasy of the whipped and the bitten. With Dickens, the sadistic and masochistic pleasures are rendered much more subtly and terrifyingly by their more conventional settings. An article of 1947 concludes that the sadist and masochist are the predominant "character-types" in Dickens' novels.[27] The group, which reaches its fullest manifestation in Miss Havisham and Estella, is indeed impressively large. Such an account of resemblances might explain some of the delight Swinburne found in Jonas Chuzzlewit, Miss Havisham, and Rogue Riderhood, but because it depends upon more recent interpretations of Dickens' work, there is, of course, no sign of it in Swinburne's essay.

After his early absorption in Dickens' novels, Swinburne passed on to other writers: Balzac, Scott, Hugo, Stendhal, Fielding, Thackeray, the Brontës, and Austen. Of all Victorian poets he became the best informed reader of prose fiction. In the process, he did not abandon his early affection for the creator of Mrs. Gamp (the latter he could quote "unwearyingly"), and it was his habit to read through the

novels during his last years, was not so much alarmed as she was puzzled. She herself had no use for Dickens' books: "I belong to a generation which has set up other demigods, the worship of whom would be regarded by the true Dickensian as mere idolatry." That a man with Swinburne's "classical equipment" should have come under Dickens' "thraldom" was a great mystery to her. She decided that it was because Swinburne, being Dickens' contemporary, had "breathed his atmosphere. We others are mentally too removed from it to enjoy it." *The Home Life of Swinburne* (1922), pp. 136-139.

entire set of Dickens' works every three years, often reading them aloud to Watts-Dunton. "This was his favourite reading," as Gosse, a fellow devotee, reports.[28]

As might be expected from such a background, the most striking feature of Swinburne's essay is its violence. Tirades against "the blatant boobies" who prefer "the bisexual George Eliot," especially that "pseudosophical quack" G. H. Lewes, are matched with superlatives in honor of "a great tragic and comic poet."[29] Under the howls and yells of the surface, however, is a reasonable appraisal of Dickens' greatness. Unlike Chesterton, Swinburne admires the early and late novels with equal intensity (the evolution of old Dorrit he likens to the best of Balzac). And although he will not allow others to criticize Dickens, including that "Triton of the minnows" Matthew Arnold, he himself does have several reservations to air. His reservations about the "bookish and stagey" language of Louisa Gradgrind's speech to her father (after she has fled from her husband) are excellent—doubly excellent from so flashy a rhetorician as Swinburne. "On the literary and sentimental side of his work Dickens was but a type of his generation and his class: on the comic and pathetic, the tragic and the creative side, 'he was not for an age, but for all time.'"

Such an evaluation of Dickens is not only reasonable; it is almost conventional. What made the essay important was its having been written by a supposed avant-garde author. That the poet who published *Poems and Ballads* could unblushingly announce his esteem for a novelist who "never . . . aspired to wallow in metaphysics or in filth" was praise indeed.

The "golden-haired lad of the Swinburnes" (as in his boyhood he was described by Dickens) was thirty-three years old when Dickens died. G. K. Chesterton was not born until 1874. Yet of the two, it is Chesterton rather than Swinburne who seems to be Dickens' contemporary. Whatever Chesterton's faults as a critic of the Victorians, he had an admirable flair for treating the age as if it were alive.

In his *Charles Dickens: A Critical Study* (1906), in his introductions to individual novels, and in an extensive number of essays,[30] Chesterton hammered out an interpretation of

Dickens which has probably been more potent and widespread than any other and which continues to hover in the background whenever Dickens' novels are being discussed. Its potency was once brought vividly to my attention when a Frenchman related that having read Chesterton's book (in translation), he at once set out to learn English so that he would be able to read Dickens in the original tongue. Not many critics receive tributes of this kind. If the test of a great critic is a capacity to lure readers back to his subject, then Chesterton is indeed a great critic. In some respects, he can be more aptly called a great salesman.* Like many successful salesmen, he combined a firm and sincere conviction in the unique value of his product with a capacity to choose the arguments which would have the most telling effect upon his prospective customers. Swinburnian tantrums, as he rightly realized, would not do.[31] Instead, Chesterton relies upon an appeal to what seems to be common sense (although much of it is not common and some of it is not sense).† He also sweeps us along with a display of patter so dazzling that we have the beery and breezy feeling we are spending Christmas at Dingley Dell with Mr. Pickwick. Above all, we have an exhilarating sense that the reader who does not enjoy Micawber ought to be consulting not a literary critic but a good psychiatrist. It is almost as if we were reading an essay about Dickens written by one of his own characters. No other critic (Dickens' contemporaries included) has conveyed so well the conviction that to miss the fun of Dickens is to miss the Greatest Show on Earth.

The salesmanship is superb, but once the reader has been lured into the tent where he continues to listen to the great voice booming away with its endless reassurances, he may

* Chesterton's belief that criticism ought to consist of saying things about an author "that would have made him jump out of his boots" seems to be borne out here. His fondness for America was limited, and to be likened to an American prototype—the salesman—would probably have irked him excessively.

† Typical of Chesterton's least effective manner is the introduction he wrote for *David Copperfield*. The critic's Little Englandism and his theories of marriage are obtrusively (if divertingly) aired at the expense of any profitable discussion of the novel or the author. See *Appreciations and Criticisms of Dickens* (New York, 1911), pp. 129-139.

wonder whether he is going to see the whole show, or whether the bulky figure of G. K. C. is hiding something from him. What sort of Dickens is Chesterton's Dickens? Most prominently he is the Christmas card Dickens, the one enjoyed by readers of *Pickwick* in 1837 and treasured by later generations of Dickensians. That Chesterton became president of the Dickens Fellowship was most appropriate. Not only is Dickens shown to be cosy, but also to be constantly cheerful. The popular impression of his novels, held by the general public when he died, was reinforced by Chesterton's insistence upon his healthy optimism: "Abandon hopelessness, all ye who enter here."[32] It was suggested earlier that when Bernard Shaw hugged Dickens, he had squeezed the object of his affections out of shape. Shaw's Dickens is the thin man's Dickens. Chesterton, an equally strong personality, does not squeeze his subject so much as he stuffs him out of shape by overfeeding him. Chesterton's Dickens is the stout man's Dickens, the traditional Dickens, the early Dickens. *Bleak House* and the other later novels are, he admits, better constructed and more free from faults than *Nicholas Nickleby*. "But do not, if you are in the company of any ardent adorers of Dickens . . . insist too urgently . . . on the splendour of Dickens's last works, or they will discover that you do not like him."[33]

The most prominent feature of Chesterton's discussions of Dickens is certainly the exclusive emphasis he places on the Santa Claus Dickens, and contemporary criticism also finds absent from these discussions any adequate consideration of Dickens' art. He goes so far as to say that the novels "are simply lengths cut from the flowing and mixed substance called Dickens" rather than novels—a very unpromising approach.[34] Yet Chesterton, I suspect, knew what he was doing, and his instinct was sound. Instead of attempting to reply to Lewes or Saintsbury by demonstrating that Dickens' novels *do* conform to the requirements of The Novel, he said, in effect, No they do not. They belong to a different category and their probability must be judged by different, and older, standards. "Dickens was a mythologist rather than a novelist;

he was the last of the mythologists and perhaps the greatest."[35] This slashing of theoretical preconceptions was, in reality, Chesterton's major contribution towards an understanding of Dickens. His point has been effectively restated by F. R. Leavis who notes that "in our preconceptions about 'the novel,' we may miss, within the field of fictional prose, possibilities of concentration and flexibility in the interpretation of life such as we associate with Shakespearian drama."[36] As a biographer, Chesterton disappoints because he did not look closely enough at Dickens' bitterness. As a critic, he exasperates by his obtrusive lectures on the Middle Ages and on marriage customs. But that in 1906 he saw a way out of the maze, into which so much novel-criticism had stumbled, compensates for all of his exasperating habits. In one essay, he even had the perception to suggest that unity in a novel may be obtained not only by unity of construction but by unity of mood and atmosphere.[37]

Dickens makes strange bedfellows. One would rarely couple Chesterton's name with that of George Santayana, but the latter's essay on Dickens (1921) is in Chesterton's predominant strain of Christmas cheer, holly berries, and love of one's fellow creatures, however absurd the latter may be. Inspired to an intensive reading of Dickens during his residence in England throughout the first War, Santayana found in the novels the kind of consolation that John Stuart Mill found in Wordsworth's poetry at a time when abstract thought was uncongenial.[38] This essay by a non-unionized Dickensian is a wise and very beautiful tribute to the novelist's healing power, as is evident in its final, Chesterton-like sentence:

> In every English-speaking home, in the four quarters of the globe, parents and children will do well to read Dickens aloud of a winter's evening; they will love winter, and one another, and God the better for it. What a wreath that will be . . . thick with bright berries, to hang to this poet's memory.

Because Dickens is aware of appearance and reality, Santayana calls him a "good philosopher," although, on such grounds, it might have been more appropriate to call him a good writer of prose fiction, for Santayana recognizes that it is the function of Dickens' humor to pierce the mask of appearance under which social realities are hidden. "When people say Dickens exaggerates, it seems to me they can have no eyes and no ears. They probably have only *notions* of what things and people are."[39]

J. B. Priestley is yet another who has continued to present the stout man's Dickens, although somewhat attenuated by Mr. Priestley's impatience when confronted by the "outrage" of Dickensian sentiment and the "tedium" of Dickensian plots.[40] His novel, *The Good Companions*, is often said to be Dickens-like, but it is really closer to Dickens' models, the eighteenth-century novelists, than to Dickens himself. Mr. Priestley deplores in twentieth-century taste what he calls a "fixed mood of self-pity,"[41] and although few Dickensians of the healthy school will admit it, this is a mood which may be as much a part of Dickens' books as it is of such incongruously assorted writers as Ernest Hemingway, Middleton Murry, and Graham Greene. What remains for Mr. Priestley to treasure is Dickens' success in creating a world which "is terrifically alive and terrifically individual."[42] In a mechanical universe he argues (as Shelley argued on behalf of poetry), Dickens' characters keep the imagination exercised.

Chesterton's reading of Dickens reappears also in the critical writings of Sir Arthur Quiller-Couch, Sir Osbert Sitwell, and Stephen Leacock.[43] As a final example of its persistence, an essay by Desmond Fitzgerald in *World Review* (October, 1950) may be cited. Once again, Dickens' novels are used to disprove an imported naturalistic theory of fiction, this time, the theory of Jean Paul Sartre. Sartre's method, says the essayist, is to assume that reality is obtained by treating every living human being in a novel with the same scrupulous analysis, mental and physical. Dickens' method consists, instead, of dividing the world into heroes, villains, grotesques. But how do we see ourselves? Mr. Fitzgerald asks. If we are honest, he says, our own world is found to be made up of one hero, one David Copperfield, to whom everything that happens is important. "My life, then, even at its dullest, is resolved not into a realistic novel, but into an artificial melo-drama."

I V

The third general pattern of Dickens criticism since 1872 is represented by George Gissing, a realist, but a realist sympathetic to Dickens. Although Gissing (like Bennett) is a typical figure in the transition from the Victorian to the twentieth-century novel, he seems to have been untypical in his earnest attempt to make a full reappraisal of the Dickensian novel. In some respects, his critical study anticipates the work of Edmund Wilson (who considers Gissing the best of Dickens' critics), but there are many areas in which the two are poles apart.

Chesterton's opinion was that Gissing misunderstood Dickens, but even Chesterton never hinted that Gissing did not revere Dickens. It has been said that when he began to write, the novel to Gissing *was* Dickens.[44] In his letters and essays, he always speaks of his great predecessor with love.[45] Yet his was a love of the maturest variety, the Jane Austen variety, in which absurdities are frankly admitted without undermining the love itself.

An awareness of these absurdities is attributable partly to Gissing's reading of other novelists such as Balzac and Dostoevsky, and partly to his own objectives as a novelist. With critical antennae directed towards the continent, he became one of the most sensitive receptors for the new fashions in fiction during the eighties and nineties. In the light of these new conventions, Gissing had to admit, reluctantly, that Howells and other realistic critics were right about his beloved English novelist. "So great a change has come over the theory and practice of fiction in the England of our times that we must needs treat of Dickens as, in many respects, antiquated."[46] Most antiquated of all, for Gissing, was the Master's reckless habit, shared by Hardy, of abusing coincidence. Of *Bleak House*, he writes: "It seems never to have occurred to him, thus far in his career, that novels and fairy tales (or his favourite *Arabian Nights*) should obey different laws in the matter of incident."[47] Equally quaint, in Gissing's eyes, was Dickens' fondness for improbable pictures of the poor.[48]

That Gissing was especially sensitive to such improbabilities was owing not only to his more intimate knowledge of the London poor but to his own aims as a novelist. At the outset of his career, he announced: "I mean to carry home to people the ghastly condition (material, mental, and moral) of our poor classes."[49] In his first novel, *Workers in the Dawn*, he portrays a feast at the Pettindund boarding-house which is startlingly different from the dinner at Todgers's or even the accounts of American boarding-houses in *Martin Chuzzlewit*. The sordid bestiality of the Pettindund scene is never relieved for a moment. Satire, sympathy, humor—all are absent. Later novels such as *The Nether World* also serve as commentaries upon Dickens' distortions. The peripheral scene of the drunken brickmaker's family in *Bleak House* becomes, in Gissing's novels, the central scene. The world of *La bête humaine* is imported by him to a London setting.*

As a critic and as a devoted reader of Dickens, Gissing's task was to salvage what he could from a flood which seemed to be washing away everything of the earlier novelist except perhaps his humor. What he saved was a great deal. His two books on Dickens consist, essentially, of fresh explorations of the problem of literary probability. He deals with it in two ways. First of all, he contends that there is a very considerable quantity of Dickens' writing that consistently adheres to the conventions of realism and for which no explanation is necessary. Anthony Chuzzlewit's funeral, for example,

---

* Gissing often criticized Dickens for failing to record realistically the coarse language of underworld characters such as Sikes, yet he was still bound by the conventions himself. In *The Nether World*, we are often told that Clem Peckover screamed obscenities at her husband, but we never learn what they were. As Gissing comments, she "made the room ring with foul abuse, that vituperative vernacular of the nether world, which has never yet been exhibited by typography, and presumably never will be." Gissing died in 1903, too early to foresee that his conventions would eventually seem as quaint as those of Dickens seemed to him.

contains not the slightest hint of "extravagance"—the scene is "such realism as no other novelist ever came near unto; for it is mere straightforward describing and narrating, without a hint of effort; and there stands the thing for ever."[50] To say that a scene is not extravagant is, from Gissing, the highest of compliments. It is typical that the fantastic Sapsea inscription in *Edwin Drood*, which provoked Chesterton to raptures, drew from Gissing a severe judgment against such a "piece of exaggeration altogether exceeding the limits of art."[51] His praise of what is unexaggerated is, however, abundant, especially in his delightful discussion of Dickens' gallery of "detestable widows, wives, and spinsters." That Gissing himself felt strongly about the motiveless shrewishness of "women who are the curse of their husbands' lives" is evident, and he gathers together an extraordinary collection including Mrs. Bumble, Mrs. Sowerberry, Mrs. Varden, Mrs. Gargery, Miss Miggs, Mrs. Gummidge, Mrs. Jellyby, Mrs. Pocket, Mrs. Weller, and Mrs. Snagsby. Of these, he says, "not a word, not a gesture, goes beyond the very truth."[52] Similar praise is also bestowed upon the portrait of old Dorrit in a novel which Gissing admired not like Shaw for its social criticism, but for the mature artistic power of its parts.

Gissing's attempt to answer Lewes by decking Dickens out in the drab colors of realism was a helpful corrective in criticism, but, as he himself recognized, it was by no means the whole story. There remained the great bulk of Dickens' writing which obviously violated realistic conventions for the novel. Gissing's solution was to abandon some of it as childish or as merely sensational. Mysteries and murders, for example, were of little interest to him; *Edwin Drood* he considered a mistake. What remained he labelled with the same term which had been used by David Masson in 1851. He called it "idealized" art and then set out to make an interesting explanation of it in terms of public taste.

His explanation is as revealing, in its way, as his appreciation of Dickens' scolding women. From his own lack of popularity as a novelist, and from his observation of the reading public even during the hey-day of realism, Gissing came to the conclusion that few readers can enjoy the objective presentation of the dullness of life.* As one of his novelist characters remarks in *New Grub Street*: "If it were anything *but* tedious it would be untrue." Humor, he realized, distorts reality, but it makes at least some degree of reality palatable to the reading public. A scene such as the half-starving of the Marchioness by Sally Brass, if presented in the purely realistic vein, would be intolerable in its unpleasantness (as Gissing's own novels can illustrate). But presented with Dickens' "inextricable blending of horrors and jocosity," the scene becomes enjoyable and powerfully effective for most readers (including Gissing himself).[53]

Gissing's dilemma in this part of his discussion is painful enough to be felt. As a novelist he was committed to one attitude towards literature. Its basic premise was that whether the reader finds a book repulsive or tedious does not matter, and Gissing was therefore deeply disturbed by Dickens' habit of distorting reality so as to please his readers. Yet judging by the event, by the work itself, he was equally disturbed by how often this "idealization" was appropriate and artistic. His solution for the dilemma was impressionistic. Sometimes Dickens' "idealism," especially his theatricality, he shows to be painfully incredible; on other occasions it is functional and beyond question. Of Falstaff and Mrs. Gamp, he writes:

> The literary power exhibited . . . is of the same kind; the same perfect method of idealism is put to use in converting to a source of pleasure things that in life repel or nauseate and in both cases the sublimation of character, of circumstance, is effected by a humour which seems unsurpassable.[54]

An earnest and unexuberant scholar, Gissing wrote the most reasonable and thoughtful appraisal of Dickens' achievement. The modest good sense of his argument does not make him a favorite with Dickensians, but many of the critical questions he raised are with us still. The tendency of all

---

* Part IV of Dostoevsky's *The Idiot* opens with an interesting discussion of this same problem.

critics to shape Dickens after their own preconceptions is not, of course, absent from his studies. Like almost any reader of good sense in his day, he had little use for the symbolical or allegorical, and he assumed that it would be pointless to look for such qualities in Dickens' work. Hugo, he said, was a master of "symbolic art"; Dickens was no such thing.[55] "Heaven forbid that I should attribute to Dickens a deliberate allegory," he writes.[56] In the light of more recent criticism, Gissing's assumption has itself, in turn, become antiquated. We may find it to be the comment of a more literal-minded than a literary-minded critic. Also somewhat quaint is his reluctance to regard Dickens' novels, even the later ones, as containing any bitterness of spirit. One scene in *Little Dorrit* seemed to him completely untypical because it was spirit-crushing, and even the fog in *Bleak House* he considered to be "rather cheerful than otherwise."[57] The legend (as it seems to later readers) of Dickens' unquenchable cheerfulness could not be more tellingly illustrated than by Gissing's overlooking the "contemptible and hateful" persons who people the world of *Bleak House* and *Our Mutual Friend* just as they people the world of *Le père Goriot* and *Le cousin Pons*.[58]

V

However admirable Gissing's reply to Lewes' attack may be, it leads to a dead end in criticism. For Gissing's attitude towards reality and towards the novel was virtually the same as that of Lewes himself. He answers Lewes in Lewes' own terms. Critical descendants of the two groups of admirers and non-admirers could go on endlessly replying to each other like Tweedledum and Tweedledee. What was needed was a different approach to fiction and to the world which fiction represents. Among the last group of critical readers who remain to be discussed, there is to be sensed, in various degrees, a significant shift away from the very premises upon which Lewes' objections rest. Kipling once predicted that as time passed Dickens' novels would become more and more modern.[59] His accurate prediction meant, I suppose, that the apprehension of experience by later generations would correspond more closely to Dickens' imagined world than to the point of view of Kipling's contemporaries.

As has been indicated, G. K. Chesterton anticipated the shift, but his eccentric wheedling and his incapacity to taste the acrid ingredients in Dickens' bitter-sweet mixture have obscured his flashes of insight. It is interesting to compare him, on this point, with a later writer and co-religionist, Graham Greene. Instead of concentrating upon the face-values of the plot of *Oliver Twist*, Mr. Greene discusses the real impact of the book: its capacity to arouse the reader's fear of a Manichean universe in which goodness seems helpless before the reality of evil:

> Is it too fantastic to imagine that in this novel, as in many of his later books, creeps in, unrecognized by the author, the eternal and alluring taint of the Manichee, with its simple and terrible explanation of our plight, how the world was made by Satan and not by God, lulling us with the music of despair?[60]

In Edmund Wilson's essays, which first appeared in 1940, this awareness of the bitterness in Dickens' novels, especially the later ones, is more fully developed. That the whole range of Dickens is not adequately explored by such an approach has been subsequently admitted by Mr. Wilson,[61] but the corrective value of his sober portrait of the man and of his writings remains evident. For the question raised is not whether Dickens' books are optimistic or pessimistic (a question dear to the hearts of the luncheon clubs), but whether they represent life in such a way that the mature reader may find in them mature satisfactions. What Kipling meant by the word *modern* is not clear. It rarely is. But most contemporary readers would agree on at least one denominator: that after the Buchenwald decades, a writer who remains as blissfully unaware of the power of human evil as some of the Christmas-card admirers would have us believe Dickens remained would deserve only our most casual attention.

The recognition that Dickens' world might be closer to that of Swift than to that of Samuel Smiles was an essential preliminary. In part, of course, Mr. Wilson's interpretation was anticipated by the insistence of both Shaw and T. A. Jackson upon Dickens' importance as a social critic, but with the aid of later biographical information, he goes further. He explores the root causes of Dickens' dissatisfactions as a man and the complexities of his themes as a social critic. The words *complexity* and *depth* are the key words in his discussion. He sees Dickens as the writer most antagonistic to the Victorian age (or what is usually assumed to have been the Victorian age), who enjoyed, in the creation of his criminals and rebels, an outlet for his antagonisms.[62]

Although Mr. Wilson's study is primarily a fresh portrait of the man, it also employs a fresh approach to the novels. He is aware, first of all, that we are dealing with a great novelist, rather than with a political economist, whose function is to make the reader share experiences through concrete persons and concrete objects. Moreover, in Dickens, the persons and objects may also have symbolic function:

> The people who talk about the symbols of Kafka and Mann and Joyce have been discouraged from looking for anything of the kind in Dickens, and usually have not read him, at least with mature minds. But even when we think we do know Dickens, we may be surprised to return to him and find in him a symbolism of a more complicated reference and deeper implication than these metaphors that hang as emblems over the door. The Russians themselves, in this respect, appear to have learned from Dickens.[63]

Mr. Wilson's lead has been followed up, somewhat belligerently, by Jack Lindsay who speaks of

> Dickens's power to draw characters in a method of intense poetic simplification, which makes them simultaneously social emblems, emotional symbols, and visually precise individuals. This is the method of so-called exaggeration or caricature, for which he has been berated by thin-blooded intellectuals, philistine nat-

uralists, and those for whom "psychology" means introspection.[64]

Edmund Wilson's application of such a reading to single novels, especially to *Bleak House*, *Little Dorrit*, and *Our Mutual Friend*, marks a turning point in the discussion of Dickens' status. The fog in *Bleak House*, which to the literal-minded can be dismissed as a superfluous display of descriptive detail, is shown to be an indispensable device for unifying the theme of obfuscation into the structure of the whole story. Later essays by other critics have followed a similar method of analysis, and it becomes apparent that whether or not Dickens was a stone age artist, he was most certainly a great artist. F. R. Leavis, in his brilliant analysis of *Hard Times*, refers repeatedly to the rightness of an art by which "the symbolic intention emerges out of metaphor and the vivid evocation of the concrete."[65] The method reappears in a study of *Oliver Twist* by Arnold Kettle in 1951. Dr. Kettle is not troubled by Dr. Leavis' scruples concerning Dickens' "place." He ranks him, in fact, as "the greatest of the English novelists."[66] His essay is another attempt to penetrate below the face-values of the plot to seek the meaning and method of a Dickens novel.

> What distinguishes the opening chapters of *Oliver Twist* from, on the one side, a social history and, on the other side, *Emma*, is that they are symbolic. It is not a sense of participation in the personal emotions of any of the characters that engages our imagination but a sense of participation in a world that is strikingly, appallingly relevant to our world.[67]

Similarly, in Dorothy Van Ghent's excellent essay on the function of Dickens' imagery, especially the imagery of *Great Expectations*, and in Robert Morse's discussion of *Our Mutual Friend*, we encounter other striking examples of the valuable insights that can be obtained by applying this method of penetration.[68] In *Charles Dickens: His Tragedy and Triumph* (1952), by Edgar Johnson, which has effectively brought together many of the findings of recent criticism, the word *symbolic* recurs again and again, and the author's best critical analyses are centered on such symbolic devices as the ice in *Dombey and Son* or on the resemblances between the richly mythological Thames setting of *Our Mutual Friend* and that of T. S. Eliot's *Waste Land*. In *The Cult of Power* (1947), Rex Warner likens Dickens' method to Dostoevsky's in that both novelists seek symbols to link the criminal to the acquisitive drives of respectable society, and in his essay on "The Allegorical Method," he singles out *Bleak House* as an admirable example of such art.[69] A year later, in an essay by Edward Sackville-West, there is praise of Dickens as the forerunner of Kafka.[70]

What we are witnessing in these studies is a critical revolution, or, more exactly, a counter-revolution. The reader who remains entirely hostile to Dickens' work may assert that all that has really happened is the development of some new critical terms, a kind of mumbo jumbo, and that Lewes' case against the Dickens novel remains untouched. But the new vocabulary is really only a reflection of a more profound shift. In brief, it would seem that the effort of late nineteenth-century novel-critics to set up criteria which would consistently differentiate the novel from poetry and from drama was a necessary effort but one which has now spent its force. As the wave has receded, there has been a need to reassess those aspects of Dickens' work which had not conformed to a rigid conception of The Novel, and to restore him to the status he held among his more perceptive contemporaries.

In the midst of this reassessment, critics have been fond of drawing parallels between Dickens and Joyce, or Lawrence, or Dostoevsky (as has already been indicated), or Kafka. We may sometimes want to protest that Dickens is more like Dickens than he is like any other writer. His note is surely distinctive enough. Yet the urge to draw these comparisons is understandable. It is a protest against the kind of reader who still wishes to confine him to the level of a childhood classic. Moreover, the four novelists cited are appropriately chosen not because each has been the idol of various cults in England during recent decades, but because all four have a similar attitude towards the possible range of prose fiction.

Joyce seems the least promising for comparison. In the Oxen of the Sun passages in *Ulysses*, there is a rollicking parody of the sentimental prose in which the death of Dora in *David Copperfield* had been described.[71] Yet *Ulysses*, with its elaborate blending of symbolistic and realistic narrative, its emphasis upon the myths of basic human experience, did more towards preparing for the reinterpretation of Dickens than did Bennett's *Old Wives' Tale* or J. B. Priestley's *The Good Companions*. I mean that such novelists as Joyce and Lawrence anticipated the counter-revolution in criticism which we have been tracing, and that criticism, in devising ways of coping with their narratives, has been aided in coping with those of Dickens.

Even more than Joyce, D. H. Lawrence is obviously a bull in the novel shop. His almost excessive vitality, his animism, and his conception of the novel as a "lively chaos" make such a work as *The Rainbow* unclassifiable. "He so surcharges his characters with vitality that they seem like persons who have taken something to drink; and as they burst into the more decorous society delineated by other English novelists, there is a cry raised for the critical police."[72] This judgment, passed upon Dickens in 1867, I have requoted here because it sounds very familiar; word for word it could be transposed to almost any review of Lawrence's experimental fiction.

That Kafka, like Dostoevsky, was directly indebted to Dickens we know from the testimony of his diary. He could be critical of Dickens' faults, and it is interesting that his complaints might be applied equally well to the work of Lawrence. He refers to "Dickens' opulence and great, careless prodigality, but in consequence passages of awful insipidity in which he wearily works over effects he has already achieved. Gives one a barbaric impression . . . that I . . . thanks to my weakness . . . have been able to avoid."[73] If Kafka's novels resemble those of Dickens, it is not in any overflowing Lawrence-like vitalism. He himself speaks of valuing Dickens' "method." The opening chapter of his novel

America he describes as "a sheer imitation of Dickens," and the whole projected novel, he says, was "even more so." Kafka specifies *David Copperfield* as his source although the incorrigible innocence of the hero of *America* may remind us equally often of Oliver Twist. After listing several parallels, he adds: "It was my intention, as I now see, to write a Dickens novel, but enhanced by the sharper lights I should have taken from the times and the duller ones I should have got from myself."[74] Although Kafka's reputation in England may have passed its peak,[75] there must still be many readers to whom these words would be a potent recommendation for a reexploration of Dickens' "method."

One way of pointing up the parallels very briefly is to consider three novels which are concerned with the Law. James G. Cozzens' *The Just and the Unjust* contains several scenes in which the nature of Law is discussed as it is also discussed in the interview between Richard Carstone and Mr. Vholes in *Bleak House* and between Joseph K. and the chaplain in Kafka's *The Trial.* But the similarity is one of situation only, for if Mr. Cozzens' scenes are examined more closely, we become aware of an immense gap. His scenes are admirable examples of conventional realism. We get from them a wise and sensible report concerning various difficulties in the administration of justice. The novelist is aware of these difficulties, but he is never really bewildered by them for a moment. Neither is his reader. *The Just and the Unjust* thus consists of straightforward narrative without a trace of incongruous humor, or of poetry, or of any kind of symbolical overtones. In *Bleak House*, as was suggested earlier, we have the same *kind* of feeling in listening to Mr. Vholes as we have in listening to Kafka's priest or to the lawyers who reply to K.'s enquiries. There is a sense of endlessly bewildering muddle, a muddle so immense that it becomes painfully funny. It is in this sense that *Bleak House* and *The Trial* obviously belong in one category, and *The Just and the Unjust* in another.

On the other hand, because Kafka is primarily concerned with the apparent muddle of Divine Law, and Dickens with the actual muddle of human law, there are also inevitable differences in their methods. Kafka's method is closer to allegory, and hence his law courts are further removed from the law courts in Mr. Cozzens' novel than are those of Dickens. What is symbolical is always literally true, and the symbolical significance can be passed over if the reader wishes (the fog in *Bleak House* is real fog, and the snow in Joyce's story "The Dead" is real snow; as such they are typical symbols). What is allegorical may be more convincing or vivid as a nightmare is convincing or vivid, but literal correspondence to ordinary experience is not required, and the reader can hardly escape the realization that the narrative is moving on two levels (at least two levels). *A Christmas Carol* might be cited as a kind of Dickensian allegory, but his usual preference is for the symbolical. With Kafka, the preference is reversed. Although *The Castle* is more sophisticated than *Pilgrim's Progress*, it is evident that its method is much closer to Bunyan's than Dickens ever came. *Bleak House* therefore represents a mid-point between the method of *Pilgrim's Progress* at one extreme and *The Just and the Unjust* at the other.

This discussion has been raised partly to reinforce the platitude that Dickens is Dickens and that Kafka is Kafka. The resemblances are, however, important reminders. Once again the experiments of a respected twentieth-century novelist prepared the ground for the crop of critical studies of Dickens' art which we have been considering. Dickens' demonstration of the variety of methods open to the novelist—a variety suggested by these comparisons to such a mixed assortment of other novelists—seems to derive from a richer conception of fiction than the premises held by Lewes and his ilk. In a sense, some of Lewes' objections to Dickens have been not so much answered (as Gissing tried to do) but by-passed. Like Kipling, Chesterton once remarked upon the challenge that Dickens offers to later readers: "Thackeray has become classical; but Dickens has done more: he has remained modern."[76] Chesterton's verdict was written in 1911. Over forty years later, it seems more readily applicable and more firmly based upon developments in modern literature and criticism.

The example of Chesterton's contemporary, Paul Elmer More, will further illustrate this development. In an essay of 1908, More speaks of his deep affection for Dickens' novels and of his enjoying an "orgy of tears and laughter" while devouring a set of these writings. Yet More's was a strange kind of blind love. He was quite literally afraid that if he exerted his critical faculties while reading Dickens, the love would evaporate. His books, he decided, "will not bear analysis."[77] Perhaps the most refreshing aspect of the more recent study of Dickens is the repeated demonstration that his novels can thrive upon analysis, and that his vitality is not a kind of fake vitality, a midnight mask of life which vanishes under the sober daylight of the breakfast-cups.

V I

In many respects the present study could have been appropriately entitled "The Variety of Dickens," for it is the infinite variety of his writings which is responsible for the seemingly infinite variety of ways in which they have been read since 1836. Jeffrey and Landor were among the earliest to compare him to Shakespeare, and the comparison has since become commonplace whenever the gallery of Dickens' characters is being discussed. It was a comparison that raised the fastidious hackles of George Meredith and other readers, but there is one sense in which it is less disputable. In an article entitled "Why Dickens is Popular," a simple answer is arrived at: "because he has something for everybody."[78] Just as Shakespeare's readers include, at one extreme, the kind who relish Polonius as the embodiment of infinite wisdom, and, at the opposite extreme, such subtle critical analysts as Wilson Knight, so the millions of readers who have laughed, or cried, or yawned their way through Dickens' books have responded in a wide variety of ways, each under the impression that his *Little Dorrit* is *the Little Dorrit*. To judge from the comments passed after a concert, one may sometimes wonder whether the individuals who made up the audience were listening to the same piece of music.

The picture of Dickens' overall qualities is also a various one. T. S. Eliot has noted that in the twentieth century there has emerged a fatigued Shakespeare, a messianic Shakespeare, a ferocious Shakespeare, and a Socialist journalist Shakespeare.[79] There is likewise a messianic Dickens (the discovery of G. B. Shaw), a ferocious Dickens (appearing in Jack Lindsay's study), and a Socialist journalist Dickens whose appearances are frequent. As yet, no one has produced a fatigued Dickens; there would be certain obvious difficulties, but there is always a benevolent and cheerful Dickens as well as a gloomy Dickens whose books fill us with despair. As Auden wrote after the death of Yeats:

> The words of a dead man
> Are modified in the guts of the living.

To the critical dogmatist, such variety must seem a deplorable anarchy. It is actually one of the surest signs of literary immortality. Even to be misunderstood is a privilege accorded only to the greatest writers. Viewed from the perspective of the present survey, what is equally remarkable is the diversity of readers who have esteemed his work. Alice Meynell and T. A. Jackson, Francis Jeffrey and the editor of the *People's Journal*, G. B. Shaw and G. K. Chesterton, William Ewart Gladstone and Algernon Swinburne, H. G. Wells and Feodor Dostoevsky, George Orwell and Katherine Mansfield, Benjamin Jowett and William Randolph Hearst—what a strange arkful do these pairs make!

That harmony would reign in such an ark is hardly to be expected. If Dickens had left only his *Pickwick Papers* and no *Little Dorrit*, or only *Little Dorrit* and no *Pickwick Papers*, it might more easily have been achieved. As it is, the variety of ways in which his books have been read indicates why, of all our novelists, he is the most difficult to assess adequately. As Robert Morse noted in 1949: "It is harder to sum up Dickens in a phrase or two than almost any other writer except Shakespeare or Dante."[80]

An awareness of this variety may sometimes make the task of synthesis seem too overwhelming a challenge for criticism, because it may increase the difficulties to the point of discouragement. Yet the risk is worth taking. To be suspicious of the critical arrogance which finds in one phase of Dickens' novels the whole of Dickens is an essential step towards synthesis. He had, for example, more than his fair share of moral indignation, but the reports of what such readers as Chesterton enjoyed in his books remind us that any critic, however well disposed, who singles out moral indignation as the exclusive quality of Dickens' writings is obviously misleading us. Similarly, to review what other earlier readers have found helps us to discredit other kinds of distortion and caricature, especially those of the moral and aesthetic dogmatists who labor to set up some prescribed concept of The Novel in which there is no place for Dickens' Gothic masterpieces. Any eccentric account of the tradition of the English novel which finds no place for them will be glaringly incomplete as an account of the pleasures of prose fiction.

What seems to be needed for future discussions of Dickens is the capacity to apply an awareness of the various qualities of his work to a further close reading of individual novels. Here again, as often happens, one of his Victorian admirers provides a suggestion. In 1889, a group of visitors to Burne-Jones' studio were comparing Zola with some earlier English novelists. It was affirmed that readers were tired of Dickens and Thackeray, having read them too much. "No, they haven't read them too much," replied the Dickensian host, "but they hurry through them and don't see how good they are."[81]

APPENDIX

DICKENS' AWARENESS OF REVIEWS

THE following is a collection of some of Dickens' scattered references to reviews, notices, and essays, which contain discussions of his writings. In view of his fondness for reading such publications as the *Athenaeum*, the *Examiner*, the *Illustrated London News*, and *The Times*, it is likely that his eye fell upon many other notices for which we have no record. On January 7, 1846, he wrote to Miss Coutts: "I see almost daily in those sources of intelligence [newspapers] the most prodigious accounts of my occupations, invitations &c. &c., which are all so new to me that they make my hair stand on end." If he stumbled upon such items of biographical information, it must have been difficult for him, despite his heroic resolution taken in 1838, to avoid stumbling upon some critical notices as well.

Herein is the principal value of the following collection. By exposing a few outcroppings of the vein, we become aware that it must have been a more extensive one than has hitherto been supposed.

A second problem, that of specifying what reviews were responsible for the defensive tactics displayed in Dickens' prefaces, has not been attempted here. Occasionally his prefaces make specific references (G. H. Lewes' articles in the *Leader*, for example, are replied to in the Preface to *Bleak House*), but usually one would have to rely upon guesswork. See above pp. 50-54.

References to the Nonesuch edition of Dickens' letters, from which most of the following derives, are indicated by volume number and page. At the conclusion of each entry, I have tried to indicate the likelihood of Dickens' having himself actually *read* the review or notice.

1. *Sketches by Boz.*   By George Hogarth, *Morning Chronicle* (February 5, 1836). Ref. February 11, 1836 (i, 65) to "Hogarth's beautiful notice." Definite.

2. *Sketches by Boz.*   Three notices, unspecified. Ref. February 14, 1836 (I, 65). Possible.

3. *Sketches by Boz.*   The *Morning Post* (March 12, 1836). Ref. April 1836 (I, 69). Definite.

4. *The Village Coquettes.*   The *Examiner, Sunday Times, Dispatch,* and *Satirist.* Ref. December 11, 1836 (I, 93). The latter three "blow their little trumpets against me, most lustily." Definite.

5. *Pickwick Papers.*   *Fraser's Magazine* (1836). Ref. 1836 (I, 72). Definite.

6. *Pickwick Papers.*   By John Forster, *Examiner* (July 2, 1837). Ref. July 2, 1837 (I, 115). Definite.

7. *Pickwick Papers.*   By Abraham Hayward, *Quarterly*, LIX (October 1837), 484-518. Ref. October, and November 3, 1837 (I, 131). Hoped that creation of Nancy would defy Hayward and all his works. Definite.

8. General.   By Harrison Ainsworth, preface to *Rookwood* (1837). Ref. October 30, 1837 (I, 134). Contains discussion of Dickens' promise. Definite.

9. General.   Review not specified, 1839. Ref. Edgar Johnson, *Charles Dickens*, I, 226. After reading a review attacking his lack of originality, Dickens is reported to have exclaimed: "They shall eat their words!" Definite.

10. *The Old Curiosity Shop.*   By Thomas Hood, *Athenaeum* (November 7, 1840). Ref. March 18, 1845 (I, 665). Definite.

11. *American Notes.*   *Fraser's* (November 1842), pp. 617-629. Ref. December 31, 1842 (I, 497) to the "miserable creature" who wrote this attack. Dickens implies that he has not the "diseased curiosity" to have read the review, but we know that he did read the *Blackwood's* review mentioned in the same letter. Possible.

12. *American Notes.*   By Samuel Warren, *Blackwood's* (December 1842), pp. 783-801. Ref. December 31, 1842 (I, 497). Dickens' indignant reply appears in *The Times*, July 16, 1843, p. 5. Definite.

13. *American Notes.*   By James Spedding, *Edinburgh* (January 1843), pp. 497-522. Ref. January 21, 1843 (I, 504, 507, 509). A letter of protest to Napier. Definite.

14. *American Notes.*   *North American Review* (January 1843), pp. 58-62. Ref. March 2, 1843 (I, 509). Definite.

15. General.   By John Lockhart, "Theodore Hook: A Sketch," *Quarterly* (June 1843). Ref. June 2, 1843 (I, 524). Contains comparison of Hook with Dickens. Definite.

16. *Martin Chuzzlewit.*   Unspecified reviews. Ref. November 2, 1843 (I, 545-546) to "knaves and idiots" having delayed the sale of the novel. Probable.

17. *A Christmas Carol.* By Thackeray, *Fraser's* (February 1844), pp. 153-169. Ref. *Letters of Thackeray*, II, 135, 165. Definite.

18. General. R. H. Horne, *A New Spirit of the Age* (1844). Ref. March 19, 1844 (I, 583). Dickens referred to the seventy-four page essay on himself. He found the book "syncretic" but said that he had no objection to the essay except for its portrait. It was rumored, however, that he was dissatisfied. See *Letters of Browning to Elizabeth Barrett*, I, 69. Definite.

19. *A Christmas Carol* and other works. In a review of Horne's *A New Spirit of the Age* in the *Westminster Review*, XLI (June 1844), 185-187. Ref. October 1844 (I, 632) to *Westminster's* having "considered Scrooge's presentation of the turkey to Bob Cratchit as grossly incompatible with political economy." The Utilitarian reviewer had noted: "Who went without turkey and punch in order that Bob Cratchit might get them . . . is a disagreeable reflection kept wholly out of sight [by Dickens]." Definite.

20. *A Christmas Carol.* By Douglas Jerrold in *Punch*. Ref. November 16, 1844 (I, 638) to the "affectionate mention of the Carol." Definite.

21. *The Cricket on the Hearth.* American reviews, not specified. Ref. March 4, 1846 (I, 740) to reviews which have begun to praise him again. Unread; only learned general gist.

22. *The Battle of Life.* By Samuel Phillips, *The Times* (January 2, 1847). Ref. January 5, 1847 (II, 3, 20, 207) to "another touch of a blunt razor." Definite.

23. *Dombey and Son.* By Charles Kent in the *Sun* (April 13, 1848). Ref. April 14, 1848 (II, 78-79). Definite.

24. *David Copperfield* and other works. By David Masson, *North British Review* (May 1851), pp. 57-89. On May 9, Dickens wrote to Masson thanking him. See Flora Masson, *Victorians All* (1931), p. 9. Definite.

25. *Bleak House.* *Illustrated London News* (September 24, 1853), p. 247. Ref. October 24, 1859 (III, 129-130) to paragraph concerning Skimpole. Possible.

26. *Hard Times.* *Illustrated London News* (1854, not traced). Ref. March 11, 1854 (II, 545-546). The date assigned in Nonesuch may be an error. Definite.

27. General. Report of Thackeray's lecture in *The Times* (March 23, 1855). Ref. same date (II, 645). Definite.

28. *Little Dorrit* and general. *Blackwood's* (April 1857), pp. 490-503. Ref. July 1857 (II, 861) to his having encountered an extract from the review in the *Globe*, including a reference to *Dorrit* as "twaddle." Definite.

29. *Little Dorrit.* By Fitzjames Stephen, *Edinburgh* (July

1857), pp. 124-156. Ref. a reply by Dickens in *Household Words* (August 1, 1857). Definite.

30. General.   J. Cordy Jeaffreson, *Novels and Novelists* (1858), 2 vols. Jeaffreson later reported that Dickens wrote him two or three letters in 1858. Although he does not quote from the letters, it seems highly likely that Dickens must have written them after reading Jeaffreson's important discussion of his novels. See J. C. Jeaffreson, *A Book of Recollections* (1894), I, 272. Very probable.

31. General.   Unspecified notices. Ref. August 2, 1859 (III, 114) to "coarse and unreasonable attacks I have seen on myself personally." See also "A Fly-Leaf on Life," in *The Uncommercial Traveller*. The reference may be to his domestic situation or to the offensive tactics of the *Saturday Review*. Definite.

32. *Our Mutual Friend.*   By H. F. Chorley, *Athenaeum* (October 28, 1865). Ref. same date (III, 441). Definite.

33. Public readings.   Edinburgh newspapers. Ref. April 19, 1866 (III, 468) to "commonplaces" usually written by newspapers concerning his success as a reader. Definite.

34. General.   Percy Fitzgerald, *Charles Lamb* (1866), pp. 221-229. Ref. February 2, 1866 (III, 459) to Fitzgerald's discussion of Dickens. Definite.

CHAPTER 1

THE PROSPERING OF PICKWICK

1. According to Anthony Trollope, 800,000 copies of *Pickwick* were sold in England before copyright expired. See "Novel-Reading," *Nineteenth Century*, v (1879), 33. See also Mowbray Morris, "Charles Dickens," *Fortnightly Review*, n.s. XXXII (1882), 762; F. G. Kitton, "The True Story of Pickwick," *Temple Bar*, LXXIX (1887), 380-381, and "The Immortal Pickwick," *Library Review*, 1892, p. 158.

2. F. G. Kitton, *Charles Dickens by Pen and Pencil* (1890), p. 145.

3. See the *Dickensian*, XXXII (1936), 43-50; *Southern Literary Messenger*, II (June 1836), 458; and also Gerald G. Grubb's three articles on Poe and Dickens in *Nineteenth-Century Fiction*, v, 1950.

4. James T. Hillhouse, *The Waverley Novels and their Critics* (Minneapolis, 1936), p. 248.

5. *Quarterly Review*, LXIV (1839), 84.

6. Hesketh Pearson, *The Smith of Smiths* (1948), p. 345.

7. See Thomas A. Trollope, *What I Remember* (1887), II, 110; *The Friendships of Mary Russell Mitford*, ed. A. G. L'Estrange (1882), II, 26.

8. See Irma Rantavaara, *Dickens in the Light of English Criticism* (Helsinki, 1944), p. 25.

9. Lady Rosina Bulwer, *Cheveley* (1839), II, 144.

10. *The Life of Mary Russell Mitford*, ed. A. G. L'Estrange (1870), III, 78.—In his introduction to *The Heart of Midlothian*, Scott comments with amusement upon the surreptitious reading of novels by judges on the bench.

11. See the *Dickensian*, XXVIII (1932), 240; *Fraserian Papers of William Maginn*, ed. R. S. Mackenzie (New York, 1857), p. 331.

12. G. O. Trevelyan, *Life and Letters of Lord Macaulay* (New York, 1876), I, 405. According to Amy Cruse, the whole English colony in India anxiously awaited the arrival of numbers of *Pickwick*. See *The Victorians and their Reading* (Boston, 1936), p. 153.

13. Herman Merivale, "About Two Great Novelists," *Temple Bar*, LXXXIII (1888), 201.

14. *Works of Ruskin*, XXXV, 303. On the other hand, the *Edinburgh* reviewer considered the Wellers untypical, and Tony, in particular, to be archaic. The *Quarterly* reviewer complained because of the literary allusions in their speeches.

15. *The Memories of Dean Hole*, 1892, p. 89.

16. "Remonstrance with Dickens," *Blackwood's Edinburgh Magazine*, LXXXI (1857), 491.

17. *National Magazine* (December 1837), quoted by W. Miller and E. H. Strange, *A Centenary Bibliography of the Pickwick Papers* (1936), p. 167.

18. *Quarterly Review*, LIX (1837), 484.

19. *London Quarterly Review*, XXXV (1871), 268.

20. *Athenaeum*, December 3, 1836, p. 841.

21. E. P. Whipple attributed its success to its "freshness" after the public had become surfeited by a diet of silver fork novels. Whipple's explanation has some merit but overlooks the existence of the more vigorous writings of Hook, Egan, and Surtees which shared popularity with the Silver Fork School during the 1830's. See "Charles Dickens," *North American Review,* LXIX (1849), 392.

22. J. B. Priestley, *The English Comic Characters* (1925), p. 201.

23. Letter to Dickens published by the New York *Daily Tribune,* October 7, 1883.

24. Pierce Egan, *Finish to the Adventures of Tom, Jerry, and Logic* (1887), p. 21. The phrases used by Egan in his Preface were coined by one of his imitators.

25. In the *Eclectic Review* (April 1837) a complaint was raised that *Pickwick* contained "some jokes, incidents and allusions, which could hardly be read by a modest woman without blushing." Quoted in *Dickensiana,* p. xiv.

26. *Edinburgh Review,* LXVIII (1838), 77.

27. A review of the opening number in the *Spectator* (April 16, 1836) notes that Boz "makes butts of some Cockneys" by ridicule.

28. Irving's letter to Dickens (May 20, 1841) published in the New York *Daily Tribune,* October 7, 1883.—A detailed discussion of the resemblance between Mr. Pickwick and Don Quixote was developed by Matthew Browne in the *Contemporary Review,* XXXVIII (1880), 162-176.

29. The reviewer found Dickens' "*come-and-go* characters" convincing, but not the "*standing*" characters. Mr. Pickwick "commences as a butt and ends as a hero" and is therefore "*not* like the men and the women of the real world." *Fraser's,* XXI (April 1840), 382, 391.

30. I am grateful to Howard D. Roelofs for this report of Mr. Auden's address which was delivered in New York, 1951.

31. *Edinburgh Review,* LXVIII (1838), 76.

32. *Quarterly Review,* LIX (1837), 507. Similar praise of Dickens appears in Harrison Ainsworth's Preface to *Rookwood* (October 18, 1837).

33. James Thurber, *The Beast in Me* (New York, 1948), p. 74.

34. Richard Aldington, *Four English Portraits* (1948), p. 175. See Flaubert's *Correspondance* (Paris, 1926-30), no. 1312 (July 12, 1872).

35. *Westminster Review,* XXVI (1864), 415.

CHAPTER 2

POPULARITIES AND CONVENTIONS

1. *North British Review,* III (1845), 66.—I have the impression that a higher proportion of authorial comment is to be found in *Oliver Twist* than in most of Dickens' novels.

2. Nonesuch, I, 647-648.

3. *Speeches,* pp. 146-147.

4. See Nonesuch, II, 797.

5. J. W. Cross, *George Eliot's Life as Related in her Letters and Journals* (New York, n.d.), II, 65, 192, and III, 36, 62.

6. *Ibid.*, II, 68.

7. *Scribner's Magazine*, IV (1888), 126.

8. Calverley's examination paper has been reprinted in the *Dickensian*, XXXII (1936), 51-54. The second prize was won by Walter Besant (1836-1901), who later put his knowledge of *Pickwick* to profitable use when he became a popular imitator of Dickens' novels.

9. *Lady John Russell: A Memoir*, ed. Desmond MacCarthy (1910), p. 108.

10. *The Letters of Maurice Hewlett*, ed. Laurence Binyon (1926), p. 191.

11. See J. B. Van Amerongen, *The Actor in Dickens* (1926).

12. *Speeches*, p. 296.

13. See Edward Wagenknecht, *Cavalcade of the English Novel* (New York, 1947), p. 227.

14. Nonesuch, II, 825. It is significant that although Dickens often groaned about the difficulties of periodical publication, only once did he seriously consider abandoning it. See Nonesuch, I, 340, 554; and III, 187, and Postscript to *Our Mutual Friend*.

15. Nonesuch, II, 891.

16. J. W. T. Ley, *The Dickens Circle* (New York, 1919), p. 81.

17. *Speeches*, p. 332.

18. Hugh Blair, *Lectures on Rhetoric and Belles Lettres* (Philadelphia, 1833), pp. 417-420.

19. "Oliver Goldsmith," *North British Review*, IX (1848), 193-194. De Quincey's writings were much admired by Dickens.

20. *Quarterly Review*, LXXI (1843), 504.

21. *Forms of Modern Fiction*, ed. William Van O'Connor (Minneapolis, 1948), p. 45.

22. G. S. Haight, *George Eliot and John Chapman* (New Haven, 1940), p. 246.

23. Francis Jeffrey, *Contributions to the Edinburgh Review* (1846), III, 2.

24. See David Masson, *British Novelists* (1859), p. 212; *TLS*, August 24, 1951, p. xviii. I cannot vouch for the accuracy of the figure given for 1864 which I obtained from an unidentified newspaper clipping in the Forster Collection.

25. [Justin McCarthy] "Novels with a Purpose," *Westminster Review*, XXVI (1864), 25-26.

26. "D'Israeli's Novels," *Edinburgh Review*, LXVI (1837), 62.

27. "Recent English Romances," *Edinburgh Review*, LXV (April 1837), 186. See also *Fraser's Magazine*, XXI (1840), 381-382.

28. *Dublin University Magazine*, XLI (1853), 77.

29. E.g., see the attack upon Scott in *The Student's Guide* (rev. edn., 1836) by the Reverend John Todd. In replying to this treatise, Ruskin made fun of the kind of moral tale which catered to puritan tastes. One of these tales, which he had read as a boy, was Mrs. Sher-

wood's *Lady of the Mirror*, "a very awful book to me, because of the stories in it of wicked girls who had gone to balls, dying immediately after of fever." *Works of Ruskin*, I, 362n.

30. *Athenaeum*, November 16, 1833, p. 810 (italics mine). For an informed but overly-sprightly account of maidenly taboos, see R. P. Utter and G. B. Needham, *Pamela's Daughters* (New York, 1937), chaps. III, VI, X.

31. *Quarterly Review*, LXXI (1843), 504.

32. *Blackwood's Edinburgh Magazine*, CII (1867), 257-258, 275.

33. Nonesuch, II, 679.

34. Bruce McCullough, usually a perceptive critic, complains that the treatment of Emily by Steerforth is improbable because the latter "has never shown any unusual weakness for women." Such an observation seems to indicate that the role of Rosa Dartle, who is virtually a symbol of Steerforth's treatment of women, has been misunderstood. Also missed, incidentally, is one of Steerforth's first speeches asking David Copperfield whether he has a sister: "I should have liked to know her," he says. See *Representative English Novelists* (New York, 1946), pp. 144-145.

35. R. H. Horne, *A New Spirit of the Age* (1844), p. 12.

36. See J. T. Hillhouse, *The Waverley Novels and their Critics* (Minneapolis, 1936), chap. III.

37. [J. G. Lockhart,] "*Lives of the Novelists*. By Sir Walter Scott," *Quarterly Review*, XXXIV (1826), 372. Lockhart's essay is a sensible defense of the novel, which, he notes, is "among the least studied" of all departments of literature.

38. *English Review*, X (1848), 274.

39. Horne, *A New Spirit of the Age*, II, 215. Of a character in *Dorrit*, Dickens remarked in his Notebook that he hoped the presentation might "lead some men to reflect, and change a little." See Nonesuch, III, 785. Concerning *The Chimes*, see I, 646.

40. *The Letters of Thackeray*, ed. Gordon N. Ray (Cambridge, U.S.A., 1945), II, 282.

41. F. T. Blanchard, *Fielding the Novelist* (New Haven, 1926), p. 370.

42. Quoted by Amy Cruse, *The Victorians and their Reading* (Boston, 1936), p. 152.

43. "Hard Times," *Gentleman's Magazine*, LXII (1854), 277.

44. *The Reinterpretation of Victorian Literature*, ed. Joseph E. Baker (Princeton, 1950), p. 70.

45. E.g., see Sir William Robertson Nicoll, *Dickens's Own Story* (New York, n.d.), pp. 6-7, 93. In the midst of his admiration of Dickens, Nicoll shows distress concerning the Master's "antipathy to the Dissenters."

CHAPTER 3

SKYROCKET AND STICK

1. William I. Knapp, *Life . . . of George Borrow* (1899), II, 287; and see Clement Shorter, *George Borrow and his Circle* (1913), pp. 345-347.

2. *Athenaeum*, December 31, 1836, p. 916.

3. See Walter C. Phillips, *Dickens, Reade, and Collins* (New York, 1919), p. 137.

4. Quoted in *Dickensiana*, p. 94, from *The Christian Remembrancer* (1842).

5. "The Temper of Modern Fiction," *TLS*, August 24, 1951, p. xxviii.

6. *Scribner's Magazine*, IV (1888), 127.

7. *Scottish Review*, III (1883), 146.

8. Nonesuch, I, 767.

9. See Graham Greene, "The Young Dickens," in *The Lost Childhood and Other Essays* (1951).

10. Nonesuch, II, 150.

11. *Memorials of Thomas Hood* (1860), II, 41.

12. Sir Joseph Arnould, *Memoir of Thomas, First Lord Denman* (1873), II, 90.

13. Elizabeth Barrett Browning, *Charles Dickens and Other 'Spirits of the Age'* (1919, privately printed), pp. 11-12.

14. One exception is Malcolm Elwin, a learned critic who believes that Ainsworth might be revived as Trollope has been revived. See his *Victorian Wallflowers* (1934), p. 176.

15. See his essay "Going to See a Man Hanged," (August 1840), in *The Book of Snobs* (1869), pp. 382-383.

16. For Dickens' own account of his obsession, of which Edmund Wilson has made much use, see Nonesuch, III, 678, 681, 718-719.

17. *Catherine*, ch. XIII. In Thackeray's opening chapter, Fagin is mentioned together with Turpin and Jack Sheppard.

18. Phillips, *op.cit.*, pp. 102-106.

19. E.g., J. S. LeFanu felt that his work had been slanderously degraded when a critic referred to him (quite correctly) as a sensation writer. See Lewis Melville, *Victorian Novelists* (1906), pp. 227-228; and R. A. Watson, *George Gilfillan* (1892), p. 275.

20. The Earl of Ilchester, *Chronicles of Holland House* (1937), p. 245.

21. *Quarterly Review*, LXIV (June 1839), 87.

22. *British Quarterly Review*, XXXV (1862), 137.

23. *Henry Crabb Robinson on Books and Their Writers*, ed. Edith J. Morley (1938), II, 542, 558.

24. *Ibid.*, pp. 543, 559, 599, 590.

25. *Quarterly Review*, LXIV (June 1839), 83-102. Ford concedes, at one point, that "Boz is . . . never vulgar when treating on subjects which are avowedly vulgar." Other reviews included the *Athenaeum*, November 17, 1838, an insignificant notice; the *Edinburgh Review*

(October 1838), which preferred *Oliver Twist* to *Pickwick*; the *Monthly Review* (January 1839), which complained that Dickens had failed to exalt and refine the reader by "the inculcation of moral sentiments" and by "lessons that refine while they delight."

26. Forster, p. 113. A late Victorian critic is equally ambiguous. "In 'Oliver Twist' he specially addresses the lower orders in London, although all classes have perhaps equally admired it." See A. S. G. Canning, *The Philosophy of Dickens* (1880), p. 92.

27. *Quarterly Review*, LIX (1837), 518. Of the review as a whole, Dickens remarked: "I find little fault with it." He hoped, however, that Nancy, in *Oliver Twist*, would be excellent enough to "defy" Hayward's prediction. See Nonesuch, I, 131, and Forster, p. 96. The review has sometimes been erroneously attributed to Lockhart and also to Croker.

28. Forster, p. 302, and Edgar Johnson, *Charles Dickens* (New York, 1952), I, 304, 345.

29. By 1870, its sales were exceeded only by those of *Pickwick* and *Copperfield*. Forster, p. 302.

30. See the extract from his letter to Miss Burdett-Coutts (September 8, 1843), printed in Parke-Bernet Galleries sale catalogue, October 30, 1950.

31. *Athenaeum*, July 20, 1844, p. 666. In America, the *Knickerbocker* (XXIV, 1844, 274-277) was mildly tolerant of Dickens' lapses, but the *Southern Literary Messenger* (X, 1844, 124-125) was extremely abusive.

32. E.g., see the *Westminster Review*, XL (1843), 242-243; the *Monthly Review*, III, (1844), 137.

33. *North British Review*, III (1845), 73.

33a. *The Heart of Charles Dickens*, ed. Edgar Johnson (New York, 1952), p. 55.

34. Quoted by Lionel Stevenson, *Dr. Quicksilver: The Life of Charles Lever* (1939), p. 154.

35. Gissing, *Critical Studies of the Works of Charles Dickens* (New York, 1924), p. 73.

36. Ada B. Nisbet, "The Mystery of 'Martin Chuzzlewit,'" in *Essays Dedicated to Lily B. Campbell* (Los Angeles, 1950), pp. 204-205.

37. In the Forster Collection at the Victoria and Albert Museum, there is a volume of clippings from the American reviews. Some of them are surprisingly tolerant.

38. *Edinburgh Review*, LXXVI (1843), 497-522. See also the *London University Magazine* review quoted by Rantavaara, pp. 97-98.

39. Nonesuch, I, 504. See also *Correspondence of the Late Macvey Napier* (1879), pp. 416-418.

40. *Quarterly Review*, LXXI (1843), 505. A few months later, Croker (prompted by an American attack on the book) spoke more kindly of *American Notes*. See *Quarterly Review*, LXXIII (December 1843), 129-142.

41. Quoted from the *National Review* by J. A. Hammerton, *The Dickens Companion* (1910), p. 313.

42. See Trollope's *The Warden*, ch. xv.

43. *Ainsworth's Magazine*, v (1844), 85. (Italics mine.)

44. Forster, p. 311.

45. *Henry Crabb Robinson on Books*, ii, 645.

46. *Ibid.*, pp. 598-599.

47. *North British Review*, iii (1845), 72.

48. *Westminster Review*, xl (December 1843), 242.

49. Nonesuch, i, 544-545, 554.

50. Nonesuch, i, 791-792, and Jack Lindsay, *Charles Dickens* (New York, 1950), p. 264.

51. Forster, p. 464.

52. Nonesuch, i, 522.

53. Preface to the 1840 edition of *Pelham*.

54. *The Letters of Thackeray*, ed. Gordon Ray, iv, 125. Concerning Lever, see Lionel Stevenson, *Dr. Quicksilver* (1939), p. 186.

55. Quoted by S. M. Ellis, *The Solitary Horseman* (1927), pp. 72-73.

56. Nonesuch, i, 545-546.

57. *The Letters of Anthony Trollope*, ed. Bradford Booth (Oxford, 1951), p. 291.

58. Hesketh Pearson, *Charles Dickens* (New York, 1949), pp. 159-160.

59. Nonesuch, ii, 861.

60. See Mathilde Parlett, "The Influence of Contemporary Criticism on George Eliot," *Studies in Philology*, xxx (1933), 103-132.

61. Nonesuch, i, 93.

62. *The Times*, December 27, 1845, p. 6.

63. *The Times*, December 27, 1845, p. 6; June 1, 1846, p. 7; and January 2, 1847, p. 6.

64. *The Times*, December 27, 1845, p. 6.

65. Quoted from a French newspaper by *The Times*, June 14, 1870, p. 12.

66. Lord Cockburn, *Life of Lord Jeffrey* (Edinburgh, 1852), ii, 408.

CHAPTER 4

LITTLE NELL: THE LIMITS OF EXPLANATORY CRITICISM

1. Quoted by Hesketh Pearson, *Oscar Wilde* (New York, 1946), p. 208.

2. Nonesuch, ii, 560. *Humphrey Clinker*, with its tender scenes, was his favorite. Cf. F. W. Boege, *Smollett's Reputation as a Novelist* (Princeton, 1947), pp. 97-100.

3. Nonesuch, ii, 767-768; 785.

4. See S. M. Ellis, *The Solitary Horseman* (1927), p. 258.

5. Quoted by J. W. T. Ley, *The Dickens Circle* (New York, 1919), p. 72. See also *The Christian Remembrancer*, iv (1842), 591-593.

6. *Speeches*, p. 66.

7. Quoted in *Dickensiana*, p. 430.

8. *Letters of Edward Fitzgerald* (1907), I, 174.

9. Smith's letters show his response to Dickens' pathos as well as to his humor and satire. See Lady Holland, *A Memoir of the Reverend Sydney Smith* (1855), II, 412, 482, 490.

10. In a Preface to *The Old Curiosity Shop*, Dickens speaks with gratitude of Hood's review which had appeared in the *Athenaeum*, November 7, 1840, pp. 887-888. See also *The Heart of Charles Dickens*, ed. Edgar Johnson (New York, 1952), p. 67.

11. *Henry Crabb Robinson on Books and their Writers*, II, 593. See also John Forster, *Walter Savage Landor* (1869), II, 459-460.

12. Forster, p. 174.

13. J. C. Young, *A Memoir of Charles Mayne Young* (1871), II, 110-111.

14. Nonesuch, I, 295, and II, 103.

15. See F. G. Kitton, *The Novels of Charles Dickens* (1897), p. 64.

16. Lord Cockburn, *The Life of Lord Jeffrey* (Edinburgh, 1852), II, 425.

17. Nonesuch, I, 823.

18. *Dictionary of National Biography*, V, 927.

19. Cockburn, *Jeffrey*, II, 410.

20. *Ibid.*, 380-381.

21. *The Letters of Thackeray*, ed. Gordon Ray, II, 267n.

22. Forster, p. 480n.

23. Nonesuch, I, 791-792.

24. *The Heart of Charles Dickens*, ed. Edgar Johnson, p. 118.

25. Ada B. Nisbet, "The Mystery of 'Martin Chuzzlewit,'" in *Essays Dedicated to Lily B. Campbell* (Los Angeles, 1950), p. 207.

26. Quoted *ibid.* Dickens himself seems to have sensed what had happened. In a letter remarking upon the small sale of *Copperfield*, he makes a defense of the high quality of *Dombey* against its detractors. See Nonesuch, II, 173.

27. Forster, p. 563.

28. *Poetical and Prose Remains of Edward Marsh Heavisides* (1850), p. 11. Similar praise of Nell can be found in John Hollingshead's *Essays and Miscellanies* (1865), pp. 277-283, and in E. P. Whipple's essay on Dickens in the *North American Review*, LXIX (1849), 404. Whipple was one of the most sensitive and sensible of Dickens' early critics.

29. E.g., see the *Saturday Review*, May 8, 1858, pp. 474-475; *Westminster Review*, XXVI (1864), 429-434; *Spectator*, XLII (1869), 474-475; *Contemporary Review*, X (1869), 221.

30. Quoted by J. D. Jump, *"Weekly Reviewing in the Eighteen-Fifties,"* RES, XXIV (1948), 45.

31. James, *Views and Reviews* (Boston, 1908), p. 156.

32. Stephen, *Cambridge Essays* (1855), pp. 154, 174n., 175.

33. See *Henry Crabb Robinson on Books and their Writers*, II, 815.

34. See Mrs. Margaret Oliphant, *The Victorian Age in Literature*

(New York, 1892), pp. 258-259, and *Annals of a Publishing House* (Edinburgh, 1898), III. See also her essay on Dickens in *Blackwood's*, CIX (1871), 673-695.

35. *Fortnightly Review*, XVII (1872), 154.

36. *Contemporary Review*, XXXVII (1880), 81.

37. From unidentified newspaper accounts in the Dickens House collection.

38. Chesterton, *Appreciations and Criticisms of Dickens* (New York, 1911), p. 54.

39. More, *Shelburne Essays: Fifth Series* (New York, 1908), pp. 34, 77.

40. Huxley, *Vulgarity in Literature* (1930), pp. 54-59.

41. Osbert Sitwell, *Dickens* (1932), pp. 27-28.

42. Miller, *The Colossus of Maroussi* (Norfolk, Conn., n.d.), p. 115.

43. W. J. Dawson, *Quest and Vision* (1886), quoted by C. W. Moulton, *The Library of Literary Criticism* (Buffalo, 1904), VI, 589.

44. Nonesuch, I, 283-284.

45. Quoted by Hesketh Pearson, *Charles Dickens* (New York, 1949), p. 48.

46. Nonesuch, I, 360.

47. Nonesuch, II, 716.

48. Cecil, *Early Victorian Novelists* (1934), p. 30.

49. Lindsay, *Charles Dickens* (New York, 1950), p. 122. Cf. Lionel Trilling, *The Liberal Imagination* (New York, 1951), p. 56.

50. J. M. S. Tompkins, *The Popular Novel in England: 1770-1800* (1932), pp. 92-93.

51. See David Cecil, *The Young Melbourne* (Indianapolis, 1939), p. 14, for a discussion of the uninhibited "manly tear" of the Whig aristocracy.

52. *Life and Letters of Macaulay* (New York, 1876), II, 186.

53. Nonesuch, III, 59.

54. Nonesuch, III, 48.

55. See R. P. Utter and G. B. Needham, *Pamela's Daughters* (New York, 1937), ch. VI.

56. Pearson, *Charles Dickens*, p. 86. Cf. Jack Lindsay, *op. cit.*, pp. 199-201.

57. See E. K. Brown in *Forms of Modern Fiction*, ed. W. Van O'Connor (Minneapolis, 1948), p. 172. See also Rex Warner's novel *The Professor* (1938) which includes a discussion of the twentieth century's abnormal distaste for grief as something that "impairs efficiency." (Chapter VII).

58. Pottle, *The Idiom of Poetry* (Ithaca, New York, 1941), pp. 13-18; 22-41.

59. Henley, "Some Notes on Charles Dickens," *Pall Mall Magazine*, XVIII (1899), 577.

60. Nonesuch, II, 6.

61. Also interesting for comparison are the lives and deaths of Paul Dombey and of Little Hanno in Thomas Mann's *Buddenbrooks*.

62. One of Bulwer-Lytton's admirers, George Gilfillan, considered that authorial comment was the highest test of an author's greatness, and added that "Dickens, when ever he moralizes, in his own person, becomes insufferably tame and feeble."—*A Second Gallery of Literary Portraits* (Edinburgh, 1850), p. 163. See also *Charles Kingsley: His Letters and Memories of his Life* (1877), II, 40-41.

63. Joseph Conrad, *A Personal Record* [1912] (1925), p. xx.

64. "Dickens and Daudet," *Cornhill Magazine*, n.s., XVII (1891), 407.

CHAPTER 5

THE CRITIC OF SOCIETY

1. F. P. Rolfe, "Letters of Charles Lever to his Wife and Daughter," *Huntington Library Bulletin*, x (1936), 164.

2. Nonesuch, II, 394.

3. Forster, 571, 807n; and Nonesuch, II, 483, 741.

4. See *The Heart of Charles Dickens*, ed. Edgar Johnson (New York, 1952), p. 366. By 1869, *All the Year Round* had a circulation of 300,000 copies.

5. Charles and Mary Cowden Clarke, *Recollections of Writers* (New York, n.d.), p. 93.

6. For an account of Dickens' meeting such a reader in America, see Nonesuch, III, 614.

7. See *The Autobiography of Sir Walter Besant* (1902), pp. 91-96.

8. *Mrs. J. Comyns Carr's Reminiscences*, ed. Eve Adam (n.d.), p. 52.

9. *Speeches*, p. 147.

10. W. D. Howells, *My Literary Passions* (New York, 1895), pp. 88-103.

11. *Speeches*, p. 100n.

12. *Ward and Lock's Penny Books for the People: The Life of Charles Dickens* [1870]. Similar praise appears in a review of *The Chimes* in *The Apprentice*, II (1844), 178-180.

13. Nonesuch, III, 48, 717.

14. James Payn, "Some Literary Recollections," *Cornhill*, n.s., II (1884), 588.

15. See John W. Dodds, *The Age of Paradox* (New York, 1952), p. 130.

16. *Ibid.*, pp. 126-128.

17. *The Tomahawk: A Saturday Journal of Satire* [London], June 25, 1870, pp. 245-246.

18. *The People's Journal*, I, (1846), p. 11.

19. H. F. Dickens, "Why Dickens is Popular," *The Book Monthly*, February 1920, p. 86.

20. *Westminster*, n.s., XXVI (1864), 417. The author was Justin McCarthy.

21. See *ibid.*, pp. 431-439.

22. Quoted by Irma Rantavaara, *Dickens* (Helsinki, 1944), pp. 111-112.

23. *Speeches*, p. 98. Cf. the red-faced gentleman's lament for the "Old Times" in part I of *The Chimes*.

24. See e.g., *Bleak House*, ch. LV; *Dombey and Son*, ch. XX.

25. See Augustus Hare, *The Story of My Life* (New York, 1896), II, 14.

26. C. W. Moulton, *The Library of Literary Criticism* (Buffalo, 1904), VI, 590.

27. Quoted by the *Dickensian*, XXVIII (1932), 330.

28. Quoted by Moulton, *op. cit.*, p. 586.

29. *The Heart of Charles Dickens*, ed. Johnson, p. 370.

30. Payn, "Some Literary Recollections," p. 587.

31. Nonesuch, II, 203 and 620-621. See also III, 297, 460.

32. *Saturday Review*, IV (1857), 15.

33. "A Fly-Leaf on Life," [1869] in *The Uncommercial Traveller*.

34. *Dickensiana*, p. 408.

35. See Alfredo Obertello, *Carlyle's Critical Theories* (Geneva, 1948), p. 4.

36. See J. W. Dodds, *The Age of Paradox*, p. 377.

37. Francis Espinasse, *Literary Recollections* (1893), p. 216.

38. *Life and Memoirs of John Churton Collins* (1912), p. 44.

39. See James T. Hillhouse, *The Waverley Novels and their Critics* (Minneapolis, 1936), p. 214ff.

40. *William Allingham: A Diary* (1907), p. 208.

41. Espinasse, *op. cit.*, p. 215.

42. D. A. Wilson, *Carlyle at his Zenith* (1927), p. 126.

43. Wilson, *Carlyle to Threescore-and-Ten*, p. 430.

44. *Anne Gilchrist: Her Life and Writings*, ed. H. H. Gilchrist (1897), p. 81.

45. See Emory Neff, *Carlyle* (New York, 1932), p. 216.

46. "Charles Dickens and David Copperfield," reprinted in the *Eclectic Magazine*, XXII (1851), 255-257.

47. Nonesuch, II, 567.

48. Quoted in *The Works of Ruskin* (1903-1912), XVIII, p. xlvi.

49. Wilson, *Carlyle to Threescore-and-Ten*, p. 211.

50. Nonesuch, III, 348.

51. *The Works of Ruskin*, I, 365.

52. *Ibid.*, XXXIV, 370

53. *Ibid.*, XI, 173.

54. *Ibid.*, XXXVI, 431-432.

55. *Ibid.*, XXVIII, 189-191.

56. *Ibid.*, XXXVII, 10.

57. *Ibid.*, XVII, 31n.

58. *Ibid.*, XXXVII, 10.

59. *Ibid.*, XXXIV, 609.

60. *Ibid.*, XXXVII, 7.

61. *Ibid.*, XXXIV, 374-376. Cf. VI, 397-398.

62. *Ibid.*, XXXVI, 26 (letter of June 6, 1841).

63. *Ibid.*, xxxiv, 275.

64. *Ibid.*, pp. 271-272.

65. *Ibid.*, xxxv, 303.

66. *The Letters of Matthew Arnold to Arthur Hugh Clough* (Oxford, 1932), p. 133. See also his letter to J. T. Rawlings, June 11, 1881.

67. *North British Review*, iii (1845), 85.

68. See *Letters to Clough*, pp. 132-133; letter to Mrs. Forster, April 14, 1853; and "Haworth Churchyard" with its tribute to Emily Brontë. See also *The Notebooks of Matthew Arnold*, ed. H. F. Lowry, Karl Young, and W. H. Dunn (Oxford, 1952), pp. 551-627.

69. See Kenneth Robinson, *Wilkie Collins* (New York, 1952), pp. 260-261.

70. *Letters of Benjamin Disraeli to Frances Anne Marchioness of Londonderry* (1936), p. 164. See also Edmund Yates, *Recollections* (1884), ii, 140.

71. *The Letters of J. R. Lowell* (New York, 1893), ii, 334.

72. Carl Van Doren, *The Life of Thomas Love Peacock* (1911), p. 255.

73. *The Works of Matthew Arnold* (1904), xi, 58-59.

74. See *Notebooks*, p. 551, and letter to J. G. Fitch, October 14, 1880.

75. *Works*, xi, 58.

76. *Ibid.*, p. 59.

77. *Ibid.*, p. 67.

78. *Ibid.*, x, 303.

79. *Ibid.*, iv, 245. For Arnold's extracts from Taine, which include some criticism of Dickens, see *Notebooks*, pp. 359-363.

80. *Works*, iv, 247.

81. Jeaffreson, *Novels and Novelists* (1858), ii, 320-321.

82. *Ibid.*, pp. 325-326.

83. *Blackwood's*, lxxxi (1857), 495-496.

84. *Ibid.*, p. 497.

85. *Saturday Review*, iv (July 1857), 15.

86. *Dickensian*, xxviii (1931), 43.

87. [Elizabeth Rigby], "*Vanity Fair* and *Jane Eyre*," *Quarterly Review*, lxxiv (1849), 173.

88. *Aurora Leigh*, book iv.

89. Trevelyan, *Life and Letters of Macaulay* (New York, 1876), ii, 320.

90. *Blackwood's*, lxxvii (1855), 453. Cf. "Hard Times," *Gentleman's Magazine*, n.s., xlii (1854), 276-278.

91. "Dickens's Hard Times," *Atlantic Monthly*, xxxix (1877), 357. (Italics mine.)

92. *Ibid.*, p. 353. Whipple admired Dickens as a novelist, but being committed to an economic dogma he could be only bewildered by Dickens as a social critic. G. M. Young has analyzed brilliantly and sympathetically the comparable circular reasoning which led even the well-disposed Victorian employer to hardness and tyranny. See *Early Victorian England*, ii, 426.

93. *Harper's New Monthly Magazine*, XII (1856), 383.

94. *Dickensiana*, pp. 285-286.

95. *St. James Magazine*, n.s., V (1870), 696-697.

96. *Saturday Review*, VIII (December 1859), 741. See also Stephen's review of *Little Dorrit* and his general article on Dickens. Vol. IV (July 1857), 15-16; vol. V (May 1858), 474-475.

97. Stephen, *Cambridge Essays* (1855), p. 192.

98. *Ibid.*, p. 166. See also his remarks on Little Nell quoted above, ch. 4, pp. 60-61.

99. *Saturday Review*, VIII, 742.

100. *Ibid.*, p. 741.

101. *Ibid.*, p. 743.

102. See Leslie Stephen, *Life of Sir James Fitzjames Stephen* (1895), p. 159.

103. *Edinburgh Review*, CVI (1857), 134.

104. Sale Catalogue of Ifan Kyrle Fletcher (London). Number 146.

105. Trollope, *An Autobiography*, ed. Bradford Booth (Los Angeles, 1947), pp. 207-208. Cf. Trollope's obituary essay on Thackeray in the *Cornhill Magazine*, IX (1864), 134-137.

106. Trollope, "Charles Dickens," *St. Paul's Magazine*, VI (1870), 374.

107. *Autobiography*, p. 211.

108. Trollope, "Novel Reading," *Nineteenth Century*, V (1879), 33-35.

109. *Autobiography*, p. 208.

110. See Ernest Boll, "The Infusions of Dickens in Trollope," *The Trollopian*, I (1946), 11-24.

111. *The Letters of Anthony Trollope*, ed. Bradford Booth (Oxford, 1951), p. 291.

112. Trollope, "Charles Dickens," p. 374.

113. "Trollope and 'Little Dorrit,'" *The Trollopian*, II (1948), 237-240. The review itself has not been traced.

114. Concerning Victorian variety, see Jerome H. Buckley's corrective study: *The Victorian Temper* (Cambridge, U.S.A., 1951).

115. See Leslie A. Marchand, *The Athenaeum* (Chapel Hill, 1941), pp. 306-309.

116. *The Letters of Queen Victoria: Second Series* (1926), II, 21. Cf. the *Annual Register* (1870), p. 153.

117. Edwin Hodder, *Life of the Seventh Earl of Shaftesbury* (1886), III, 298. For his comments on Dotheboys Hall, see Barbara Blackburn, *Noble Lord* (1949), p. 18.

118. *The Times*, June 20, 1870, p. 14.

119. See the Rev. William Kirkus, *Miscellaneous Essays* (1863), p. 5 and p. 63; and also Marchand, *op. cit.*, p. 146, and *Dickensiana*, pp. 274-275; 286, 506.

120. *The Times*, June 20, 1870, p. 14.

CHAPTER 6

THE ARTIST

1. W. A. Sibbald, "Charles Dickens Revisited," *Westminster Review*, January 1907, pp. 62-63.

2. Lewes, *Ranthorpe* (1847), p. 110.

3. *Saturday Review*, IV (1857), 15.

4. Masson, *British Novelists and their Styles* (Cambridge, 1859), p. 252.

5. Andrew Lang, *The Life and Letters of John Gibson Lockhart* (1897), II, 310.

6. *Letters and Memorials of Jane Welsh Carlyle*, ed. J. A. Froude (New York, 1883), I, 296.

7. Leslie Marchand, *The Athenaeum* (Chapel Hill, 1941), p. 315.

8. E.g., see J. G. Lockhart's *Theodore Hook* (1852), p. 98.

9. Lord Lytton, *The Life of Edward Bulwer* (1913), II, 13, 74.

10. *Ibid.*, p. 412.

11. See Kenneth W. Hooker, *The Fortunes of Victor Hugo in England* (New York, 1938), chapters V and VII.

12. *The Letters of Robert Browning and Elizabeth Barrett* (New York, 1899), II, 107, 113. Another important admirer of Balzac was Swinburne. *Lesbia Brandon* includes a lively discussion at a country house, in 1850, concerning Balzac's greatness and of his superiority to his "chief imitator" in England. The imitator referred to is clearly Thackeray, although Swinburne's editor, Mr. Hughes, states that the reference seems to be about Dickens but is, in reality, about Charles Reade. See *Lesbia Brandon*, ed. Randolph Hughes (1952), pp. 70-72; 542-544.

13. Howells, *My Literary Passions* (New York, 1895), p. 96.

14. Benson, "Charles Dickens," *North American Review*, CXCV (1912), 382.

15. Greene, *The Lost Childhood and other Essays* (1951), pp. 52-53.

16. *Quarterly Review*, LXIV (1839), 92.

17. "Charles Dickens and David Copperfield," reprinted in the *Eclectic Magazine*, XXII (1851), 248.

18. Quoted by A. W. Secord, "Our Indispensable Eighteenth Century," *JEGP*, LXV (1946), 163.

19. *Saturday Review*, V (1858), 474-475.

20. *North British Review*, III (1845), 76.

21. See H. A. Taine, *History of English Literature* (New York, 1879), II, 344.

22. G. S. Layard, *The Life, Letters, and Diaries of Shirley Brooks* (1907), p. 555.

23. "Mr. Thackeray's New Novel," *The Times*, December 22, 1852, p. 8. See also "Popular Serial Literature," *North British Review*, VII (1847), 119.

24. George Barnett Smith, *Poets and Novelists* (1875), p. 12.

25. Masson, " 'David Copperfield.' 'History of Pendennis.' " *North*

British Review, May 1851, reprinted in *Littell's Living Age*, July 19, 1851, p. 97.

26. *Ibid.*, p. 102.

27. *Ibid.*, p. 104.

28. Masson, *British Novelists and their Styles*, p. 249.

29. *Littell's Living Age*, p. 100.

30. *Ibid.*, p. 104.

31. *British Novelists and their Styles*, p. 250.

32. *Littell's Living Age*, p. 104. See also the *British Journal*, I (1852), 138.

33. *Ibid.*, p. 102.

34. See Flora Masson, *Victorians All* (1931), pp. 9-12.

35. *The Letters of Thackeray*, ed. Gordon N. Ray (Cambridge, U.S.A., 1945), II, 772-773.

36. *Barnaby Rudge* is the only novel of this period to which Thackeray seems to have made no recorded reference.

37. Various comments on Dickens are included in Thackeray's review of *A Christmas Carol* in "A Box of Novels" (*Fraser's*, February 1844, pp. 153-169); and in such essays as "Dickens in France," "Going to See a Man Hanged," and "Charity and Humour."

38. "On Some French Fashionable Novels: With a Plea for Romances in General," *The Paris Sketch Book* (1869), p. 86.

39. See Miriam M. H. Thrall, *Rebellious Fraser's* (New York, 1934), pp. 73-77.

40. *Letters of Thackeray*, II, 308. Concerning Hayward's review of *Vanity Fair*, see also pp. 312-313, 334, 449.

41. Gordon S. Haight, *George Eliot and John Chapman* (New Haven, 1940), pp. 178-179.

42. *Letters of Thackeray*, II, 266, 267n., 533, 535, 588, 648. See also "Brown the Younger at a Club" in *Sketches and Travels in London*.

43. *Ibid.*, III, 37. See also William Allingham, *A Diary* (1907), p. 78.

44. Yates, *Recollections* (1884), II, 32-33.

45. *Letters of Thackeray*, III, 288.

46. "A Pictorial Rhapsody: Concluded," *Ballads and Critical Reviews* (New York, 1903), p. 342.

47. Quoted by Hugh Kingsmill, *The Sentimental Journey* (Bristol, 1934), p. 169.

48. See *Charles Kingsley: His Letters and Memories of his Life* (1901), II, 25; Arabella Kenealy, *Memoirs of Edward Vaughan Kenealy* (1898), p. 227; F. T. Blanchard, *Fielding the Novelist* (New Haven, 1926), p. 424.

49. Charles Tennyson, *Alfred Tennyson* (New York, 1949), pp. 373, 515; and *Alfred Lord Tennyson: A Memoir* (1897), II, 371-372.

50. *Letters of Browning and Elizabeth Barrett*, II, 116.

51. *Alfred Lord Tennyson: A Memoir*, II, 371.

52. Hammerton, *Dickens Companion*, p. 338.

53. Charles Tennyson, *Alfred Tennyson*, p. 389.

54. *Ibid.*, p. 347.

55. E.g., "Which is the Nobler Writer—Dickens or Thackeray?" *The British Controversialist*, VI (1858).

56. "Vanity Fair," *The Times*, July 10, 1848, p. 10.

57. Serjeant Ballantine, *Some Experiences of a Barrister's Life* (1882), I, 135-139.

58. Frederic Harrison, *Autobiographic Memoirs*, I, 184.

59. *Letters of Thackeray*, II, 531, 535. In *Hard Times* Thackeray also found traces of his own influence (*ibid.*, III, 363). Lionel Stevenson suggests that the Dedlock scenes in *Bleak House* also owe something to Thackeray ("Dickens's Dark Novels," pp. 404-405).

60. *Prospective Review*, VII (1851), 158.

61. *National Review*, I (1855), 337.

62. *Our Mutual Friend*, Postscript. For studies of Dickens and serialization, see Gerald G. Grubb, "Dickens's Pattern of Weekly Serialization," *ELH*, IX (1942), 141-156; John Butt, "Dickens at Work," *Durham University Journal*, XL (1948), 65-77; John Butt and Kathleen Tillotson, "Dickens at Work on *Dombey and Son*," *Essays and Studies Collected for the English Association*, n.s., IV (1951), 70-93.

63. *Dickensiana*, p. 70.

64. Percy Lubbock, *The Craft of Fiction* (1935), pp. 128-134; 213-219. See also Fred W. Boege, "Point of View in Dickens," *PMLA*, LXV (1950), 90-105.

65. Nonesuch, II, 619.

66. Stevenson, "Dickens's Dark Novels," p. 403.

67. Nonesuch, II, 776.

68. "Mr. Thackeray's New Novel," *The Times*, December 22, 1852, p. 8.

69. George Brimley, *Essays* (Cambridge, 1858), pp. 290-291.

70. *Ibid.*, pp. 290-300.

71. Robert Chambers, *Cyclopaedia of English Literature* (Edinburgh, 1844), II, 633; and 1858, II, 647-650.

72. *Illustrated London News*, XXIII (September 24, 1853), 247.

73. "Mr. Dickens's Last Novel," *Dublin University Magazine*, LVIII (1861), 685.

74. See J. W. Mackail, *The Life of William Morris* (1899), I, 220-221.

75. Reprinted from *Fraser's* in the *Eclectic Magazine*, XXII (1851), p. 252.

76. *Harriet Martineau's Autobiography* (Boston, 1877), II, 62.

77. *Prospective Review*, VII (1851), 157-191.

CHAPTER 7

THE POET AND THE CRITICS

OF PROBABILITY

1. G. H. Lewes, "Criticism in Relation to Novels," *Fortnightly Review*, III (1866), 355. Cf. Henry James' discussion of romance and probability in his Preface to *The American*.

2. Sean O'Faolain, "Dickens and Thackeray," in *The English Novelists*, ed. D. Verschoyle (1936), p. 149.

3. Nonesuch, II, 385; III, 268-269.

4. Wolfgang Wickhardt, *Die Formen der Perspektive in Charles Dickens' Romanen* (Berlin, 1933), p. 9.

5. *Harriet Martineau's Autobiography* (Boston, 1877), II, 62. Miss Martineau added that it would be a "curious speculation" to discover how much "the foreign conception of English character" would be affected by reading Dickens. In such countries as Soviet Russia, his continued popularity has apparently had marked effects.

6. Edward H. Dering, *Memoirs of Georgiana, Lady Chatterton* (1878), p. 137.

7. See Miss Washburn's thesis, p. 196, and David Masson, *British Novelists*, pp. 257-258.

8. J. M. S. Tompkins, *The Popular Novel in England* (1932), pp. 18-19.

9. *Athenaeum*, September 25, 1841, p. 740 (quoted by Miss Washburn, p. 27). Cf. the *British Quarterly Review*, XXXV (1862), 135-136. For a useful discussion of the quarrel about realism among critics of poetry, see R. G. Cox, "Victorian Criticism of Poetry: The Minority Tradition," *Scrutiny*, XVIII (1951), 2-17.

10. *Contemporary Review*, X (1869), 207.

11. *Edinburgh Review*, CVI (1857), 127.

12. "The Haunted Man," *The Times*, December 21, 1848, p. 8.

13. Forster, p. 88.

14. Charles Kent, "Dombey and Son," *The Sun*, April 13, 1848, p. 4.

15. Nonesuch, II, 653.

16. Nonesuch, I, 555.

17. Forster, pp. 727-728.

18. Nonesuch, II, 352.

19. Oliver Elton, *A Survey of English Literature 1830-1880* (1948), II, 217.

20. Orwell, *Inside the Whale* (1940), p. 69.—That *all* great novels "are essentially lavish of particulars" is discussed by José Ortega Y Gasset in his *The Dehumanization of Art and Notes on the Novel* (Princeton, 1948), pp. 97-103.

21. Forster, p. 744.

22. James, *Partial Portraits* (1888), p. 318.

23. Nonesuch, I, 782.

24. Forster, p. 734.

25. Nonesuch, III, 284; and II, 852. On another occasion, he advised Collins: "I think the probabilities here and there require a little more respect than you are disposed to show them." Nonesuch, II, 435-436.

26. Letter to Richard Woodhouse, October 27, 1818.

27. Nonesuch, II, 17-18.

28. Quoted by Edward H. Carr, *Dostoevsky* (1949), p. 205.

29. Edwin Muir, *The Structure of the Novel* (1946), p. 26.

30. J. W. T. Ley, *The Dickens Circle* (New York, 1919), p. 87.

31. Muir, *op. cit.*, pp. 63, 81-84.

32. Nonesuch, II, 850 (italics mine).

33. Nonesuch, III, 462.

34. Cather, *On Writing* (New York, 1949), pp. 35-37.

35. *Ibid.*, p. 40.

36. Forster, p. 721.

37. H. Taine, "Charles Dickens," *Revue des Deux Mondes*, 1 février, 1856, pp. 621, 647.

38. Whipple, "The Genius of Dickens," *Atlantic Monthly*, XIX (1867), 549. Although, like Bagehot, Whipple deplored the lack of "great natures" in Dickens, he considered that the "exaggeration rather increases than diminishes our sense of the reality of his personages."

39. Floris Delattre, *Dickens et la France* (Paris, 1927), pp. 62-67; M. G. Devonshire, *The English Novel in France: 1830-1870* (1929), chs. XVII, XIX.

40. H. Taine, *History of English Literature* (New York, 1879), II, 340, 347, 352.

41. *Ibid.*, pp. 343-344.

42. *Works of Walter Bagehot*, ed. Mrs. Barrington (1915), III, 85. The essay appeared originally in the *National Review* (October 1858).

43. Cazamian, *Criticism in the Making* (1929), pp. 63-80.

44. Bagehot, *op. cit.*, pp. 78, 85.

45. *Ibid.*, pp. 106-107.

46. *Ibid.*, pp. 78-79; 81, 89, 103-105.

47. *Ibid.*, p. 105.

48. Hutton, *Brief Literary Criticisms* (1906). See his essays on "The Genius of Dickens," "What is Humour?" and "Bookishness in Literature."

49. Morris Greenhut, "G. H. Lewes as a Critic of the Novel." *Studies in Philology*, XLV (1948), 491. Lewes contributed to the *Leader*, *Athenaeum*, *Pall Mall Gazette*, *Saturday Review*, and *Fortnightly Review*.

50. Lewes, *The Principles of Success in Literature* (Boston, 1894), pp. 137-138.

51. Lewes, "Criticism in Relation to Novels," *Fortnightly Review*, III (1866), 352-353.

52. *Principles of Success in Literature*, pp. 83-84.

53. *Ibid.*, p. 40.

54. Greenhut, *op. cit.*, p. 495.

55. Lubbock, *The Craft of Fiction*, p. 9.

56. Lewes, "Dickens in Relation to Criticism," *Fortnightly Review*, XVII (1872), 151-154. Lewes speaks of having pleased Dickens by something he had written about *Pickwick*. I have been unable to trace this review or letter.

57. *Principles of Success in Literature*, pp. 32-33.

58. See Greenhut, *op. cit.*, p. 503.

59. "Dickens in Relation to Criticism," p. 144.

60. *Loc. cit.*

61. *Ibid.*, pp. 145, 148.

62. Flaubert, *Correspondance* (Paris, 1926-1930), no. 951 [1868?]; and Lionel Trilling, "Art and Neurosis," in *The Liberal Imagination* (New York, 1951), pp. 160-180.

63. "Dickens in Relation to Criticism," pp. 145-146.
64. *Ibid.*, p. 147.
65. *Ibid.*, pp. 148-149.
66. *Ibid.*, p. 146.

CHAPTER 8

BIOGRAPHY

1. From an unidentified newspaper in the Dickens House collection.
2. E.g., John C. Camden, *Charles Dickens: The Story of his Life* (1870); R. S. Mackenzie, *Life of Charles Dickens* (Philadelphia, 1870); George Sala, *Charles Dickens* (1870).
3. See *English Institute Essays: 1946* (New York, 1947), and René Wellek and Austin Warren, *Theory of Literature* (New York, 1949), pp. 67-74.
4. See Aldous Huxley, *Point Counter Point*, ch. x.
5. Aylmer Maude, *The Life of Tolstoy* (Oxford, 1929), I, 177.
6. Nonesuch, III, 15.
7. *Complete Works of Swinburne* (1927), XVIII, 345.
8. Lewes, *Ranthorpe* (1847), pp. 42-43.
9. *Leeds Mercury*, November 15, 1872.
10. "The Life of Charles Dickens," *Temple Bar*, 1873, p. 185.
11. Hall, *A Book of Memories*, third edn., n.d., p. 458.
12. Nonesuch, III, 550.
13. *The Times*, December 26, 1871, p. 4, and November 28, 1872, p. 6. See also William J. Linton, *Recollections* (1895), p. 161.
14. *British Quarterly Review*, LVII (1873), 230; and the *Spectator*, XLVII (1874), 174-176.
15. "Who Wrote Dickens's Novels?" *Cornhill Magazine*, n.s., XI (1888), 114. Andrew Lang wrote a similar skit in 1886 in which he argued that Herbert Spencer must have written the novels. See *Macmillan's Magazine*, LIV, 112-115.
16. Katherine Mansfield, e.g., was disillusioned to learn from Forster that Dickens was killed by a desire for money. See her letters (ed. J. M. Murry), 1928, II, 21.
17. Forster, p. 836.
18. For a more detailed account of the biographers between Forster and Wright, such as Kitton, Leacock, Strauss, and Maurois, see Irma Rantavaara, *Dickens in the Light of English Criticism* (Helsinki, 1944), pp. 61-73. Concerning Chesterton and Gissing, see below, ch. 12, and also Morton D. Zabel, "Dickens: The Reputation Revised," *The Nation*, September 17, 1949, pp. 279-281. Concerning Ellen Ternan, it has always been assumed that the only reference to her in Forster is in the reprinting of Dickens' will. There seems to be another reference to her under the initial "E.," when Dickens was describing one of his dreams. See Forster, p. 841.
19. *Letters of Geraldine Jewsbury to Jane Welsh Carlyle* (1892), p. 338.

20. Blanchard Jerrold, "Charles Dickens. In Memoriam," *The Gentleman's Magazine*, n.s., v (1870), 228.

21. Corelli, "Why Dickens is Popular," *The Book Monthly*, February 1920, p. 87.

22. *Works of Walter Bagehot*, III, 94.

23. *The Times*, June 20, 1870, p. 14.

24. Browning, e.g., hints in a letter that Ellen Ternan was Dickens' mistress. See *Dearest Isa*, ed. E. C. McAleer (Austin, Texas, 1951), pp. 348-349.

25. M. M. Bevington, *The Saturday Review* (New York, 1941), pp. 166-167.

26. Sala, *Life and Adventures of George Augustus Sala* (1895), I, 382.

27. *Dickensiana*, pp. 63-64.

28. Mrs. Lynn Linton, "Landor, Dickens, Thackeray," *Woman at Home*, January 1896, p. 345.

29. *The Tribune* (London), February 3 and 5, 1906; *Charles Dickens and Maria Beadnell* (Boston, privately printed, 1908). The latter documents were exploited at length by Ralph Strauss in his *Charles Dickens* (New York, 1928), and by J. H. Stonehouse, *Green Leaves* (1931).

30. Gladys Storey, *Dickens and Daughter* (1939), p. 94. For some later articles and correspondence concerning the reliability of this work, see the Sunday *Times*, March 8, 15, 22 (1953).

31. See the *Dickensian*, XXXII (1936), 306-307. Professor Gilbert Norwood's attack on Dickens was stimulated not by Wright but by Stephen Leacock's biography of Dickens. The latter, which ought to have been a fine book, is a pot-boiler.

32. Bush, *Mythology and the Romantic Tradition* (Cambridge, U.S.A., 1937), p. 56.

33. Woolf, *The Moment* (New York, 1948), pp. 76-80.

34. Julian Symons, *Charles Dickens* (1951), pp. 8, 24-29.

35. Edward Wagenknecht, *The Man Charles Dickens* (Cambridge, U.S.A., 1929), p. 248.

CHAPTER 9

THE COMMON READER

1. William S. Lilly, *Four English Humourists* (1895), pp. 27-32. See also P. G. Thomas, *Aspects of Literary Theory and Practice* (1931), p. 189.

2. *London Quarterly Review*, XXXV (1871), 273. See also Charles D. Yonge, *Three Centuries of English Literature* (1872), pp. 622-677.

3. Gissing, p. 182.

4. Mallock, "Are Scott, Dickens, and Thackeray Obsolete?" *The Forum*, XIV (1893), 503-506.

5. Mowbray Morris, "Charles Dickens," *Fortnightly Review*, n.s., XXXII (1882), 762. See also Clement Shorter, *Victorian Literature: Sixty Years of Books and Bookmen* (1897), pp. 42-44; Arthur Waugh,

"How Dickens Sells," *Book Monthly*, III (1906), 773-776; Arthur Waugh, *A Hundred Years of Publishing* (1930), pp. 177-179; 201-203. The statistics show that *Pickwick.Papers* was temporarily superseded by *A Tale of Two Cities* in having the largest sale after the turn of the century. Martin Harvey's *The Only Way* was apparently responsible for moving the latter novel up from the seventh place which it held in the eighties. *David Copperfield* remained a close second, but *Great Expectations* dropped from fifth to fourteenth place. See also Arthur Adrian's statistics in *Modern Language Quarterly*, XI (1950), 330-331.

6. Waugh, *A Hundred Years of Publishing*, p. 201.

7. See Irma Rantavaara, p. 144.

8. *Dickensian*, XL (1944), 81-82.

9. Aldington, *Four English Portraits* (1948), p. 189.

10. *The Times*, May 19, 1922, p. 16.

11. Graves, *The Real David Copperfield* (1933), p. 6.

12. Arnold Bennett, *Fame and Fiction* (1901), p. 225.

13. Justin McCarthy, *A History of Our Own Times* (1879), II, 392. In C. W. Moulton's *Library of Literary Criticism*, VI, 589-593, there are listed a number of tributes to Dickens' cheerfulness. Clement Shorter noted in 1897 that thousands "have found in his writings the aid to a cheery optimism which has made life more tolerable amid adverse conditions."

14. Anthony Trollope, "Novel Reading," *Nineteenth Century*, V (1879), 33.

15. *The Recollections of Sir Henry Dickens* (1934), pp. 340-342. Cf. the *Dickensian*, I (1905), p. 80.

16. See Walter Dexter's article in the *Dickensian*, XL (1943), p. 26.

17. Calhoun and Heaney, "Dickensiana in the Rough," *Papers of the Bibliographical Society of America*, XLI (1947), p. 293.

18. *The Book Monthly*, III (1906), 775.

19. Kenneth Robinson has shown that despite the inferiority of his later novels, Collins retained a firm hold of his public. In the eighties, the *Pall Mall Gazette* discovered, by ballot, that he was still the most popular author.—*Wilkie Collins* (New York, 1952), pp. 276, 306.

20. In Collins' later novels, problem and purpose are as important as suspense. In this development, he again shows some indebtedness to Dickens, but more to Charles Reade. Reade, in turn, learned much from Collins, and, like the latter, he narrowed the scope of the Dickensian novel. Concerning the intricacies of their relationship, see W. C. Phillips, *Dickens, Reade, and Collins* (New York, 1919), and Henry Milley's unpublished Ph.D. dissertation on Collins (Yale, 1941).

21. Elwin, *Victorian Wallflowers* (1934), p. 312.

22. George Santayana, *Soliloquies in England* (New York, 1934), p. 62.

CHAPTER 10

THE DISCOVERY OF THE SOUL

1. Quoted by J. A. Hammerton, *George Meredith* (1909), p. 341.
2. *Letters of Thackeray*, III, 363.
3. Reginald Viscount Esher, *Ionicus* (New York, 1924), pp. 54-55.
4. Anna T. Kitchel, *George Lewes and George Eliot* (New York, 1933), p. 186.
5. J. W. Cross, *George Eliot's Life* (New York, n.d.), I, 36-39.
6. *Ibid.*, I, 143-144.
7. To the horror of Henry James, she describes *Père Goriot* as a "hateful book" because of its apparent lack of sentiment (by which she did not mean "lachrymosity.") See *Essays and Reviews by George Eliot* (Boston, 1877), pp. 18, 182; Henry James, *Partial Portraits* (1888), pp. 49-50.
8. *Essays and Reviews*, pp. 14-15.
9. Cross, *op. cit.*, I, 219.
10. E. T., *D. H. Lawrence: A Personal Record* (1935), p. 105.
11. E.g., see F. T. Blanchard, *Fielding the Novelist*, pp. 453-457.
12. H. D. Traill, *The New Fiction* (1897), p. 144.
13. "The Natural History of German Life," in George Eliot's *Works* (New York, n.d.), VI, 161-162.
14. Brimley, *Essays* (Cambridge, 1858), pp. 295-298.
15. J. W. Cross, *op. cit.*, II, 6, 90; and Nonesuch, III, 4, 110. After becoming acquainted with Dickens, Eliot was impressed by the "strain of real seriousness" in his conversation.
16. R. E. Francillon, *Mid-Victorian Memories* (n.d.), p. 108.
17. *The Times*, April 12, 1859, p. 5.
18. Quoted by Franklin P. Rolfe, *The Huntington Library Bulletin*, October 10, 1936, pp. 182-183.
19. See Mathilde Parlett, "The Influence of Contemporary Criticism on George Eliot," *Studies in Philology*, XXX (1933), 103-132.
20. Quoted by Hammerton, *George Meredith*, p. 150.
21. Horatio F. Brown, *John Addington Symonds* (1895), II, 19-20. In another letter of 1868, Symonds likened her to Shakespeare. "Who else has made men and women like Tito, Romola, Maggie, Silas . . . ? I cannot criticize her." See Margaret Symonds, *Out of the Past* (1925), p. 119. During the same period, the *Spectator* was also speaking of Eliot as the greatest living novelist. See J. D. Jump, "Weekly Reviewing in the Eighteen-Sixties," *Review of English Studies*, n.s., III (1952), 251-252.
22. Sidney Lanier, *The English Novel and the Principle of its Development* [1883], Centennial edition (Baltimore, 1945).
23. Shorter, *Victorian Literature* (1897), p. 53, and see also *Lady John Russell, A Memoir* (1910), p. 286. According to S. C. Chew, an American literary historian, George Eliot was still "little read" in 1948 by comparison with other major Victorian novelists. Recent studies indicate, however, a marked revival of interest in her work,

especially in *Middlemarch*. Cf. A. C. Baugh, *A Literary History of England* (New York, 1948), p. 1378.

24. *Letters of Gerard Manly Hopkins to Robert Bridges* (Oxford, 1935), p. 239; Edward Fitzgerald, *Letters* (1910), II, 190; *The Works of Swinburne* (Bonchurch edition), XIV, 6-10; Oswald Doughty, *Dante G. Rossetti* (1949), p. 563.

25. James A. Noble, *Morality in English Fiction* (Liverpool, 1886), pp. 31-37; *Impressions and Memories* (1895), pp. 105-115.

26. *Works of Arnold*, IV, 189.

27. *Letters of Hopkins to Bridges*, p. 262.

28. Quoted by Siegfried Sassoon, *Meredith* (New York, 1948), p. 80.

29. *Letters of George Meredith* (New York, 1912), I, 206.

30. Edward Clodd, "George Meredith: Some Recollections," *Fortnightly Review*, n.s., LXXXVI (1909), 27. Meredith's touchstones as a critic included Stendhal as well as Cervantes. See *Letters*, I, 163-164.

31. Alice Meynell, "Charles Dickens as a Man of Letters," *Atlantic Monthly*, XCI (1903), 52-59.

32. *Letters from George Meredith to Alice Meynell* (1923), p. 63.

33. See *Letters*, I, 156-157: "Little writers should be realistic."

34. See Ernest A. Baker, *The History of the English Novel from the Brontës to Meredith* (1937), pp. 303, 328-329; Hammerton, *George Meredith*, p. 163. Together with these comparisons, it should be noted that Meredith considered the pathetic fallacy to be a major Dickensian failing although the device is common enough in his own novels.

35. *The Tragic Comedians*, ch. VIII.

36. Quoted by René Galland, *George Meredith and British Criticism: 1851-1909* (Paris, 1923), p. 34.

37. *An Essay on Comedy* (New York, 1897), p. 99.

38. See Galland, *op. cit.*, pp. 115-117. Sassoon notes that in the early twentieth century, some of Meredith's novels did reach a wide public through sixpenny versions (*op. cit.*, p. 260).

39. Galland, *op. cit.*, p. x.

40. Hammerton, *George Meredith*, p. 28.

41. F. T. Blanchard, *op. cit.*, p. 533.

42. Quoted by Sassoon, *op. cit.*, p. 33.

43. Concerning the quaintness of his prose style, see J. W. Beach, *The Technique of Thomas Hardy* (Chicago, 1922), p. 12.

44. Florence E. Hardy, *The Early Life of Thomas Hardy* (New York, 1928), pp. 129, 305.

45. *Ibid.*, pp. 232, 268; cf. pp. 243, 189, 285.

46. Hardy, *Life and Art* (New York, 1925), pp. 64, 58.

47. Albert J. Guerard, *Thomas Hardy* (Cambridge, U.S.A., 1949), pp. 3-4.

48. *Ibid.*, pp. 4, 39.

49. Quoted by Helen Muchnic, *Dostoevsky's English Reputation (1881-1936)*, *Smith College Studies in Modern Languages*, XX (1939), p. 86.

50. Charles D. Yonge, *Three Centuries of English Literature* (1872), p. 569.

51. Maugham, *A Writer's Notebook* (1949), p. 145.

52. Forster, *Aspects of the Novel* (1927), p. 16.

53. Clifford Bax, *The Poetry of the Brownings* (1947), pp. 153-154.

54. See Royal Alfred Gettman, *Turgenev in England and America*, *University of Illinois Studies in Language and Literature*, XXVII (1941).

55. James, *French Poets and Novelists* (1884), p. 216.

56. James, *Partial Portraits*, pp. 299-300, 318.—The book sale catalogue of Dickens' library indicates that Turgenev in 1862 addressed a copy of his *Récits d'un Chasseur* "To Charles Dickens, one of his greatest admirers, the author." Cf. Ford Madox Ford, *The English Novel* (Philadelphia, 1929), pp. 110-115, and *Portraits from Life* (Boston, 1937), p. 162; and Gettman, *op. cit.*, p. 165.

57. *The Complete Works of Swinburne*, XVIII, 477; Hammerton, *The Dickens Companion*, p. 347; Aylmer Maude, *The Life of Tolstoy* (Oxford, 1929), I, 177.

58. Swinburne, *loc.cit.*

59. T. de Wyzewa, "A propos d'une nouvelle biographie de Dickens," *Revue des Deux Mondes*, XII (1902), 462-463.

60. T. de Wyzewa, "Un nouveau romancier allemand," *Revue des Deux Mondes*, XI (1902), 459.

61. Concerning Tolstoy's blindness to *King Lear*, see George Orwell, *Shooting an Elephant* (New York, 1935), pp. 32-52.

62. *The Works of Tolstoy* (Oxford, 1929), XVIII, 242-243, 265.

63. Huxley, *Vulgarity in Literature* (1930), p. 57.

64. F. M. Dostoievsky, *The Diary of a Writer* (New York, 1949), I, 75, 343, 350. Concerning Dickens' popularity in Russia, see *Dickensian*, XLI, 204. Between 1894 and 1944, 3,000,000 copies were printed.

65. *Letters of Dostoevsky* (1917), p. 269.

66. E. H. Carr, *op. cit.*, p. 84. For a sympathetic discussion of Dostoevsky's humor, see V. S. Pritchett, *The Living Novel* (New York, 1947), pp. 235-240.

67. Muchnic, *op. cit.*, pp. 19-20.

68. Quoted *ibid.*

69. Gissing, p. 222.

70. George Katkov, "Steerforth and Stavrogin," *Slavonic and East European Review*, XXVII (1949), 469-488.

71. Gissing, pp. 223-224.

72. Symons, *Charles Dickens* (1951), p. 82. See also Stefan Zweig's *Three Masters: Balzac, Dickens, Dostoeffsky* (New York, 1930)—a superficial study. Cf. Walter Allen's excellent review in *The New Statesman and Nation*, September 17, 1949, pp. 306-307.

73. Woolf, "The Russian Point of View," in *The Common Reader* (New York, 1925), p. 250.

74. See Walter Neuschäffer, *Dostojewskijs Einfluss auf den englischen Roman* (Heidelberg, 1935).

75. "Dostoevsky and the Novel," *TLS*, XXIX (1930), p. 465.

76. Woolf, "Modern Fiction," in *The Common Reader*, p. 214.

77. Woolf, *The Death of the Moth* (New York, 1942), p. 177; *The Moment* (New York, 1948), pp. 76-80.

78. Wilson, *The Wound and the Bow* (Cambridge, U.S.A., 1941), p. 1.

79. Edward Dowden, "Victorian Literature," *Fortnightly Review*, n.s., XLI (1887), 843.

80. Leavis, *The Great Tradition* (New York, n.d.), p. 19.

81. Symons, *op. cit.*, p. 83.

82. Woolf, *The Moment*, p. 75.

83. Elizabeth Bowen, *Collected Impressions* (1950), pp. 265-266.

84. Wilson, *The Triple Thinkers* (New York, 1948), p. ix.

85. *Letters of Dostoevsky*, p. 241.

86. Woolf, *The Common Reader*, p. 237.

CHAPTER 11

THE HIGH AESTHETIC LINE

1. Green, *Pack My Bag* (1952), pp. 210-211. Cf. Raphael Cor, *Un romancier de la vertu et un peintre du vice: Charles Dickens, Marcel Proust* (Paris, n.d.).

2. White, *Letters to Three Friends* (Oxford, 1924), pp. 71-72.

3. Francillon, *Mid-Victorian Memories* (n.d.), pp. 304-305.

4. Lang, *Letters to Dead Authors* (1886), p. 16.

5. Quoted by Irma Rantavaara, p. 132.

6. *The Book Monthly*, III (1906), 235.

7. Crawford, *The Novel: What it Is* (1893), p. 9.

8. Henry James, *Partial Portraits* (1888), p. 376.

9. By William Lyon Phelps (New York, 1916).

10. W. D. Howells, *Criticism and Fiction* (1891), pp. 174-176. Elsewhere Howells is slightly more sympathetic and mentions, "with a thousand reservations," that Dickens was a "masterful artist." See *My Literary Passions* (New York, 1895), p. 88, and *Harper's Monthly Magazine*, CV (1902), 308-312, and *The Rise of Silas Lapham*, ch. XIV.

11. See Wilbur L. Cross, "The Return to Dickens," *Yale Review*, n.s., II (1912), 144.

12. Stevenson, *Memories and Portraits* (1887), p. 298, and also "A Note on Realism," in *Essays in the Art of Writing* (1905), pp. 91-107.

13. See *The Letters of Robert Louis Stevenson* (1911), III, 42-43; *Memories and Portraits*, p. 228.

14. Stevenson, "Some Gentlemen in Fiction," *Scribner's Magazine*, III (1888), 767.

15. James, *A Small Boy and Others* (New York, 1913), pp. 118-119.

16. *Ibid.*, pp. 116-120.

17. See *The Notebooks of Henry James* (New York, 1947), p. 319; *Notes of a Son and Brother* (New York, 1914), pp. 252-255.

18. James, *Views and Reviews* (Boston, 1908 [1865]), pp. 157-159.

19. James, *Partial Portraits* (1888 [1884]), pp. 300, 318.
20. James, *French Poets and Novelists* (1884), p. 213.
21. See *ibid.*, pp. 197-210; Rebecca West, *Henry James* (New York, n.d.), pp. 64-65. The later essay on Flaubert in *Notes on Novelists* (1914) is in a vein of full reverence.
22. *Partial Portraits*, pp. 124-125.
23. *Ibid.*, p. 100.
24. *French Poets and Novelists*, p. 147.
25. Preface to *The Tragic Muse* in *The Art of the Novel*, ed. R. P. Blackmur, p. 84.
26. Blackmur, "The Loose and Baggy Monsters of Henry James," *Accent* (Summer, 1951), pp. 132-133.
27. *The Letters of Maurice Hewlett* (1926), p. 22.
28. Bowen, *Anthony Trollope* (Oxford, 1946), p. 6.
29. E.g., J. W. Beach, *The Method of Henry James* (New Haven, 1918); Percy Lubbock, *The Craft of Fiction* (1921); Morris Roberts, *Henry James's Criticism* (1929).
30. *The Question of Henry James*, ed. F. W. Dupee (New York, 1945), pp. 254-266.
31. Henry James, *The Middle Years* (New York, 1917), pp. 58-59 (italics mine). Cf. the reference to the "sinister" prison in *The Princess Casamassima*, ch. III.
32. F. O. Matthiessen, *Henry James: The Major Phase* (Oxford, 1944), p. xiv.
33. See Lionel Trilling, *E. M. Forster* (Norfolk, Conn., 1943), p. 19; and *The Liberal Imagination* (New York, 1951), pp. 88-89. See also Stephen Spender's essay in *Hound and Horn*, April 1934, pp. 431-433.
34. *Partial Portraits*, p. 223.
35. *Ibid.*, p. 222.
36. James, *Notes on Novelists* (New York, 1914), pp. 438-443.
37. Leavis, *The Great Tradition*, pp. 132-134.
38. See "The Last of the Dickensians: William De Morgan," *TLS*, November 18, 1939, p. 673.
39. *The Question of Henry James*, pp. 258-259.
40. Joseph Conrad, *A Personal Record* (1925), p. 71.
41. *Ibid.*, p. 124; and the *Dickensian*, XXVIII (1931), 40-41.
42. For other parallels between Conrad and Dickens, see F. R. Leavis, *The Great Tradition*, pp. 17-19, 208, 210.
43. The following sentence from *Lord Jim*, ch. XXXIV, sounds almost as if it were a parody: "It was a strange and melancholy illusion, evolved half-consciously like all our illusions, which I suspect only to be visions of remote unattainable truth, seen dimly."
44. Conrad's independence is suggested by David Daiches' remarking upon the lack of either factory or drawing room in his novels. See *The Novel and the Modern World* (Chicago, 1939), p. 48. Actually Conrad did portray the drawing room as in *Suspense*, but the industrial scenes, dear to the naturalist, are certainly absent.
45. Yvor Winters, in *The Foundations of Modern Literary Judgment*, ed. Schorer, Miles, McKenzie (New York, 1948), p. 292.

46. Quoted by Henry James, *Essays in London* (1893), p. 129.

47. Aylmer Maude, *The Life of Tolstoy* (Oxford, 1929), I, 177.

48. See Desmond Pacey, "Flaubert and his Victorian Critics," *University of Toronto Quarterly*, XVI (1946), 74-84; Clarence R. Decker, "Balzac's Literary Reputation in Victorian Society," *PMLA*, XLVII (1932), 1150-1157, and "Zola's Literary Reputation in England," *PMLA*, XLIX (1934), 1140-1153.

49. See H. D. Traill, *The New Fiction* (1897), p. 17.

50. See "Dickens and Daudet," *Cornhill Magazine*, n.s., XVII (1891), 400-415. Some reviewers recommended not only Dickens but the comparative delicacy of Russian novels to offset the grossness of the French.

51. D. F. Hannigan, quoted by Pacey, *op. cit.*, p. 82.

52. Flaubert was critical of Dickens' lack of careful construction (see above, ch. 1, note 35), but his usual tone is one of respect. E.g., see his *Correspondance* (Paris, 1926-1930), no. 609, June 15, 1859, and no. 729, July 1862.

53. Concerning Dickens' extraordinary popularity in Germany, see the thorough study by Ellis N. Gummer, *Dickens' Works in Germany: 1837-1937* (Oxford, 1940).

54. Moore, *Confessions of a Young Man* (New York, 1923), p. 362.

55. Moore, *A Modern Lover* (1883), I, 78.

56. Beerbohm, *A Christmas Garland* (New York, 1913), p. 183.

57. *Confessions of a Young Man*, p. 455.

58. See Joseph Hone, *The Life of George Moore* (1936), p. 96. Concerning the reception of Moore's novels, see A. J. Farmer, *Le mouvement esthétique et "décadent" en Angleterre: 1873-1900* (Paris, 1931), p. 87 ff.

59. John Freeman, *A Portrait of George Moore* (1922), p. 111.

60. *Ibid.*, p. 116.

61. Bennett, *Fame and Fiction* (1901), pp. 223, 186-187.

62. *The Journals of Arnold Bennett* (1932), I, 158.

63. See *ibid.*, pp. 68, 85. See also J. B. Simons' chapter on literary influences in his *Arnold Bennett* (Oxford, 1936), pp. 29-98.

64. See the *Dickensian*, XXXIII (1937), p. 68. Bennett's attack on Dickens in *Literary Heresies* (1904) was replied to in an article in the *Amalgamated Engineers' Journal*, October 1904, pp. 9-11. The reply is typical of the kind of popular support which Dickens' novels continued to receive.

65. Bennett, *Literary Taste* (1909), p. 104. Scott is ranked second to Dickens (with five novels).

66. Bennett, *The Author's Craft* (New York, 1914), pp. 47-51, 57-58.

67. E.g., see Walter Allen, *Arnold Bennett* (1948), pp. 46, 60, 97.

68. *Journals*, III, p. 52.

69. For this passage, I am indebted to an unpublished paper by Lawrence J. Hynes.

70. Wells, *Experiment in Autobiography* (1934), II, 506.

71. See Geoffrey West, *H. G. Wells* (1930), p. 31.

72. *A Modern Utopia* [1904] (1925), p. 223.

73. West, *op. cit.*, Appendix II.

74. E. Wagenknecht, *Cavalcade of the English Novel* (New York, 1943), p. 469.

75. V. S. Pritchett, *The Living Novel* (New York, 1947), pp. 87-88.

76. *Tono-Bungay*, bk. II, ch. II.

77. Norman Nicholson, *H. G. Wells* (1950), pp. 46-47. See also W. Y. Tindall, *Forces in Modern British Literature* (New York, 1947), p. 174; E. M. Forster, *Aspects of the Novel* (1927), pp. 27-30; Wagenknecht, *op. cit.*, p. 460n., and West, *op. cit.*, p. 298.

78. *Autobiography*, II, 508.

79. *Ibid.*, p. 500.

80. *Ibid.*, pp. 618-619.

81. *The Letters of Henry James*, ed. Lubbock (New York, 1920), II, 138.

82. Wells, "The Contemporary Novel," *Atlantic Monthly*, CIX (1912), 1-11.

83. See Joyce Cary, "Including Mr. Micawber," *New York Times Book Review*, April 15, 1951; Somerset Maugham, "Charles Dickens," *Atlantic Monthly*, CLXXXII (1948), 50-56.

84. See Henry Reid, *The Novel Since 1939* (1948), pp. 9-10; Henry James, *Partial Portraits*, pp. 245-246.

85. J. W. Beach, *The Technique of Thomas Hardy* (Chicago, 1922), pp. 86-87. Cf. F. Dubrez Fawcett, *Dickens the Dramatist* (1952).

86. Forster, *Aspects of the Novel*, pp. 107-109. Cf. Allen Tate in *Forms of Modern Fiction*, ed. W. O'Connor (Minneapolis, 1948), p. 30.

87. Maugham, *The Summing Up* (New York, 1939), p. 218.

88. C. E. Montague, *A Writer's Notes on his Trade* (Pelican Books, 1949), pp. 36, 42-43.

89. See above, ch. 6, p. 124.

90. Bentley, *Some Observations on the Art of Narrative* (New York, 1948), p. 16.

91. An interesting preliminary study is F. W. Boege's "Point of View in Dickens," *PMLA*, LXV (1950), 90-105.

92. *The Letters of Katherine Mansfield*, ed. J. M. Murry (1928), I, 114, 118, 131, 212.

CHAPTER 12

THE UNCOMMON READER

1. Warner, *The Cult of Power* (Philadelphia, 1947), p. 29.

2. Trilling, "The Measure of Dickens," *The Griffin*, II (1952), 1.

3. Chesterton, *Charles Dickens: A Critical Study* (New York, 1913), pp. 15-19.

4. See Lubbock, *The Craft of Fiction* (1926), p. 204.

5. See the *New Yorker*, January 10, 1953, pp. 81-88.

6. Saintsbury, *Corrected Impressions* (1895), pp. 128-131.

7. Saintsbury, *The English Novel* (1913), p. 229.

8. E.g., see his *History of Criticism* (Edinburgh, 1904), III, 253-254.

9. *The Cambridge History of English Literature* (New York, 1917), XIII, 336.

10. *Ibid.*, p. 346.

11. Hoffman, *Freudianism and the Literary Mind* (Baton Rouge, Louisiana, 1945), p. 72.

12. Quoted by the *Dickensian*, XXXII (1936), 226. Cf. R. J. Cruikshank, *Charles Dickens and Early Victorian England* (1949), pp. 270-273.

13. *Letters of Alexander Woollcott* (Toronto, 1944), p. 109.

14. *The Bookman*, LXXXIX (1934), 209.

15. Shaw, *Pen Portraits and Reviews* (1949), p. 222.

16. *Ibid.*, pp. 155, 222.

17. See J. B. Priestley's remarks on Shaw and Dickens in the *Dickensian*, XXVIII (1932), 139.

18. Frank Harris, *Bernard Shaw* (New York, 1931), pp. 114-115, 317.

19. See the *Dickensian*, XXVIII (1931), p. 41.

20. *The Letters of Stevenson* (1911), III, 41.

21. *The Bookman*, LXXXIX (1934), 209.

22. See Edwin Pugh, *Charles Dickens: The Apostle of the People*; Cumberland Clark, *Dickens and Democracy* (1930); McEwan Lawson, *Challenge to Oppression: The Story of Charles Dickens* (1947).

23. Fox, *The Novel and the People* (New York, 1937), pp. 63-71.

24. Priestley, *The English Novel* (1935) [1927], p. 3. See also his *The English Comic Characters* (1925) and *Fools and Philosophers* (1926).

25. See Jerome H. Buckley, *William Ernest Henley* (Princeton, 1945), a useful corrective to conventional accounts of the aesthetic period. Henley's articles on Dickens appeared in *The Outlook*, March 5, 1898, pp. 134-135, and in the *Pall Mall Magazine*, August 1899, pp. 573-579.

26. See Paul de Reul, *L'oeuvre de Swinburne* (Brussels, 1922), pp. 458-459.

27. See Jared Wenger's article, *PMLA*, LXII (1947), 220-232.

28. Edmund Gosse, *The Life of Swinburne* in the *Complete Works of Swinburne* (Bonchurch edition), XIX, 227, 291.

29. See the *Complete Works of Swinburne*, XIV, 57-88.

30. See, e.g., his chapter contributed to *The Outline of Literature*, ed. John Drinkwater (n.d.), and his *Autobiography* (New York, 1936), pp. 12-20.

31. See Chesterton, *Charles Dickens: A Critical Study*, p. 293.

32. *Ibid.*, p. 23.

33. *Ibid.*, p. 185.

34. *Ibid.*, p. 81.

35. *Ibid.*, p. 87.

36. F. R. Leavis, *The Great Tradition*, p. 241.

37. Chesterton, *Appreciations and Criticisms of Dickens* (New York, 1911), pp. 62-63.

38. See Santayana, *The Middle Span* (New York, 1945), p. 90.

39. See Santayana, *Soliloquies in England* (New York, 1922), pp. 65-66.

40. Priestley, *The English Novel*, p. 62.

41. See the *New York Times Book Review*, April 22, 1951.

42. Priestley in the *Dickensian*, XXVIII (1932), 140.

43. Leacock's best essay on Dickens is his "Fiction and Reality" which appears in his *Essays and Literary Studies* (1916), pp. 159-188. Sir Osbert Sitwell's *Dickens* (1932) and *Trio* (1937) seem to be merely charming after-dinner speeches, but by insinuating that Dickens was worthy of a critic's serious attention, they were a helpful corrective.

44. Robert Shafer, introduction to *Workers in the Dawn* by George Gissing (New York, 1935), p. xxxix.

45. See *Letters of Gissing to Members of his Family* (1927), p. 55.

46. Gissing, p. 63.

47. *Ibid.*, p. 57.

48. The account of Kit and his family at Astley's, which is only slightly discolored by sympathy, seemed to Gissing magnificent, but the refined portrait of Lizzie Hexam in *Our Mutual Friend* seemed to him a discreditable "misrepresentation of social facts," and typical of misguided authors who "delight in idealizing girls of the . . . lowest class." See *ibid.*, pp. 77, 150. See also Gissing's *Critical Studies of the Works of Charles Dickens* (New York, 1924), p. 132.

49. *Letters to his Family*, p. 83.

50. Gissing, pp. 189-190.

51. *Ibid.*, p. 124.

52. *Ibid.*, pp. 133, 141, 155.

53. *Ibid.*, pp. 169, 114.

54. *Ibid.*, pp. 171-172.

55. *Ibid.*, p. 220.

56. *Ibid.*, p. 177.

57. *Ibid.*, pp. 190-191.

58. See *ibid.*, p. 218.

59. Concerning Dickens' profound influence on Kipling, see Ann Matlack Weygandt, *Kipling's Reading and its Influence on his Poetry* (Philadelphia, 1939), pp. 88-89. Cf. Ernest Baker, *History of the English Novel* (1939), x, 109-110.

60. Greene, *The Lost Childhood* (1951), p. 57. Henry James also speaks of having had a similar impression from *Oliver Twist*. See *A Small Boy and Others* (New York, 1913), p. 120.

61. See Wilson, *The Triple Thinkers* (New York, 1948), pp. vii-ix.

62. Wilson, *The Wound and the Bow* (Cambridge, U.S.A., 1941), p. 29. Cf. E. E. Stoll, *From Shakespeare to Joyce* (New York, 1944), pp. 346-347.

63. *Ibid.*, pp. 37-38.

64. Lindsay, *Charles Dickens* (New York, 1950), p. 170.

65. Leavis, *The Great Tradition* (New York, n.d.), pp. 230-231.

66. Kettle, *An Introduction to the English Novel* (1951), p. 8.

67. *Ibid.*, p. 126.

68. Van Ghent, "The Dickens World," *Sewanee Review*, LVIII

(1950), 419-438; and Morse, "Our Mutual Friend," *Partisan Review*, xvi (1949), 277-289.

69. Warner, *The Cult of Power*, pp. 35-36, 133-135.

70. See Edward Sackville-West, in the *New Statesman and Nation*, December 11, 1948, p. 527.

71. Joyce, *Ulysses* (New York, 1937), pp. 413-414. Concerning the parallels between Mr. Jingle in *Pickwick* and Mr. Bloom in *Ulysses*, see Harry Levin, *James Joyce* (Norfolk, Conn., 1941), pp. 92-93.

72. See above ch. 7, p. 146. Concerning Dickens' impact on Lawrence, see F. R. Leavis, *D. H. Lawrence* (Cambridge, 1930), p. 14.

73. *The Diaries of Franz Kafka: 1914-1923* (New York, 1949), pp. 188-189.

74. *Loc. cit.* See also Rudolf Vasăta on Kafka and Dickens in *The Kafka Problem*, ed. Angel Flores (New York, 1946), pp. 134-139.

75. See *TLS*, February 8, 1952, "More New Writing."

76. Chesterton, *Appreciations and Criticisms of Dickens*, p. xiii.

77. More, *Shelburne Essays: Fifth Series* (New York, 1908), pp. 42-43.

78. J. Cuming Walters in the *Book Monthly*, February 1920, p. 91.

79. See Eliot, *Selected Essays* (1932), pp. 126-127.

80. Morse in *Partisan Review*, xvi (1949), 288.

81. *Memorials of Edward Burne-Jones* (New York, 1906), ii, 190.

BIBLIOGRAPHY

Note: It seems unnecessary to reprint here the kind of Dickens bibliography which is readily accessible elsewhere. The following lists are therefore restricted to studies which relate to the history of novel-criticism or to the reputations of individual novelists. All other works, including biographies, reviews, letters, and diaries, are referred to in the footnotes only.

PART I: THE REPUTATION OF NOVELISTS AND THE HISTORY OF NOVEL-CRITICISM

BENNETT, ARNOLD, *Fame and Fiction: An Inquiry into Certain Popularities*. 1901.

BLANCHARD, F. T., *Fielding the Novelist; A Study in Historical Criticism*. New Haven, 1926.

BOEGE, FRED W., *Smollett's Reputation as a Novelist*. Princeton, 1947.

BROWN, ROLLO WALTER, *The Writer's Art*. Cambridge, U.S.A., 1921.

BURKE, KENNETH, "Psychology and Form." *The Dial*, LXXIX (July 1925), 34-46.

CRUSE, AMY, *The Victorians and their Books*. 1935.

———, *After the Victorians*. 1938.

DECKER, CLARENCE R., "Balzac's Literary Reputation in Victorian Society." *PMLA*, XLVII (1932), 1150-1157.

———, "Zola's Literary Reputation in England." *PMLA*, XLIX (1934), 1140-1153.

DEVONSHIRE, M. G., *The English Novel in France: 1830-1870*. 1929.

ERNLE, ROWLAND E. P., *The Light Reading of our Ancestors*. Oxford, 1921.

GALLAND, RENÉ, *George Meredith and British Criticism: 1851-1909*. Paris, 1923.

GETTMAN, ROYAL ALFRED, *Turgenev in England and America*. University of Illinois Studies in Language and Literature, XXVII (1941).

GIBSON, BYRON HALL, *The History, from 1800 to 1832, of English Criticism of Prose Fiction*. Urbana, Illinois, 1931. An abstract.

GUÉRARD, ALBERT, *Literature and Society*. Boston, 1935.

HILLHOUSE, JAMES T., *The Waverley Novels and their Critics*. Minneapolis, 1936.

HOOKER, KENNETH WARD, *The Fortunes of Victor Hugo in England*. New York, 1938.

HUGHES, HELEN S., "The Middle-Class Reader and the English Novel." *JEGP*, XXV (1926), 362-378.

JOHNSON, R. BRIMLEY, *Novelists on Novels, From the Duchess of Newcastle to George Eliot*. 1928.

JUMP, J. D., "Weekly Reviewing in the Eighteen-Fifties." *RES*, XXIV (1948), 42-57.

———, "Weekly Reviewing in the Eighteen-Sixties." *RES*, n.s., III (1952), 244-262.

LEAVIS, Q. D., *Fiction and the Reading Public*. 1932.

MARCHAND, LESLIE, *The Athenaeum: A Mirror of Victorian Culture*. Chapel Hill, North Carolina, 1941.

MUCHNIC, HELEN, *Dostoevsky's English Reputation: 1881-1936*. Smith College Studies in Modern Languages, XX (1939).

NEUSCHÄFFER, WALTER, *Dostojewskijs Einfluss auf den englischen Roman*. Heidelberg, 1935.

PACEY, DESMOND, "Flaubert and his Victorian Critics." *University of Toronto Quarterly*, XVI (1946), 74-84.

PARLETT, MATHILDE, "The Influence of Contemporary Criticism on George Eliot." *SP*, XXX (1933), 103-132.

PEYRE, HENRI, *Writers and their Critics: A Study of Misunderstanding*. Ithaca, New York, 1944.

SCHORER, MARK, Foreword to *Critiques and Essays on Modern Fiction: 1920-1951*. Ed. J. W. Aldridge, New York, 1952.

TAYLOR, JOHN TINNON, *Early Opposition to the English Novel . . . 1760-1830*. New York, 1943.

TOMPKINS, J. M. S., *The Popular Novel in England: 1770-1800*. 1932.

WASHBURN, CAROLYN, "The History, from 1832 to 1860, of British Criticism of Prose Fiction." University of Illinois Ph.D. dissertation. Abstract published at Urbana, Illinois, 1937.

WOLFF, MAX L., *Geschichte der Romantheorie*. Nürnberg, 1915.

PART II: STUDIES OF DICKENS' REPUTATION

ADRIAN, ARTHUR A., *"David Copperfield*: A Century of Critical and Popular Acclaim." *MLQ*, XI (1950), 325-331.

CALHOUN, PHILO, AND HOWELL J. HEANEY, "Dickensiana in the Rough." *Papers of the Bibliographical Society of America*, XLI (1947), 293-320.

CROSS, WILBUR L., "The Return to Dickens." *Yale Review*, n.s., II (1912), 142-162.

DARTON, F. J. HARVEY, "Charles Dickens" in F. W. Bateson's *The Cambridge Bibliography of English Literature*. New York, 1941, III, 435-455.

DARWIN, BERNARD, "Return to Dickens." *St. Martin's Review* (February 1940), pp. 30-33.

DELATTRE, FLORIS, *Dickens et la France*. Paris, 1927.

DEXTER, WALTER, "How Press and Public Received 'The Pickwick Papers.'" *The Nineteenth Century and After*, CXIX (1936), 318-329.

FREWER, L. B., AND OTHERS, "The Influence of Dickens: Collected from Recent Books." *The Dickensian*, XXVIII (1932), 40-45, and in successive issues.

GUMMER, ELLIS N., *Dickens' Works in Germany: 1837-1937*. Oxford, 1940.

HAMMERTON, J. A., *The Dickens Companion*. n.d. [1910].

KITTON, FRED. G., *Dickensiana: A Bibliography of the Literature Relating to Charles Dickens and his Writings*. 1886.

LEY, J. W. T., *The Dickens Circle*. 1918.

MALLOCK, W. H., "Are Scott, Dickens, and Thackeray Obsolete?" *The Forum*, XIV (1893), 503-513.

MAURICE, ARTHUR B., "Famous Novels and their Contemporary Critics." *The Bookman*, XVII (1903), 130-138.

MILLER, W., AND E. H. STRANGE, *A Centenary Bibliography of the Pickwick Papers*. 1936.

MILLER, WILLIAM, *The Dickens Student and Collector*. Cambridge, U.S.A., 1946.

MOULTON, CHARLES W., *The Library of Literary Criticism*. Buffalo, New York, 1902-04, vol. VI.

MURRY, JOHN MIDDLETON, "The Dickens Revival." *The Times* (May 19, 1922), p. 16.

NISBET, ADA B., "The Mystery of 'Martin Chuzzlewit,'" in *Essays Critical and Historical Dedicated to Lily B. Campbell*. . . . Berkeley, California, 1950, pp. 201-216.

RANTAVAARA, IRMA, *Dickens in the Light of English Criticism*. Helsinki, 1944.

SHORTER, CLEMENT, *Victorian Literature: Sixty Years of Books and Bookmen*. 1897.

ZABEL, MORTON D., "Dickens: The Reputation Revised." *The Nation* (September 17, 1949), pp. 279-281.

PART III: SOME VICTORIAN ESSAYS ON FICTION

BESANT, WALTER, The Art of Fiction. 1884.

BULWER-LYTTON, EDWARD. For a useful summary of his scattered essays and prefaces, see H. H. Watts, "Lytton's Theories of Prose Fiction." *PMLA*, L (1935), 274-289.

CRAWFORD, F. MARION, *The Novel: What it Is*. 1893.

ELIOT, GEORGE, "Silly Novels by Lady Novelists." *Westminster Review*, LXVI (1856), 442-461.

GREEN, THOMAS HILL, "An Estimate of the Value and Influence of Works of Fiction in Modern Times" (1862), in *The Works of T. H. Green*. 1906, III, 20-45.

HARDY, THOMAS, "The Profitable Reading of Fiction" (1888), in *Life and Art*. New York, 1925, pp. 56-74.

HOWELLS, W. D., *Criticism and Fiction*. 1891.

JAMES, HENRY, "The Art of Fiction," in *Partial Portraits*. 1888, pp. 375-408.

JEAFFRESON, JOHN C., *Novels and Novelists, from Elizabeth to Victoria*. 1858, 2 vols.

LEWES, GEORGE H., "Criticism in Relation to Novels." *The Fortnightly Review*, III (1866), 325-361.

MASSON, DAVID, *British Novelists and their Styles*. Cambridge, 1859.

SENIOR, NASSAU W., *Essays on Fiction*. 1864.

STEPHEN, FITZJAMES, "The Relation of Novels to Life," in *Cambridge Essays*. 1855, pp. 148-192.

TRAILL, H. D., *The New Fiction and other Essays*. 1897.

TROLLOPE, ANTHONY, "Novel-Reading." *The Nineteenth Century*, V (1879), 24-43.

INDEX

Norton Critical Editions

Inexpensive paperbacks containing authoritative texts, carefully annotated, plus comprehensive selections of criticism and source materials.

Emily Brontë *Wuthering Heights* EDITED BY William M. Sale, Jr. N308

Samuel Clemens *Adventures of Huckleberry Finn* EDITED BY Sculley Bradley, Richmond Croom Beatty, AND E. Hudson Long N304

Joseph Conrad *Heart of Darkness* EDITED BY Robert Kimbrough N307

Stephen Crane *The Red Badge of Courage* EDITED BY Sculley Bradley, Richmond Croom Beatty, AND E. Hudson Long N305

Fyodor Dostoyevsky *Crime and Punishment* EDITED BY George Gibian N310

Gustave Flaubert *Madame Bovary* EDITED BY Paul de Man N311

Nathaniel Hawthorne *The Scarlet Letter* EDITED BY Sculley Bradley, Richmond Croom Beatty, AND E. Hudson Long N303

Henry James *The Ambassadors* EDITED BY S. P. Rosenbaum N309

William Shakespeare *Hamlet* EDITED BY Cyrus Hoy N306

William Shakespeare *Henry the Fourth, Part I* EDITED BY James L. Sanderson N302

Jonathan Swift *Gulliver's Travels* EDITED BY Robert A. Greenberg N301

Norton Anthologies

SOUNDLY EDITED • HANDSOMELY DESIGNED

The Norton Anthology of English Literature Complete
Edition in Two Volumes Major Authors Edition in
One Volume

GENERAL EDITOR: M. H. Abrams EDITORS: E. Talbot Donaldson,
Hallett Smith, Robert M. Adams, Samuel Holt Monk, George H.
Ford, AND David Daiches

The American Tradition in Literature, Revised Edition
Complete Edition in Two Volumes Shorter Edition
in One Volume

EDITED BY Sculley Bradley, Richmond Croom Beatty, AND E.
Hudson Long

The English Drama: An Anthology 900-1642

EDITED BY Edd Winfield Parks AND Richmond Croom Beatty

*The Golden Hind: An Anthology of Elizabethan Prose and
Poetry,* Revised Edition

EDITED BY Roy Lamson AND Hallett Smith

*Renaissance England: Poetry and Prose from the Reforma-
tion to the Restoration*

EDITED BY Roy Lamson AND Hallett Smith

*Enlightened England: An Anthology of English Literature
from Dryden to Blake,* Revised Edition

EDITED BY Wylie Sypher

The Great Critics: An Anthology of Literary Criticism,
Third Edition

EDITED BY James Harry Smith AND Edd Winfield Parks

World Masterpieces

GENERAL EDITOR: Maynard Mack EDITORS: Kenneth Douglas,
Howard E. Hugo, Bernard M. W. Knox, John C. McGalliard,
P. M. Pasinetti, AND René Wellek

The Continental Edition of World Masterpieces

GENERAL EDITOR: Maynard Mack EDITORS: Kenneth Douglas,
John Hollander, Howard E. Hugo, Bernard M. W. Knox, John
C. McGalliard, P. M. Pasinetti, AND René Wellek

*Eight American Writers: An Anthology of American
Literature*

GENERAL EDITORS: Norman Foerster AND Robert P. Falk. EDITED
BY Floyd Stovall, Stephen E. Whicher, Walter Harding, Richard
H. Fogle, Leon Howard, James E. Miller, Jr., AND Gladys C.
Bellamy

In the Norton Library

LITERATURE

In the Norton Library

CRITICISM AND THE HISTORY OF IDEAS